The Language
of Argument

The Language
of Argument

DANIEL McDONALD

University of South Alabama

CHANDLER PUBLISHING COMPANY
An Intext Publisher · Scranton / London / Toronto

For

Mr. and Mrs. Birger Gabrielsen

Contents

IV. ARGUMENT BY AUTHORITY

V. SEMANTIC ARGUMENT

Subjects Discussed
in This Book

EDUCATION

LANGUAGE AND LITERATURE

CONTROVERSIAL COURSES

STUDENT UNREST

LAW AND ORDER

CAUSES OF CRIME

GUNS:

POLITICS

NATIONAL AND INTERNATIONAL

THE MILITARY

RELIGION

ETHICS—ETERNAL OR SITUATIONAL

MORAL ISSUES

SCIENCE

MAN AS ANIMAL

HEALTH AND POSSIBLE HAZARDS

DRUGS:

CIGARETTES:

THE ENVIRONMENT

THE MYSTERIOUS FRONTIER

PREFACE

The purpose of this text is to teach students how to read argument and to provide materials around which they can write argumentative essays of their own. The selections cover a range of provocative issues: some are intended to be persuasive; some are not.

The editor who selects and annotates controversial articles must work to keep his own opinions out of his textbook. I *have* tried.

I must record my indebtedness to Mr. Charles Harwell, to Mrs. Polly Patterson, and to my wife Irene, for their contributions to this book.

D Mc

The Language
of Argument

1

"Truth"
and Argument

Ronald Reagan is handsome.
Capital punishment is wrong.
Pontiac is America's No. 1 Road Car.
Icksnak brack a brack disnold fleb.
Lyndon Johnson was President of the U.S.
I like pizza.

Which of these statements are true? On what evidence do you base your judgment? Are you prepared to defend it?

Before one begins to discuss such assertions, he should recognize two things: (1) Such statements cannot meaningfully be argued without a careful definition of terms, which in itself may be difficult to arrive at. (2) "Truth," whatever it may denote in a philosophical realm, usually means "a statement for which the evidence offers a high degree of probability."

Some arguments rely more on definition of terms than on evidence. When two people argue whether Ronald Reagan is handsome, they are not disagreeing about his hair, teeth, clothes, and so on, but about the definition of "handsomeness." If they agree on a definition, they will probably agree about Ronald Reagan as well. Similarly, the question of whether capital punishment is wrong hinges not so much on the character of the act (the pain, the possibility of error, the protection afforded society) as on the definition of "wrongness."

Aesthetic and moral questions are often not susceptible to evidence because disputants cannot agree on the terms of argument. The meaning of any word is what people agree that it is (e.g., a telephone is called a "telephone" because people regularly use that word to denote it), but in more abstract areas people do not agree. What is "handsomeness"? What is beauty? Theoreticians have sought objective standards, but the quest seems fruitless. Is a Greek temple more beautiful than a Gothic cathedral?

Is Whistler's Mother handsomer than da Vinci's Mona Lisa, than Andy Warhol's Marilyn Monroe? Who can say? The decision rests on a subjective judgment, which does not lend itself to argument.

Like "beauty," the idea of "goodness" is not subject to easy definition. Seeking an objective basis for moral judgments, authorities have cited Scriptural precedents; they have insisted that nature provides a moral example; they have based systems on the inalienable rights of each human being. But such definitions have won no universal acceptance. If two disputants agree that morality resides, say, in a "natural law," they might then *begin* to argue about capital punishment. But in general usage, moral terms remain so ill-defined that such issues sometimes cannot be argued meaningfully at all.

Moral and aesthetic questions are further removed from argument by the fact that they often elicit emotional responses. For example, two individuals who did agree in defining "handsomeness" might still disagree about Ronald Reagan because one objected to his political opinions. It is, of course, unreasonable to let emotions color such a judgment, but the attitude is not uncommon. Regarding capital punishment, one might be completely persuaded that the practice is cruel and barbaric — yet, at a given moment, argue that hanging is too good for a child murderer or a political assassin.

Vagueness of definition precludes argument in other areas as well. Pontiac has been advertised as "America's *No. 1 Road* Car"; Kent as America's "largest selling *premium* cigarette"; and Shenley Reserve as "the whiskey of *elegance.*" Are these claims true? Until the key words are defined, these statements are no more subject to evidence that is "Icksnak brack a brack disnold fleb."

It is only when terms are defined and mutually accepted that one can begin marshaling evidence to prove the truth of a statement. One can, for example, argue whether Bronco Nagurski or Jim Brown was the better fullback, because their records, the merits of their supporting and opposing teams, and the qualities of a good fullback are generally enough agreed on. Is it true that cigarette smoking causes lung cancer, that James Hoffa tried to fix a jury, that Volkswagen is an economical car to own? The questions can at least be argued.

One must be careful, however, about using the word "truth" in any argument. In theory, a statement is true if it conforms to reality; in practice, it is called "true" if available evidence gives it a high degree of probability. With minor exceptions, one can never be sure that any conclusion is absolutely true. Except in statements which repeat themselves ("Business is business" or "Either it is raining or it is not raining") or statements which express one's own immediate feelings ("I like pizza"), there always exists an element of doubt.

It is.routine exercise for Socratic teachers to call all their students' certainties into doubt, to demonstrate that what is called "truth" is, in fact, a high degree of probability. Can one be sure that Lyndon Johnson was President of the United States? Newspapers said he was, but newspapers frequently print error. In 1948, the *Chicago Tribune* announced that Thomas Dewey was elected President. Television showed Johnson as President, but that could have been part of a national hoax. In *Nineteen Eighty-four* the real rulers of Oceania used a fictitious Big Brother image to control the citizenry. The world agrees that Johnson was President, but there is some dissent. Inmates in mental hospitals who think they are Christ or Napoleon deny the existence of both Johnson and the twentieth century.

Despite such doubts, most people agree that Johnson was President. *And it is exactly this agreement which creates the "truth" of the statement.* Just as the words "telephone," "beauty," and "goodness" come to mean what a majority of people think they mean, so "truth" is whatever most people agree is true. Truth, as we know it, is statistically derived.

A man can insist that fire engines are red because he is expressing a general opinion. Though a "Napoleon" might call them a mass hallucination, he is sure that fire engines exist. Though the color-blind might cavil, he knows they are colored red. And though foreigners or semanticists might do otherwise, he uses the word "red." The reason he speaks the truth and the dissenters do not is that he is in the majority. If the majority did not perceive the engines, or saw them as green, or described them as "rouge," he would be locked up as a babbling, color-blind visionary. "Truth" is what people agree to call true.

To assert that moral, aesthetic, and factual arguments are statistically derived, is not to argue that there is no such thing as absolute goodness, beauty, or truth. It is to declare that these ultimate values have little relevance in practical argument. They have little relation to this book. (Much is expressed about the base of real-world argument in the story of two men in conversation: One muses, "I wonder if Rex Harrison is his real name." The other responds, "You wonder if Rex Harrison is whose real name?")

In argument, it is preferable to think in terms of probabilities and of the evidence which shapes probabilities. The following pages discuss kinds of evidence and ways of arranging evidence which give a conclusion a high or low degree of probability.

CAN ONE ARGUE THE TRUTH OF THESE STATEMENTS?

1. All men are created equal.

2. A valuable treasure chest is buried 306 feet below my chair.

3. Nothing does it like 7-Up!

4. Members of the Chicago Seven were guilty of the conspiracy charges brought against them by the federal government.

5. Springfield is the capitol of Illinois.

6. "The purest and most thoughtful minds are those which love color the most." —John Ruskin

7. Babe Ruth was a better baseball player than Dizzy Dean.

8. "The word *cohort* is always misused." —Jerome Beatty, Jr.

9. Abortion is a sin.

10. "Criminologists believe that only a stiffening of the moral fabric of the nation and a spiritual renaissance can halt the steady increase of crime." —*Newsweek*

"I switched the plates. . . ."

"I switched the plates. We'll be printing the real thing, and the
Treasury Department will be turning out counterfeits."

2

Induction

Polar bears are white.
The State Department is run by Communists.
Ban is preferred by 7 out of 10 American women.
Most labor leaders are crooks.
Women are better drivers than men.

Induction is the process of arriving at a general conclusion on the basis of incomplete information. Almost everything a person knows, he knows by induction.

One believes, for example, that polar bears are white. But because he has not seen all polar bears, his judgment is based on limited evidence. The two or three polar bears he has seen were white. Those he saw in *National Geographic* and in nature movies were white. Everyone he knows agrees they are white. From this information, he reasonably concludes that *all* polar bears are white. This process is induction. One considers evidence he has seen or heard to draw a conclusion about things he has not seen or heard. The intellectual move from limited facts — called a *sample* — to a general conviction is called an inductive leap.

Most conclusions regarding past, present, and future events are based on this kind of leap. One believes that Balboa discovered the Pacific Ocean, that taking aspirin eases a headache, that the Democrats will win the next presidential election. Because he can never secure all the evidence relating to these questions, he reasonably makes judgments from the facts he has.

It is equally reasonable, on hearing induced conclusions, to inquire about the number and kinds of facts which went into them. For a statement to be creditable, its sample must be (1) known, (2) sufficient, and (3) representative. If one is told simply that the U.S. State Department is directed by Communists, he can dismiss the charge on the ground that the sample is not *known*. No evidence is given to support the accusation. If he hears some noted person's IQ cited to demonstrate that all blacks (or whites) are intellectually inferior, he can respond that the sam-

6

ple is not *sufficient*. One example proves nothing about an entire race. And if he hears the cruelties of the Spanish Inquisition used to evidence the repressive views of Catholics in general, he can insist that the sample is not *representative*. Spanish practice in the Middle Ages is hardly typical of worldwide Catholicism today.

One frequently meets statements which simply lack evidence. Advertisements announce that "Ban is preferred by 7 out of 10 American women," that "Eight out of ten Hollywood stars use Lux toilet soap." Rumor whispers that Viceroy filters are made of harmful fiber glass and that smoking Kents may cause sterility. Such claims can safely be ignored until evidence is offered to support them.

A variation popular with sensational writers is to make an extravagant claim and point to concrete evidence—which happens to be unavailable. They charge that Warren Harding was murdered by his wife and that Franklin Roosevelt was poisoned by the Russians at Teheran—then regret that evidence is lost in the past. They affirm the existence of abominable snowmen, Atlantis, and the Loch Ness monster—then lament that proof is out of reach. They know that UFO's are extraterrestrial spaceships and that a massive conspiracy led to the assassination of President Kennedy—then insist that the U.S. Air Force, the F.B.I., and the C.I.A. are withholding crucial evidence. These too are inductions based on an absent sample.

Induction with an insufficient sample is equally common. One regularly hears charges like these:

> Most labor leaders are crooks. Look at Dave Beck, Frank Brewster, and Jimmy Hoffa.
> The peacetime draft is unfair. Let me tell you what happened to my brother.
> Don't talk to me about Puerto Ricans. I lived next to a Puerto Rican family for two years.

Clearly the indicated samples—*three* labor leaders, *one* brother, *one* family—are inadequate to justify any broad conclusion.

Spokesmen commonly try to broaden the effect of limited examples by declaring them "average" or "typical." They remain limited examples. (In argument, the word "average" deserves immediate suspicion.)

A sample is said to be unrepresentative when it is not typical of the whole class of things being studied. It is easy to see that one cannot gauge his town's attitude toward liquor taxes by polling only the citizens at the corner bar or only members of the local W.C.T.U. chapter.

But conclusions based on an unrepresentative sample can be quite deceptive on first hearing: e.g., "Women are better drivers than men; they have fewer accidents." Here the sample is large enough—a substantial body of accident statistics—but it is not broad enough to be meaningful. The conclusion concerns *all* drivers, but the sample group includes only drivers who have had accidents. To be representative (i.e., typical of the whole area under investigation), the sample must include all four groups involved:

1. men
2. women
3. drivers who had accidents
4. drivers who had no accidents.

With this broad sample one can see that there are fewer women in automobile accidents because there are fewer women driving. The isolated accident statistics are meaningless if not compared to those for all drivers.

Similarly, if one hears that 70 percent of all lung-cancer victims are moderate-to-heavy smokers, or that 80 percent of all San Quentin convicts come from homes which served liquor, he can draw no significant conclusion. The sample includes only cancer victims and convicts; there is no general data with which to make comparison. Perhaps 70 percent of *all* people are moderate smokers and 80 percent of *all* homes serve liquor; then, of course, the statistics would be completely meaningless.

Any induced conclusion is open to question, then, if its sample is too small or is unduly weighted in some way. The Nielsen rating service claims to know the audience size for American television programs. But because its data comes from 1100 audiometers (one for every 50,000 homes), the sufficiency of the sample is doubtful. The Kinsey Report was said to reveal the sexual habits of American women. But because the information came from 5940 women—most of whom were well-educated, white, non-Catholic, and Gentile, and all of whom were willing to describe their sex lives to interviewers—the representativeness of the sample is open to question. (Any poll with a selective sample—i.e., where some individuals choose to respond to it and others do not—is unrepresentative.)

A person can misuse a poll to make it substantiate a desired opinion. He can question a carefully selected group and claim that their answers represent a general view. (In 1968, before the New Hampshire primary and before he bowed out of the race, President Johnson revealed a "confidential poll" which showed him more popular in the state than any of his Republican rivals. He neglected to say his survey had been taken in a Democratic county.) He can phrase a poll question to draw the response he seeks. (In 1967 all Alabama parents were asked to respond to a questionnaire: "I [We] prefer that my [our] child shall be taught by a teacher of the following race: White. Negro. Other.") Or he can announce the results of a poll which probably never was made. (In November 1968, several days before the candidate's defeat by a 3 to 1 margin, Alabama advertisements announced "Surveys show Perry Hooper has moved out front in the U.S. Senate race.")

What is an adequate sample on which to base an induction? There is no easy answer. Size varies with the character of the question and with the degree of probability one seeks. It should be remembered, however, that a small sample—if genuinely representative—can sustain a broad conclusion. George Gallup assesses American political opinion by polling 1500 individuals. But because his sample is chosen so that every adult American has an equal chance of being interviewed, the Gallup Poll (like similar polls) is a reliable source of information. The mathematical probability is that, 95 times out of 100, a selection of 1500 anonymous people will give results no more than 3 percentage points off the figures which would be obtained by interviewing every voter. (Such induction can have disturbing implications: On the night Senator Goldwater defeated Governor Rockefeller in the 1964 California primary, CBS Television took the returns from 42 out of 32,861 precincts, fed them to a vote-analysis computer, and declared the winner 38 minutes before the last polls closed.)

Even in everyday experience, one commonly uses very limited information to draw a tentative conclusion. This is not unreasonable. If one sees an acquaintance not wearing her engagement ring and acting despondently, he may speculate that she has broken her engagement. The evidence is not sufficient for him to offer condolences, but it is enough to keep him from making jokes about marriage. If one hears from a friend that a newly opened restaurant is disappointing, he will probably choose not to eat there—at least until he hears a contrary report. His conclusion is based on a minute sample, but it is all the sample he has. As his sample grows, so will his degree of conviction.

A final point. With induction, one should remember *Occam's razor*, i.e., the maxim that when a body of evidence exists, the simplest conclusion which expresses all of it is probably the best. A perfect illustration occurred in 1967 when New Orleans district attorney James Garrison sought to prove that Clay Shaw was involved in the assassination of President Kennedy. He submitted that Shaw's address book carried the entry "Lee Odom, P.O. Box 19106, Dallas, Texas" and that the number "PO 19106," when properly decoded became "WH 15601," the unlisted phone number of Jack Ruby, the slayer of Lee Oswald. (The process involved "unscrambling" the numerals and—since P and O equal 7 and 6 on a telephone dial—subtracting 1300.) Thus, Garrison used the entry in Shaw's address book as inductive evidence leading to a sensational conclusion. But Occam's razor suggests a simpler conclusion, one which proved to be a fact: Shaw was acquainted with a businessman named Lee Odom, whose Dallas address was Box 19106.

HOW VALID ARE THESE EXAMPLES OF INDUCTION?

1. In a study of possible relationship between pornography and antisocial behavior, questionnaires went to 7500 psychiatrists and psychoanalysts, whose listing in the directory of the American Psychological Association indicated clinical experience. Over 3400 of these professionals responded. The result: 7.4 percent of the psychiatrists and psychologists had cases in which they were convinced that pornography was a causal factor in antisocial behavior; an additional 9.4 percent were suspicious; 3.2 percent did not commit themselves; and 80 percent stated they had no cases in which a causal connection was suspected.

2. "Proven most effective against colds"—Listerine Antiseptic advertisement.

3. I'm not going to sign up for Professor Dendinger's class. Several of my friends had the course and disliked it.

4. When a rating service indicated that "The Walter Winchell File" ranked low in television popularity, Mr. Winchell,

taking a letter poll of the readers of his newspaper column, declared that his was the most popular of all Friday productions.

5. Arguing that eighteenth-century English poetry was essentially prosaic, Matthew Arnold offered a passage from "Pope's verse, take it almost where you will":

   > To Hounslow Heath I point, and Banstead Down;
   > Thence comes your mutton, and these chicks my own.

6. A study of 3400 New York citizens who had had recent heart attacks showed that 70 percent of them were 10–50 pounds overweight. Clearly, obesity is a cause of heart disease.

7. "I wouldn't marry a railroad man.
   I'll tell you the reason why.
   I never knew a railroad man
   Who wouldn't tell his wife a lie."
        — lyric from "I Am a Rovin' Gambler"

A Behavioral Study of Obedience[1]

STANLEY MILGRAM[2]

Obedience is as basic an element in the structure of social life as one can point to. Some system of authority is a requirement of all communal living, and it is only the man dwelling in isolation who is not forced to respond, through defiance or submission, to the commands of others. Obedience, as a determinant of behavior, is of particular relevance to our time. It has been reliably established that from 1933–45 millions of innocent persons were systematically slaughtered on command. Gas chambers were built, death camps were guarded, daily quotas of corpses were produced with the same efficiency as the manufacture of appliances. These inhumane policies may have originated in the mind of a single person, but they could only be carried out on a massive scale if a very large number of persons obeyed orders.

Obedience is the psychological mechanism that links individual action to political purpose. It is the dispositional cement that binds men to systems of authority. Facts of recent history and observation in daily life suggest that for many persons obedience may be a deeply ingrained behavior tendency, indeed, a prepotent impulse overriding training in ethics, sympathy, and moral conduct. C. P. Snow (1961) points to its importance when he writes:

When you think of the long and gloomy history of man, you will find more hideous crimes have been committed in the name of obedience than have ever been committed in the name of rebellion. If you doubt that, read William Shirer's "Rise and Fall of the Third Reich." The German Officer Corps were brought up in the most rigorous code of obedience . . . in the name of obedience they were party to, and assisted in, the most wicked large scale actions in the history of the world [p. 24].

While the particular form of obedience dealt with in the present study has its antecedents in these episodes, it must not be

Reprinted from the October 1963 *Journal of Abnormal and Social Psychology*, pp. 379–387.

[1]This research was supported by a grant (NSF G-17916) from the National Science Foundation. Exploratory studies conducted in 1960 were supported by a grant from the Higgins Fund at Yale University. The research assistance of Alan C. Elms and Jon Wayland is gratefully acknowledged.
[2]Now at Harvard University.

thought all obedience entails acts of aggression against others. Obedience serves numerous productive functions. Indeed, the very life of society is predicated on its existence. Obedience may be ennobling and educative and refer to acts of charity and kindness, as well as to destruction.

GENERAL PROCEDURE

A procedure was devised which seems useful as a tool for studying obedience (Milgram, 1961). It consists of ordering a naive subject to administer electric shock to a victim. A simulated shock generator is used, with 30 clearly marked voltage levels that range from 15 to 450 volts. The instrument bears verbal designations that range from Slight Shock to Danger: Severe Shock. The responses of the victim, who is a trained confederate of the experimenter, are standardized. The orders to administer shocks are given to the naive subject in the context of a "learning experiment" ostensibly set up to study the effects of punishment on memory. As the experiment proceeds the naive subject is commanded to administer increasingly more intense shocks to the victim, even to the point of reaching the level marked Danger: Severe Shock. Internal resistances become stronger, and at a certain point the subject refuses to go on with the experiment. Behavior prior to this rupture is considered "obedience," in that the subject complies with the commands of the experimenter. The point of rupture is the act of disobedience. A quantitative value is assigned to the subject's performance based on the maximum intensity shock he is willing to administer before he refuses to participate further. Thus for any particular subject and for any particular experimental condition the degree of obedience may be specified with a numerical value. The crux of the study is to systematically vary the factors believed to alter the degree of obedience to the experimental commands.

The technique allows important variables to be manipulated at several points in the experiment. One may vary aspects of the source of command, content and form of command, instrumentalities for its execution, target object, general social setting, etc. The problem, therefore, is not one of designing increasingly more numerous experimental conditions, but of selecting those that best illuminate the *process* of obedience from the sociopsychological standpoint.

Related Studies

The inquiry bears an important relation to philosophic analyses of obedience and authority (Arendt, 1958; Friedrich, 1958; Weber, 1947), an early experimental study of obedience by Frank (1944), studies in "authoritarianism" (Adorno, Frenkel-Brunswik, Levinson, & Sanford, 1950; Rokeach, 1961), and a recent series of analytic and empirical studies in social power (Cartwright, 1959). It owes much to the long concern with *suggestion* in social psychology, both in its normal forms (e.g., Binet, 1900) and in its clinical manifestations (Charcot, 1881). But it derives, in the first instance, from direct observation of a social fact; the individual who is commanded by a legitimate authority oridinarily obeys. Obedience comes easily and often. It is a ubiquitous and indispensable feature of social life.

METHOD

Subjects

The subjects were 40 males between the ages of 20 and 50, drawn from New Haven and the surrounding communities. Subjects were obtained by a newspaper advertisement and direct mail solicitation. Those who responded to the appeal believed they were to participate in a study of memory and learning at Yale University. A wide range of occupations is represented in the sample. Typical subjects were postal clerks, high school teachers, salesmen, engineers, and laborers. Subjects ranged in educational level from one who had not finished elementary school, to those who had doctorate and other professional degrees. They were paid $4.50 for their participation in the experiment. However, subjects were told that payment was simply for coming to the laboratory, and that the money was theirs no matter what happened after they arrived. Table 1 shows the proportion of age and occupational types assigned to the experimental condition.

Personnel and Locale

The experiment was conducted on the grounds of Yale University in the elegant interaction laboratory. (This detail is relevant to the perceived legitimacy of the experiment. In further variations, the experiment was dissociated from the university, with consequences for performance.) The role of experimenter was played by a 31-year-old high school teacher of biology. His manner was impassive, and his appearance

TABLE 1
DISTRIBUTION OF AGE AND OCCUPATIONAL TYPES
IN THE EXPERIMENT

Occupations	20–29 years n	30–39 years n	40–50 years n	Percentage of total (Occupations)
Workers, skilled and unskilled	4	5	6	37.5
Sales, business, and white-collar	3	6	7	40.0
Professional	1	5	3	22.5
Percentage of total (Age)	20	40	40	

Note. — Total $N = 40$.

somewhat stern throughout the experiment. He was dressed in a gray technician's coat. The victim was played by a 47-year-old accountant, trained for the role; he was of Irish-American stock, whom most observers found mild-mannered and likable.

Procedure

One naive subject and one victim (an accomplice) performed in each experiment. A pretext had to be devised that would justify the administration of electric shock by the naive subject. This was effectively accomplished by the cover story. After a general introduction on the presumed relation between punishment and learning, subjects were told:

But actually, we know *very little* about the effect of punishment on learning, because almost no truly scientific studies have been made of it in human beings.

For instance, we don't know how *much* punishment is best for learning—and we don't know how much difference it makes as to who is giving the punishment, whether an adult learns best from a younger or an older person than himself—or many things of that sort.

So in this study we are bringing together a number of adults of different occupations and ages. And we're asking some of them to be teachers and some of them to be learners.

We want to find out just what effect different people have on each other as teachers and learners, and also what effect *punishment* will have on learning in this situation.

Therefore, I'm going to ask one of you to be the teacher here tonight and the other one to be the learner.

Does either of you have a preference?

Subjects then drew slips of paper from a hat to determine who would be the teacher and who would be the learner in the experiment. The drawing was rigged so that the naive subject was always the teacher and the accomplice always the learner. (Both slips contained the word "Teacher.") Immediately after the drawing, the teacher and learner were taken to an adjacent room and the learner was strapped into an "electric chair" apparatus.

The experimenter explained that the straps were to prevent excessive movement while the learner was being shocked. The effect was to make it impossible for him to escape from the situation. An electrode was attached to the learner's wrist, and electrode paste was applied "to avoid blisters and burns." Subjects were told that the electrode was attached to the shock generator in the adjoining room.

In order to improve credibility the experimenter declared, in response to a question by the learner: "Although the shocks can be extremely painful, they cause no permanent tissue damage."

Learning task. The lesson administered by the subject was a paired-associate learning task. The subject read a series of word pairs to the learner, and then read the first word of the pair along with four terms. The learner was to indicate which of the four terms had originally been paired with the first word. He communicated his answer by pressing one of four switches in front of him, which in turn lit up one of four numbered quadrants in an answer box located atop the shock generator.

Shock generator. The instrument panel consists of 30 lever switches set in a horizontal line. Each switch is clearly labeled with a voltage designation that ranges from 15 to 450 volts. There is a 15-volt increment from one switch to the next going from left to right. In addition, the following verbal designations are clearly indicated for groups of four switches going from left to right: Slight Shock, Moderate Shock, Strong Shock, Very Strong Shock, Intense Shock, Extreme Intensity Shock, Danger: Severe Shock. (Two switches after this last designation are simply marked XXX.)

Upon depressing a switch: a pilot light corresponding to each switch is illuminated in bright red; an electric buzzing is heard;

an electric blue light, labeled "voltage energizer," flashes; the dial on the voltage meter swings to the right; various relay clicks are sounded.

The upper left-hand corner of the generator is labeled Shock Generator, Type ZLB, Dyson Instrument Company, Waltham, Mass. Output 15 Volts–450 Volts.

Details of the instrument were carefully handled to insure an appearance of authenticity. The panel was engraved by precision industrial engravers, and all components were of high quality. No subject in the experiment suspected that the instrument was merely a simulated shock generator.[3]

Sample shock. Each naive subject is given a sample shock on the shock generator, prior to beginning his run as teacher. This shock is always 45 volts, and is applied by pressing the third switch of the generator. The shock is applied to the wrist of the naive subject, and has its source in a 45-volt battery wired into the generator. This further convinces the subject of the authenticity of the generator.

Shock instructions. The subject is told to administer a shock to the learner each time he gives a wrong response. Moreover — and this is the key command — the subject is instructed to "move one level higher on the shock generator each time the learner flashes a wrong answer." He is also instructed to announce the voltage level before administering a shock. This serves to continually remind subjects of the increasing intensity of shocks administered to the learner.

Preliminary and regular run. Pretests revealed that the procedure of reading words and administering shocks requires some practice before it can be handled smoothly. Therefore, immediately preceding the regular run, the teacher is given a preliminary series of 10 words to read to the learner. There are 3 neutral words in the practice series (i.e., words that the learner answers correctly), so that shocks are administered for 7 of the words, with the maximum shock at 105 volts (moderate shock).

[3]A related technique, making use of a shock generator, was reported by Buss (1961) for the study of aggression in the laboratory. Despite the considerable similarity of technical detail in the experimental procedures, both investigators proceeded in ignorance of the other's work. Milgram provided plans and photographs of his shock generator, experimental procedure, and first results in a report to the National Science Foundation in January 1961. This report received only limited circulation. Buss reported his procedure 6 months later, but to a wider audience. Subsequently, technical information and reports were exchanged. The present article was first received in the Editor's office on December 27, 1961; it was resubmitted with deletions on July 27, 1962.

Almost all subjects master the procedure by the time the preliminary run is over.

Subjects are then presented with a second list, and are told
that the procedure is the same as for the first list; the experimenter adds, however:

When you get to the bottom of the list, repeat it over again, and
continue giving shocks, until the learner has learned all the pairs
correctly.

The experimenter instructs the subject to

start from 15 volts and increase the shock level one step each time
the learner gives a wrong answer.

Feedback from the victim. In all conditions the learner gives a
predetermined set of responses to the word pair test, based on a
schedule of approximately three wrong answers to one correct
answer. In the present experimental condition no vocal response
or other sign of protest is heard from the learner until Shock Level
300 is reached. When the 300-volt shock is administered, the
learner pounds on the wall of the room in which he is bound to
the electric chair. The pounding can be heard by the subject.
From this point on, the learner's answers no longer appear on
the four-way panel.

At this juncture, subjects ordinarily turn to the experimenter
for guidance. The experimenter instructs the subject to treat
the absence of a response as a wrong answer, and to shock the
subject according to the usual schedule. He advises the subjects
to allow 5–10 seconds before considering no response as a wrong
answer, and to increase the shock level one step each time the
learner fails to respond correctly. The learner's pounding is repeated after the 315-volt shock is administered; afterwards he
is not heard from, nor do his answers reappear on the four-way
signal box.

Experimenter feedback. At various points in the experiment
the subject may turn to the experimenter for advice on whether
he should continue to administer shocks. Or he may indicate that
he does not wish to go on. It was important to standardize the
experimenter's responses to these inquiries and reactions.

If the subject indicated his unwillingness to go on, the experimenter responded with a sequence of "prods," using as many as
necessary to bring the subject into line.

Prod 1: Please continue, *or* Please go on.
Prod 2: The experiment requires that you continue.

Prod 3: It is absolutely essential that you continue.
Prod 4: You have no other choice, you *must* go on.

The prods were always made in sequence: Only if Prod 1 had
been unsuccessful, could Prod 2 be used. If the subject refused
to obey the experimenter after Prod 4, the experiment was terminated. The experimenter's tone of voice was at all times firm,
but not impolite. The sequence was begun anew on each occasion
that the subject balked or showed reluctance to follow orders.

Special prods. If the subject asked if the learner was liable
to suffer permanent physical injury, the experimenter said:

Although the shocks may be painful, there is no permanent tissue
damage, so please go on. [Followed by Prods 2, 3, and 4 if necessary.]

If the subject said that the learner did not want to go on, the
experimenter replied:

Whether the learner likes it or not, you must go on until he has
learned all the word pairs correctly. So please go on. [Followed by
Prods 2, 3, and 4 if necessary.]

Dependent Measures

The primary dependent measure for any subject is the maximum shock he administers before he refuses to go any further.
In principle this may vary from 0 (for a subject who refuses to
administer even the first shock) to 30 (for a subject who administers the highest shock on the generator). A subject who
breaks off the experiment at any point prior to administering
the thirtieth shock level is termed a *defiant* subject. One who
complies with experimental commands fully, and proceeds to
administer all shock levels commanded, is termed an *obedient*
subject.

Further records. With few exceptions, experimental sessions
were recorded on magnetic tape. Occasional photographs were
taken through one-way mirrors. Notes were kept on any unusual
behavior occurring during the course of the experiments. On
occasion, additional observers were directed to write objective
descriptions of the subjects' behavior. The latency and duration
of shocks were measured by accurate timing devices.

Interview and dehoax. Following the experiment subjects
were interviewed; open-ended questions, projective measures,
and attitude scales were employed. After the interview, procedures were undertaken to assure that the subject would leave

the laboratory in a state of well being. A friendly reconciliation was arranged between the subject and the victim, and an effort was made to reduce any tensions that arose as a result of the experiment.

RESULTS

Preliminary Notions

Before giving an account of the experimental results, it is instructive to consider how persons predict others will perform when commanded to administer powerful shocks to another person. Fourteen Yale seniors, all psychology majors, were provided with a detailed description of the experimental situation. They were asked to reflect carefully on it, and to predict the behavior of 100 hypothetical subjects. More specifically, they were instructed to plot the distribution of obedience of "100 Americans of diverse occupations, and ranging in age from 20 to 50 years," who were placed in the experimental situation.

There was considerable agreement among the respondents on the expected behavior of hypothetical subjects. All respondents predicted that only an insignificant minority would go through to the end of the shock series. (The estimates ranged from 0 to 3%; i.e., the most "pessimistic" member of the class predicted that of 100 persons, 3 would continue through to the most potent shock available on the shock generator—450 volts.) The class mean was 1.2%. The question was also posed informally to colleagues of the author, and the most general feeling was that few if any subjects would go beyond the designation Very Strong Shock.

Result of Experiment I

Subjects accept situation. With few exceptions subjects were convinced of the reality of the experimental situation, that they were administering shocks to another person, and the most potent shocks were extremely painful. In the post-experimental interview subjects were asked: "How painful to the learner were the last few shocks that you administered to him?" Subjects were instructed to indicate their answers on a printed 14-point scale ranging from "Not at all painful" to "Extremely painful." The modal response was 14 (Extremely painful) with the mean at 13.42.

Signs of extreme tension. Many subjects showed signs of nervousness in the experimental situation, and especially upon administering the more powerful shocks. In a large number of cases the degree of tension reached extremes that are rarely seen in sociopsychological laboratory studies. Subjects were observed to sweat, tremble, stutter, bite their lips, groan, and dig their fingernails into their flesh. These were characteristic rather than exceptional responses to the experiment.

One sign of tension was the regular occurrence of nervous laughing fits. Fourteen of the 40 subjects showed definite signs of nervous laughter and smiling. The laughter seemed entirely out of place, even bizarre. Full-blown, uncontrollable seizures were observed for 3 subjects. On one occasion we observed a seizure so violently convulsive that it was necessary to call a halt to the experiment. The subject, a 46-year-old encyclopedia salesman, was seriously embarrassed by his untoward and uncontrollable behavior. In the post-experimental interviews subjects took pains to point out that they were not sadistic types, and that the laughter did not mean they enjoyed shocking the victim.

Distribution of scores. It has been conjectured that persons would not, in general, agree to administer shocks beyond the level designated as Very Strong Shock. The distribution of maximum shocks for this experiment is shown in Table 2. The obtained distribution of scores deviates radically from the prediction.

Upon command of the experimenter, each of the 40 subjects went beyond the expected breakoff point. No subject stopped prior to administering Shock Level 20. (At this level — 300 volts — the victim kicks on the wall and no longer provides answers to the teacher's multiple-choice questions.)

Of the 40 subjects, 5 refused to obey the experimental commands beyond the 300-volt level. Four more subjects administered one further shock, and then refused to go on. Two broke off at the 330-volt level, and 1 each at 345, 360, and 375 volts. Thus a total of 14 subjects defied the experimenter. It is instructive to reprint their remarks at the point of defiance, as transcribed from the tape recordings:

[0124] I think he's trying to communicate, he's knocking. . . . Well it's not fair to shock the guy . . . these are terrific volts. I don't think this is very humane. . . . Oh, I can't go on with this; no, this isn't right.

TABLE 2
Distribution of Breakoff Points

Verbal designation and voltage indication	Number of subjects for whom this was maximum shock
Slight Shock	
15	0
30	0
45	0
60	0
Moderate Shock	
75	0
90	0
105	0
120	0
Strong Shock	
135	0
150	0
165	0
180	0
Very Strong Shock	
195	0
210	0
225	0
240	0
Intense Shock	
255	0
270	0
285	0
300	5
Extreme Intensity Shock	
315	4
330	2
345	1
360	1
Danger: Severe Shock	
375	1
390	0
405	0
420	0
XXX	
435	0
450	26

It's a hell of an experiment. The guy is suffering in there. No, I don't want to go on. This is crazy. [Subject refused to administer more shocks.]

[0123] He's banging in there. I'm gonna chicken out. I'd like to continue, but I can't do that to a man. . . . I'm sorry I can't do that to a man. I'll hurt his heart. You take your check. . . . No really, I couldn't do it.

These subjects were frequently in a highly agitated and even angered state. Sometimes, verbal protest was at a minimum, and the subject simply got up from his chair in front of the shock generator, and indicated that he wished to leave the laboratory.

Of the 40 subjects, 26 obeyed the orders of the experimenter to the end, proceeding to punish the victim until they reached the most potent shock available on the shock generator. At that point, the experimenter called a halt to the session. (The maximum shock is labeled 450 volts, and is two steps beyond the designation: Danger: Severe Shock.) Although obedient subjects continued to administer shocks, they often did so under extreme stress. Some expressed reluctance to administer shocks beyond the 300-volt level, and displayed fears similar to those who defied the experimenter; yet they obeyed.

After the maximum shocks had been delivered, and the experimenter called a halt to the proceedings, many obedient subjects heaved sighs of relief, mopped their brows, rubbed their fingers over their eyes, or nervously fumbled cigarettes. Some shook their heads, apparently in regret. Some subjects had remained calm throughout the experiment, and displayed only minimal signs of tension from beginning to end.

DISCUSSION

The experiment yielded two findings that were surprising. The first finding concerns the sheer strength of obedient tendencies manifested in this situation. Subjects have learned from childhood that it is a fundamental breach of moral conduct to hurt another person against his will. Yet, 26 subjects abandon this tenet in following the instructions of an authority who has no special powers to enforce his commands. To disobey would bring no material loss to the subject; no punishment would ensue. It is clear from the remarks and outward behavior of many participants that in punishing the victim they are often acting against their own values. Subjects often expressed deep disapproval of shocking a man in the face of his objections, and others denounced it as stupid and senseless. Yet the majority complied with the experimental commands. This outcome was surprising from two perspectives: first, from the standpoint of predictions made in the questionnaire described earlier. (Here, however, it is possible that the remoteness of the respondents from the actual situation, and the difficulty of conveying to them the concrete details of the experiment, could account for the serious underestimation of obedience.)

But the results were also unexpected to persons who observed the experiment in progress, through one-way mirrors. Observers often uttered expressions of disbelief upon seeing a subject administer more powerful shocks to the victim. These persons had a full acquaintance with the details of the situation, and yet systematically underestimated the amount of obedience that subjects would display.

The second unanticipated effect was the extraordinary tension generated by the procedures. One might suppose that a subject would simply break off or continue as his conscience dictated. Yet, this is very far from what happened. There were striking reactions of tension and emotional strain. One observer related:

I observed a mature and initially poised businessman enter the laboratory smiling and confident. Within 20 minutes he was reduced to a twitching, stuttering wreck, who was rapidly approaching a point of nervous collapse. He constantly pulled on his earlobe, and twisted his hands. At one point he pushed his fist into his forehead and muttered: "Oh, God, let's stop it." And yet he continued to respond to every word of the experimenter, and obeyed to the end.

Any understanding of the phenomenon of obedience must rest on an analysis of the particular conditions in which it occurs. The following features of the experiment go some distance in explaining the high amount of obedience observed in the situation.

1. The experiment is sponsored by and takes place on the grounds of an institution of unimpeachable reputation, Yale University. It may be reasonably presumed that the personnel are competent and reputable. The importance of this background authority is now being studied by conducting a series of experiments outside of New Haven, and without any visible ties to the university.

2. The experiment is, on the face of it, designed to attain a worthy purpose—advancement of knowledge about learning and memory. Obedience occurs not as an end in itself, but as an instrumental element in a situation that the subject construes

as significant, and meaningful. He may not be able to see its full significance, but he may properly assume that the experimenter does.

3. The subject perceives that the victim has voluntarily submitted to the authority system of the experimenter. He is not (at first) an unwilling captive impressed for involuntary service. He has taken the trouble to come to the laboratory presumably to aid the experimental research. That he later becomes an involuntary subject does not alter the fact that, initially, he consented to participate without qualification. Thus he has in some degree incurred an obligation toward the experimenter.

4. The subject, too, has entered the experiment voluntarily, and perceives himself under obligation to aid the experimenter. He has made a commitment, and to disrupt the experiment is a repudiation of his initial promise of aid.

5. Certain features of the procedure strengthen the subject's sense of obligation to the experimenter. For one, he has been paid for coming to the laboratory. In part this is canceled out by the experimenter's statement that:

> Of course, as in all experiments, the money is yours simply for coming to the laboratory. From this point on, no matter what happens, the money is yours.[4]

6. From the subject's standpoint, the fact that he is the teacher and the other man the learner is purely a chance consequence (it is determined by drawing lots) and he, the subject, ran the same risk as the other man in being assigned the role of learner. Since the assignment of positions in the experiment was achieved by fair means, the learner is deprived of any basis of complaint on this count. (A similar situation obtains in Army units, in which—in the absence of volunteers—a particularly dangerous mission may be assigned by drawing lots, and the unlucky soldier is expected to bear his misfortune with sportsmanship.)

7. There is, at best, ambiguity with regard to the prerogatives of a psychologist and the corresponding rights of his subject. There is a vagueness of expectation concerning what a psychologist may require of his subject, and when he is overstepping acceptable limits. Moreover, the experiment occurs in a closed setting, and thus provides no opportunity for the subject to remove these ambiguities by discussion with others. There are few

[4] Forty-three subjects, undergraduates at Yale University, were run in the experiment without payment. The results are very similar to those obtained with paid subjects.

standards that seem directly applicable to the situation, which
is a novel one for most subjects.

8. The subjects are assured that the shocks administered
to the subject are "painful but not dangerous." Thus they assume
that the discomfort caused the victim is momentary, while the
scientific gains resulting from the experiment are enduring.

9. Through Shock Level 20 the victim continues to provide
answers on the signal box. The subject may construe this as a
sign that the victim is still willing to "play the game." It is only
after Shock Level 20 that the victim repudiates the rules completely, refusing to answer further.

These features help to explain the high amount of obedience
obtained in this experiment. Many of the arguments raised need
not remain matters of speculation, but can be reduced to testable
propositions to be confirmed or disproved by further experiments.[5]

The following features of the experiment concern the nature
of the conflict which the subject faces.

10. The subject is placed in a position in which he must
respond to the competing demands of two persons: the experimenter and the victim. The conflict must be resolved by meeting
the demands of one or the other; satisfaction of the victim and
the experimenter are mutually exclusive. Moreover, the resolution must take the form of a highly visible action, that of continuing to shock the victim or breaking off the experiment. Thus
the subject is forced into a public conflict that does not permit
any completely satisfactory solution.

11. While the demands of the experimenter carry the weight
of scientific authority, the demands of the victim spring from
his personal experience of pain and suffering. The two claims
need not be regarded as equally pressing and legitimate. The
experimenter seeks an abstract scientific datum; the victim
cries out for relief from physical suffering caused by the subject's actions.

12. The experiment gives the subject little time for reflection.
The conflict comes on rapidly. It is only minutes after the subject
has been seated before the shock generator that the victim begins
his protests. Moreover, the subject perceives that he has gone
through but two-thirds of the shock levels at the time the subject's first protests are heard. Thus he understands that the
conflict will have a persistent aspect to it, and may well become

---

[5]A series of recently completed experiments employing the obedience paradigm
is reported in Milgram (1964).

more intense as increasingly more powerful shocks are required. The rapidity with which the conflict descends on the subject, and his realization that it is predictably recurrent may well be sources of tension to him.

13. At a more general level, the conflict stems from the opposition of two deeply ingrained behavior dispositions: first, the disposition not to harm other people, and second, the tendency to obey those whom we perceive to be legitimate authorities.

REFERENCES

Adorno, T., Frenkel-Brunswik, Else, Levinson, D. J., & Sanford, R. N. *The authoritarian personality.* New York: Harper, 1950.

Arendt, H. What was authority? In C. J. Friedrich (Ed.), *Authority.* Cambridge: Harvard Univer. Press, 1958. Pp. 81–112.

Binet, A. *La suggestibilité.* Paris: Schleicher, 1900.

Buss, A. H. *The psychology of aggression.* New York: Wiley, 1961.

Cartwright, S. (Ed.) *Studies in social power.* Ann Arbor: University of Michigan Institute for Social Research, 1959.

Charcot, J. M. *Oeuvres complètes.* Paris: Bureaux du Progrès Médical, 1881.

Frank, J. D. Experimental studies of personal pressure and resistance. *J. gen. Psychol.,* 1944. **30**, 23–64.

Friedrich, C. J. (Ed.) *Authority.* Cambridge: Harvard Univer. Press, 1958.

Milgram, S. Dynamics of obedience. Washington: National Science Foundation, 25 January 1961. (Mimeo)

Milgram, S. Some conditions of obedience and disobedience to authority. *Hum. Relat.,* 1964, in press.

Rokeach, M. Authority, authoritarianism, and conformity. In I. A. Berg & B. M. Bass (Eds.) *Conformity and deviation.* New York: Harper, 1961. Pp. 230–257.

Snow, C. P. Either-or. *Progressive,* 1961(Feb.) 24.

Weber, M. *The theory of social and economic organization.* Oxford: Oxford Univer. Press, 1947.

DISCUSSION QUESTIONS

1. What is the implicit conclusion of the study? To whom does it apply?

2. Why does the author contrast the results of this experiment with the result anticipated by fourteen psychology majors at Yale?

3. Can a brief experiment testing 40 persons "from New Haven and surrounding communities" lead to any reasonable conclusions about American citizens, about German history, about human nature?

4. What is the point of Table 1 [Distribution of Age and Occupational Types in the Experiment]?

5. Assuming the reader tends to relate this experiment to certain atrocity situations in recent history, comment on the purpose of notations 1–13 in the "Discussion" which concludes the article. Considering this purpose, can you mention any facts the author might have added?

6. Why does the essay relate the results of this experiment (i.e., the "cruel" actions of most of the members of the sample) to C. P. Snow's statement that "The German Officer Corps were brought up in the most rigorous code of obedience"?

7. Why does the author spell out the appearance (dress, manner, etc.) of the experimenter and of the victim? Is this different from his description of the electrical equipment?

The Armed Citizen

An armed robber was startled when Dallas, Tex., cab driver Sam Putnam refused to be robbed and instead got out of his cab. The gunman also got out and found himself staring across the car roof into the barrel of a gun held by Putnam. He surrendered to Putnam, who radioed for police. *(Dallas, Tex., Morning News)*

When a motorcycle gang of about 25 surrounded the home of Tony Palmer, Cleveland, Ohio, and threatened those inside, Mrs. Palmer grabbed a .22 rifle and fired 11 shots through windows at tires. Her hits stranded seven of the intruders, who were arrested by police. *(Cleveland, Ohio, Plain Dealer)*

When Pat King, 17, of El Monte, Calif., saw two men drive repeatedly by his father's dairy store, he laid a .38 revolver near the cash register. Soon afterward, the men entered the store. One flourished a pistol and announced that it was a stickup. King immediately opened fire, wounding both bandits. *(Pasadena, Calif., Star News)*

Two holdup men entered the Union County, Ind., home of Carl Burris, 84, bound Burris and his wife, and began to steal the couple's furniture. Burris freed himself, took a shotgun from a closet, killed one intruder and held the other until police arrived. The holdup men's gun was found to be a toy. *(Cincinnati, Ohio, Post and Times-Star)*

After two masked gunmen broke into Press Montgomery's home in Springfield, Mo., and threatened him and his wife, Montgomery ran into the bedroom to get a .38 he kept hidden there. He fired three shots through the bedroom door, frightening the men away. *(Springfield, Mo., Leader and Press)*

When two men entered Samuel Hornstein's North Philadelphia, Pa., grocery store, and demanded money at gun point, Hornstein's son Allen began a scuffle with one of the men. Hornstein drew a .38 revolver and fired at the man wrestling with his son, hitting him in the chest. The wounded man fled. He was found by police and later died. The other robber surrendered. *(Philadelphia, Pa., Evening Bulletin)*

Reprinted from *The American Rifleman* (December 1969), p. 15.

A Los Angeles widow, Mrs. Shirley Morosco, awoke before dawn to discover a burglar ransacking her home. She took a pistol from under her pillow, tried to scare him away by shouting, then fired three shots. The burglar fled and died in a driveway a block away. Police recovered $83 and a ring taken from her home. *(Los Angeles, Calif., Herald Examiner)*

Mrs. Albert Austin of Memphis, Tenn., seeing two men breaking into a neighbor's house, called police. Her husband took a shotgun and held one of the men at bay until officers arrived. The other burglar was arrested trying to leave the house. *(Memphis, Tenn., Press-Scimitar)*

Noticing two suspicious youths entering his Roxbury, Mass., grocery, Abraham Whittenberg went behind the counter to be near his gun. One of the pair shot Whittenberg in the leg. Whittenberg mortally wounded one youth. The other escaped. *(Lowell, Mass., Sun)*

As Manager A. L. Dehlinger, of a Dallas, Tex., drive-in theater prepared to make a night bank deposit, two men approached him brandishing knives. He dropped his money into the depository slot and turned, gun in hand. The knife-wielding pair fled without a word. *(Dallas, Tex., Morning News)*

Seven men noisily invaded the yard of Mrs. Lorraine Rodriguez, San Pedro, Calif., one night while she was home alone. When she went outside, they threatened to beat her. Mrs. Rodriguez fired one shot from her cal. .38 revolver. All seven men ran. *(San Pedro, Calif., News Pilot)*

Awakened before dawn by screams of a house guest, former Norfolk, Va., mayor John Gurkin, 80, found an intruder attempting to rob several guests at gunpoint. Gurkin armed himself with a shotgun and chased the intruder from the house. *(Norfolk, Va., Ledger-Star)*

When a man entered Elmer Luckac's restaurant in Franklin, N. J., and drew a snubnosed revolver, Luckac didn't respond as expected. Instead of reaching for his money, he reached for a shotgun and frightened the would-be thief away. *(New Brunswick, N. J., Home News)*

• • •

An analysis of "The Armed Citizen" for 5 years, 1963-67, recently revealed that the mere presence of a firearm prevented crime, without the firing of a shot, in 121 incidents. In 112, a would-be assailant was killed and in 92 others he was wounded. Shooting as a rule cannot be justified, it should be emphasized, except where crime constitutes an immediate, imminent threat of violence to life or limb or, in some circumstances, property.

Above are accounts from clippings sent in by NRA Members.

DISCUSSION QUESTIONS

1. What is paradoxical about enumerating incidents in which "presence of a firearm" prevented a crime?

2. What is the conclusion to which these cases seem to tend?

3. How does this evidence relate to proposed legislation which
   (a) seeks to curb the mail-order sale of guns?
   (b) seeks to prohibit the sale of guns to minors, mental defectives, known criminals, etc.?
   (c) requires registration of all new guns sold?
   (d) aims to register all American guns?
   (e) might lead to the confiscation of all privately owned guns?

4. The argumentative sample consists of
   (a) the rewritten version
   (b) of a selection of clippings chosen by *The American Rifleman*
   (c) from news-stories which NRA members culled
   (d) from newspaper descriptions
   (e) of incidents in which armed citizens prevented crime.
   Comment on the sample as known, sufficient, and representative.

5. What meaningful conclusions can be drawn from the five-year analysis of "The Armed Citizen," 1963–1967?

Extrasensory Perception in the Laboratory

ERIC J. DINGWALL and JOHN LANGDON-DAVIES

The enormous interest aroused by the earlier scientific researches into hypnotism and suggestion may be said in a way to have been a handicap to scientific psychical research. People who were determined not to believe in any paranormal phenomena, and who had had to be content hitherto with putting everything down to fraud, were now able to find an alternative explanation.

"Yes," they said. "I dare say that sort of thing happens, but it is all due to suggestion. The human mind is so suggestible that it can be fooled into believing or experiencing anything."

Needless to say, such people seldom took the trouble to examine the alleged phenomena.

There were always sufficient fraudulent cases or cases of innocent self-deception to justify a closed mind toward the whole matter. For those who felt there was something to investigate there was only one way to break down this opposition. It was to find a method of examining paranormal phenomena which equaled the laboratory technique in other kinds of scientific research.

Now, a research scientist carrying out an experiment is very often required, by his own conscience as well as by the critical attitude of his colleagues, to answer the following question: I have got the result I wanted or expected, but does this prove my theory to be correct, or is the result due to pure chance?

In many cases chance cannot be ruled out altogether, except by repeating the experiment an almost infinite number of times, which, in practice, cannot possibly be done, and then the scientist will look about for some way of estimating the odds against chance being the sole explanation for the limited number of repetitions that he can do. There is a branch of mathematics which deals with this problem. It has established laws of probability which can be used for estimating the odds against chance.

If, by using these rules, a chemist, let us say, finds that the odds are 20 to 1 or more against chance explaining his results, he will feel fairly certain that his result is a valuable one. Now

Reprinted from *The Unknown—Is It Nearer?* (New York: New American Library, 1956), pp. 45–55.

32

the problem with paranormal phenomena was that after ruling out all such things as fraud and human error, both innocent and deliberate, there was no way of ruling out coincidence. If a person dreams of an accident to the railway train on which he was going next day to Edinburgh, and puts off the journey, and if the accident actually happens to the train, there is no way of ruling out coincidence, because, for example, we cannot tell how often people put off going by a train because they have a pre-sentiment of an accident that does not take place.

The question, therefore, which sooner or later had to arise in the minds of psychical research workers was this: Can I arrange an experiment, perhaps in telepathy, in which I can estimate accurately the odds of any results being due to chance, so that I can say to my orthodox critics, "You are content with 20-to-1 odds against chance for your results; here are results in which the odds are 200, 2000 or 20,000 to 1 against chance?"

Among pioneers of this kind of experimental work four require special mention. As long ago as 1885 F. Y. Edgeworth showed how the "calculus of probabilities" could be used to show how likely or unlikely it was that any particular psychical phenomenon was due merely to chance. It is worthwhile quoting the last sentence of his paper on this: "Such is the evidence which the calculus of probabilities affords as to the existence of an agency other than mere chance. The calculus is silent as to the nature of that agency—whether it is more likely to be vulgar illusion or extraordinary law. That is a question to be decided, not by formulae and figures, but by general philosophy and common sense."

In 1888 the great French physiologist Charles Richet laid down three rules to be observed in all psychical research. All supposed paranormal phenomena are useless as evidence unless (1) the conscious good faith of all concerned is undoubted; (2) the unconscious bad faith of all concerned, including oneself, is suspected; (3) "We have no right to insist in the case of psychic phenomena on a greater probability than we do in other sciences and if the odds are above 1,000 to 1, one has a sufficiently rigorous proof."

In 1895 Mrs. A. W. Verrall did a number of card-guessing experiments which were statistically analyzed by C. P. Sanger, F.S.S. The results were divided into those where chance was a sufficient explanation and those where a further explanation was called for.

In 1928 Miss Ina Jephson, helped by R. A. Fisher, F.R.S., did a large number of statistically analyzable card experiments with very interesting results. A side effect of her work was the realization that with an ordinary pack of playing cards any extrasensory perception might be interfered with and masked by a person's preference for particular cards. This led to the substitution of the Zener pack for the usual pack of playing cards.

These and others made possible the well-known work of Dr. J. B. Rhine and his colleagues at Duke University. What Dr. Rhine added was his American genius for mass production. He saw that very large numbers of experiments must be carried through, and helped by advances in the science of statistics, he was able to devise techniques which made this possible. It is important to give Dr. Rhine due credit, because a great deal of his early work can be criticized on grounds of faulty technique. Some, though not all, of his results can be impeached only by those who are determined not to accept any existence of E.S.P. (extrasensory perception).

As we shall see later, Dr. S. G. Soal, following up and improving on Dr. Rhine's technique, has since produced results which seem to be unassailable from any point of view. As most people know, Rhine's experiments involve the use of a pack of 25 cards called Zener cards. In their original form the pack consisted of 5 "suits." There were 5 crosses, 5 squares, 5 circles, 5 stars, and 5 wavy lines. A typical experiment in its simplest form would be that the experimenter would look at each card in turn and as he looked at each card the experimental guinea-pig, known as the percipient, would write down to which suit he believed the card belonged. When all 25 cards have been guessed, the right guesses are added up and the experiment repeated *ad lib.*

The point of the experiment is that we know exactly how many right guesses to expect if there is nothing but chance behind the guess. There will be 5 right guesses per set of 25 cards. Of course, this does not mean that the exact number 5 will be guessed right on each occasion; if we toss a coin long enough it will turn up an equal number of tails and heads, but this does not mean that if we toss it ten times there will be 5 heads and 5 tails. If there is nothing but pure chance in the card guesses, as time goes on the right guesses will approximate to 1 in 5. There may never be exactly 5 right guesses in any one set of 25, but the average will come closer and closer to 5.

Now suppose that when a man has guessed through the pack 20 times it is found that his average is not, say, 4¾ or 5½ per 25 cards, but 7 or 8 or 9, can we say that there must be some other explanation besides chance? No, we cannot, because for all we know by the time he had guessed through the pack a million times (if that were possible) his average might be much closer to 5.

But there is something that we can do which is of the greatest importance. The laws of probability can provide us with a mathematical formula which tells us how unlikely it is that any particular result is due to nothing but chance. Without entering into the mathematics, anyone will see that the degree of unlikelihood will depend on two things: first, the extent to which the average deviates from 5; and, second, the total number of guesses.

Thus, if a man only guesses once through a pack and has 10 right guesses, we are not justified in drawing any conclusions, any more than we would be if a coin tossed up only ten times came down heads eight times. If after 2,500 guesses he has an average of 7, i.e., 700 right guesses instead of the expected 500, then by using the mathematical formula we can say exactly what the odds are against pure chance explaining his success. A smaller degree of success over a very long series of trials is more impressive than a larger degree in only one or two.

It will be seen that such a guessing experiment has precisely the advantage for parapsychology over most kinds of evidence that is required, if the study of paranormal phenomena is to be put on the same level as the scientific study of any other kind of phenomena.

Now, what were the results of the card-guessing experiments? In a majority of cases people who guessed through packs of Zener cards produced no significant results whatever; i.e., their average guesses were not sufficiently above or below 5 to suggest that anything but chance guided them. But quite soon some notable exceptions were found. Men and women turned up whose guesses were so far above expectation that the odds against chance were not a matter of 20 to 200 or 2,000 to 1, but a million or a million million or even 1-with-35-naughts-after-it to 1.

In what might be called the battle for respectability an entirely new situation had now arisen. Dr. Rhine could say to Dr. X the biologist, bitterly opposed to any waste of time and money on research into paranormal phenomena: "Look here, Dr. X, you got your Ph.D. with a thesis in which your experiments showed odds against chance of about 200 to 1; I can show you experiments in which the odds are millions of times those obtained in your experiments. What are you going to do about it?" Some parapsychologists have at this point been rather too hard on Dr. X. True, they can point to stronger backing from statistics for their results than many people working in Dr. X's field; but the whole of scientific method cannot be summed up in figures. Dr. X can turn around with a very strong counterattack. "Even if that is so," he can say, "I can do something which you can't do, and that is repeat my experiments with a certainty of getting the same results. I shall not be convinced until you devise a technique which includes repeatable experiments."

This is an absolutely sound criticism, but unfortunately Dr. X was not always content with it. He often criticized the work without studying it. Even so, the barrage of criticism could do nothing but good in the long run; for when it was stupid it reacted on the heads of the critics, and when it was sound it made valuable contributions to the improvement of experimental technique.

The critics soon found that it was no use attacking the statistical basis of the experiments; the few errors that they found were so very minor that they did not appreciably affect the findings. But they were sometimes able to criticize the experimental technique. For example, some of the earlier Rhine packs of cards were defective. It was possible to suppose that they were helping the percipient, or at least the percipient's unconscious, to cheat; the symbols were sometimes visible through the backs of the cards in a suitable light. There were specks and imperfections in the backs which might give clues, although the percipient would usually be perfectly unconscious of them.

Indeed, after some time, Dr. Rhine himself became convinced that the percipient must never be allowed to see the card he is guessing, back or front, and in the end the experimenter and the percipient were often housed in different rooms or even different buildings.

Whatever criticism may justly be leveled at the Rhine experiments in their early stages, as time went on many improvements in technique were made, and today we can, we hope, be sure that in the hands of a first-class investigator the technical picture can be described as follows:

Everything to do with the experiment is considered on the supposition that anybody concerned with it may be a liar, a fraud, or an unconscious faker of results.

The experiments began with two people facing one another, and the cards in sight of the percipient. This is never the case today. Often the agent and percipient are housed in different buildings and thus any chance that knowledge is being gained by marks on the backs of the cards, by unconscious whisperings, by signals conscious or unconscious, is eliminated.

Next there is the question of shuffling the cards. Is this being done properly, or is the shuffling influenced by some bias on the part of the agent which can be passed to the percipient? All kinds of mechanical shufflers have been invented, or the choice of the card order is decided by the use of random numbers, or perhaps by numbers taken from a telephone directory by someone who often does not know why he is doing it.

Great care is taken to prevent errors in scoring results and to make sure that nobody can tamper with results afterward.

When all these precautions had been taken, opponents of the reality of telepathy and clairvoyance were delighted to find that the number of percipients scoring odds-against-chance-results fell off considerably and that their scores were definitely lower than in some of the less carefully devised experiments. But one fact stands out, and it is sufficient to destroy every argument that has yet been advanced by opponents—some percipients were still able to produce results which, even though sometimes lower than some earlier results, were still giving odds of millions and billions against chance as the explanation.

In fact, we are justified in saying that E.S.P. is a fact proved by laboratory experiments and now, although it is necessary to verify it again and again, the balance of interest has shifted. Further experiments will be devoted not so much to proving it once more, but to finding out how it works, why it works so seldom, what are the best conditions for observing it, what kinds of people possess it, and how it can be controlled, until ultimately we can repeat our results at will.

Certainly no unprejudiced person can any longer deny the rank of science to psychical research. Certain phenomena have been repeatedly observed under sound laboratory conditions, and unless somebody can disprove all the results, paranormal phenomena of the sort called extrasensory perception must be accepted as certainly as the other facts of natural science. The Unknown has been taken by its unseen hand and courteously but firmly led into the science laboratory.

What comes under the heading of extrasensory perception? People used to divide the phenomena into three seemingly water-tight compartments. They are telepathy, clairvoyance, and pre-cognition. For reasons which will be clearer later, these three words are little if anything more than convenient terms to describe the results of certain kinds of experiments. However, we will simplify matters by giving the definitions which seemed good enough until recent advances altered the situation.

Telepathy is the passing of previously unknown information from one person to another without the use of the ordinary senses and means of communication. For example, if I look at the king of hearts and ask you what card I am looking at and you reply, "the king of hearts," that seems to be either pure chance or fraud or telepathy. Older experimenters believed that telepathy always involved some kind of thought transference from one mind to another, but this view is seldom held today.

Clairvoyance is the power of "seeing" a physical object, which nobody else has seen, without the use of normal senses or chan-nels of communication.

Precognition means having knowledge about an event before it has occurred. If I take several cards out of the pack one after the other without looking at them and you guess what each card is as I lay it down, and if you guess the first card to be the king of hearts and it turns out to be the jack of diamonds or some other card, and if when I lay down the second card *that* proves to be the king of hearts; if this happens a sufficient number of times to rule out chance, then we have something that may be an ex-ample of precognition. You know that I was going to put down the king of hearts before I put it down, or chose another card from the pack, or even thought of putting it down.

Precognition differs from telepathy and clairvoyance in two important ways: first, nobody was looking for it, or expected it to turn up, when in fact it did turn up under laboratory condi-tions; second, whereas telepathy and clairvoyance can, to a cer-tain limited extent, be fitted into the picture of the world which scientists have generally agreed upon, precognition seems to upset everything. It even upsets the very subject we are studying; for now that we are faced with evidence for it, as well as for telepathy and clairvoyance, we find ourselves never able to tell which of the three is being manifested in any successful experi-ment, unless very special precautions are taken. It is for this reason that we find parapsychologists more and more disinclined to use these three terms, preferring to content themselves with the general term "extrasensory perception."

So far as the laboratory is concerned, E.S.P. has been proved to exist in what can only be called emotionally boring forms. Who cares if some people can tell by telepathic or clairvoyant means which card lies on the table? Even if precognition of any sort alarms us and upsets us, we take refuge by saying, "They're only a pack of cards." Yes, but———

What has happened in the laboratories of Dr. Rhine and Dr. Soal and their colleagues is not so important in itself as in its implications. What is of outstanding importance is that we can perhaps obtain greater enlightenment in a thousand hitherto insoluble problems not only of human but of animal behavior. For example, extrasensory perception may be more valuable as a working hypothesis than "instinct" when we try to tackle such mysteries as the queen termite's control of her workers, the yearly return of swallows to their nesting places, and a thousand others.

People who explain bird migration in terms of magnetism already seem to be antediluvians from the age of Mesmer, but we are still far from saying that the problem is solved. We have only been able by careful laboratory work to bring the Unknown nearer; for we do not shut our eyes any longer to one important means of getting in closer touch with it. Our duty now is to find out how telepathy works. We do not waste time proving men have eyes, but there is an enormous amount to be learned about vision; so with telepathy we now know it exists, but there is almost everything to be learned about *how* it works.

With that we can for the moment leave telepathy, clairvoyance, and precognition as Rhine and Soal have demonstrated them, and turn to other and earlier researches which can claim to have been conducted in accordance with scientific method. There is a natural tendency at present to forget, thanks to the great success of present-day workers, that much of the earlier work was well done. The trouble was that until the crucial researches of Dr. Rhine and Dr. Soal in particular, psychical research was on the defensive. Thus people who refused to believe in it started from the assumption that telepathy did not exist, and when presented with an experiment which seemed to favor it, all they had to do was to find a way in which fraud, or error, or "suggestion" could have crept in.

Thus, if it was a case of card-guessing, all they had to do was to find out if there was a chance of the percipient seeing the backs of the cards; if there was, it followed that there might have been specks or marks useful for identification on the backs of the cards, and the percipient might have seen these and used them to memorize what suit the particular card belonged to; and if all these possibilities could be stated, then the experiment was considered worthless. It was not even necessary to prove that the percipient had used these methods; it was enough that he *could* have done so.

To somebody who has never seen a paranormal experiment, these arguments will seem very powerful, especially if there is a preconceived prejudice against telepathy and other E.S.P. phenomena; but if you have actually taken part in experiments you begin to wonder just how many ordinary people could use the specks or invent a code *without previous practice*. Thus in a remarkable series of tests carried out by the authors since this book was begun, many of the criticisms could have been raised, for no attempt to produce laboratory conditions was made; yet there was virtual certainty that none of them was valid.

When an ignorant peasant girl is asked to guess through a pack of Zener cards, and when afterward she says she had imagined it was a kind of fortune-telling so had thought all the time of her boy friend; when she *begins* by guessing 16 right out of 25, and continued with 12, 10, 13, 9, 10, 5, 9, a result of 100,000 to 1 or more against chance as the explanation, what is the good of suggesting that she had worked out a code, observed specks, or listened to unconscious whispering? When she then acts as agent and another peasant girl of fifteen acts as percipient and produces 15, 18, 12, 22, 15, 14, with three careful observers watching and failing to see any sign of code or other cheating (the cards were guessed in about a second each), one must rule out the sort of explanation which seems so obvious to a person who has never had the luck to watch such an event.

Yes, the determined skeptic will say, but why not subject these girls to laboratory conditions and see if they can repeat their results? It could be done, and indeed it has been done since by J.L.-D. and his wife; but when laboratory conditions are imposed great care has to be taken not to interfere with something essential in "psychological atmosphere." If under the new conditions the results are not repeated, this would not disprove E.S.P. It would simply tell us something more about E.S.P. — namely, that the general conditions in which an experiment takes place are an essential part of whatever reality E.S.P. may turn out to possess; that, specifically, what can happen in a peasant kitchen with two children playing round about, two girls cheering on the results and laughing with excitement, and two men with some considerable *practical* knowledge of parapsychology quietly hiding their intense excitement and watching—without giving away the fact—for any sign of cheating, cannot be duplicated in a laboratory atmosphere which to peasant girls might seem embarrassing or even alarming.

In short, the work in laboratories gives us confidence in accepting such an *experience* (let us use that word rather than *experiment*) at face value. It means that, as far as older experiments are concerned, nobody can any longer argue: There must have been fraud, because there can't be anything in it. We *can* argue: Reliable, serious investigators could see no fraud, and as no fraud was found the explanation may be exactly what it seems, that E.S.P. has now been proved to exist.

DISCUSSION QUESTIONS

1. The authors begin their article by mentioning people "who were determined not to believe in any paranormal phenomena" and end by dismissing "the determined skeptic." Are these references anything more than simple *ad hominem* arguments?

2. The essay praises the work of four "pioneers" in psychical research. What specifically is their contribution? Why mention them at all?

3. The authors praise Dr. Rhine even though "a great deal of his early work can be criticized on grounds of faulty technique." Trace references to this questionable work through the essay. Do these references invalidate any of the ESP successes mentioned?

4. In certain experiments, we are told, "the odds against chance were . . . a million or a million million or even 1-with-35-naughts-after-it to 1." How else might these numbers have been expressed? Since such experiments reach conclusions inductively, comment on the samples as known, sufficient, and representative.

5. Dr. X, the biologist, is made to say: "I can do something which you can't do, and that is repeat my experiments with a certainty of getting the same results." Is this a substantial

argument against ESP research? How do the authors answer it?

6. Submitting that ESP is "a fact proved by laboratory experiments," the authors indicate that future experiments will be devoted "not so much to proving it once more, but to finding out how it works, why it works so seldom, what are the best conditions for observing it . . . " Comment on the advantages of this form of argument.

7. How might the given examples of precognition serve to cast doubt on Zener-card experiments in general?

8. Consider the paragraphs describing the Zener-card experiments with the two peasant girls as a single inductive argument. What is the conclusion to be drawn? How acceptable is the sample?

9. In an article titled "Chance" (*Scientific American*, October 1965, pp. 44–54), A. J. Ayer considers a subject facing a kind of Zener-card test and challenges the premises of the experiment: "It is assumed that if it were merely a matter of guesswork he would be right, on the average, 20 times out of 100. . . . What reason could we have for making such an assumption antecedently to any experience? As far as I can see, none whatsoever." Is this a valid criticism of ESP research?

Wallace Fan At 1968 Rally

DISCUSSION QUESTIONS

1. In what way can this photograph be considered an example of inductive argument?

2. What is the implicit conclusion?

3. Discuss the sample as known, sufficient, and representative.

4. What inferences might be drawn from the picture of the man in the background? Would any conclusion be justified?

5. Would the photograph be equally credible if the central figure — wearing a different hat — appeared at a rally supporting Richard Nixon or Hubert Humphrey?

3

Deduction

Socrates is mortal.
You haven't registered; so you can't vote.
Richard Nixon prefers blondes.
Richard Ordway will make a fine husband.
Socrates is a cat.

Deduction is the opposite of induction. Whereas induction moves from specific facts to a general conclusion, deduction moves from a general statement to a specific application. Because there are many kinds of deduction—some quite complicated—this discussion aims to be no more than a useful oversimplification.

The vehicle of deduction is the *syllogism*. This is an argument which takes two existing truths and puts them together to produce a new truth. Here is the classical example:

MAJOR PREMISE: All men are mortal.
MINOR PREMISE: Socrates is a man.
CONCLUSION: Socrates is mortal.

In everyday affairs, one meets many examples of deductive thinking. Often, however, the syllogism is an abbreviated form, with one of the parts implied rather than stated:

You haven't registered; so you can't vote.
[IMPLICIT MAJOR PREMISE: Anyone who does not register can not vote.]
No man lives forever, you know. Even Old Harry Jackson will die someday. [IMPLICIT MINOR PREMISE: Harry Jackson is a man.]
Anyone can make a mistake. After all, Rogers is only human.
[IMPLICIT CONCLUSION: Rogers can make a mistake.]

Many informal arguments can easily be resolved into syllogistic form. One does this to more systematically judge their reliability.

A deductive argument is considered reliable if it fulfills three conditions: (1) Its premises must be true. (2) Its terms must be

45

unambiguous. (3) Its syllogistic form must be valid. These requirements will be considered in turn.

First, the premises must be true. Because the major premise of a syllogism is derived by induction (i.e., it is a general statement drawn from specific facts), one can judge its reliability by asking if the facts which produced it are known to be sufficient and representative. Here is a questionable example:

> Gentlemen prefer blondes.
> Richard Nixon is a gentleman.
> Richard Nixon prefers blondes.

The syllogism reaches an unreliable conclusion because the major premise is doubtful. The generalization exists only as a clichéd platitude (and as a title by Anita Loos); it is induced from no known sample. Political spokesmen regularly use dubious major premises (e.g., a war hero would make a good president; a divorced man would make a poor one; etc.) to produce a desired conclusion.

Second, the terms of the argument must be unambiguous. If definitions change within the syllogism, arguments can be amusingly fallacious (e.g., all cats chase mice; my wife is a cat . . .); but some can be misleading. The advertisement "See *Butch Cassidy and the Sundance Kid* — the Academy Award winning movie" is based on this syllogism:

> The Academy Award winning movie is worth seeing.
> *Butch Cassidy and the Sundance Kid* is this year's Academy
>   Award winning movie.
> *Butch Cassidy and the Sundance Kid* is worth seeing.

Here the term "Academy Award winning movie" is ambiguous. In the major premise, it refers to the movie chosen the best of the year; in the minor premise, to a movie winning one of the many minor awards given annually. *Butch Cassidy and the Sundance Kid* won the award for "cinematography."

Third, a reliable syllogism must have a valid form. This requirement introduces a complex area because there are many types of syllogisms, each with its own test for validity. Commonly, "valid form" means that the general subject or condition of the major premise must appear in the minor premise as well. It is easy to see that this argument is false:

All cats climb trees.
Squirrels climb trees.
Squirrels are cats.

But what makes the argument unreliable syllogistically is that
the major term "cat" does not appear in the minor premise. The
major premise about "all cats" can only lead to a conclusion about
cats. Here, in a different kind of syllogism, is another example of
invalid form:

If Carter loses his job, his wife will leave him.
Carter will not lose his job.
His wife will not leave him.

Here, the major premise can produce a reliable conclusion only
if Carter *does* lose his job. Because the general condition *lose his
job* does not appear in the minor premise (*not lose his job* is, of
course, something else), the argument fails. It is obvious that,
even if he keeps his job, his wife might leave him anyway.

Because these two examples of invalid form are more illus-
trative than common, it is well to consider a more familiar
argument:

The American Communist Party opposes loyalty oaths.
The Supreme Court opposes loyalty oaths.
The Supreme Court is communistic.

This kind of syllogism can discredit an individual who has any
one feature in common with an unpopular entity. But because
the major term does not appear in both premises, it is no more
valid than the argument that squirrels are cats.

These three tests, then, permit one to judge the reliability of
a deductive argument.

It should be added that because any syllogism begins with an
induced major premise, certain arguments can be analyzed as
either induction or deduction. Here is an example: "Richard
Ordway doesn't drink or smoke; he'll make some girl a fine husband." One can read this as a syllogism and attack the implicit
major premise "Anyone who does not drink or smoke will make
a fine husband." Or he can treat it as induction and argue that
the sample (the fact that Richard Ordway does not drink or
smoke) is insufficient to sustain a conclusion about his prospects
as a husband. With such arguments, it is best not to quibble
over terms; either approach is satisfactory.

And, having weighed a syllogism, it is best to judge it, not as true or false, but as reliable or unreliable. An unreliable conclusion, it must be remembered, may nevertheless be true. From the doubtful major premise ("Anyone who does not drink or smoke . . ."), one cannot reasonably deduce that Richard Ordway will make a fine husband. But he might, in fact, make a very fine husband. In rejecting the syllogism as unreliable, one simply says that the fact is not proven by *this* argument.

One can recognize the distinction between truth and a reasonable conclusion by recalling a passage from Ionesco's *Rhinoceros*: The Logician argues, "All cats die. Socrates is dead. Therefore Socrates is a cat." And his student responds, "That's true, I've got a cat named Socrates."

HOW RELIABLE ARE THESE
EXAMPLES OF DEDUCTION?

1. Of course Mrs. Clary is a poor driver. She's a woman, isn't she?

2. *Human Events* attacked the physical-fitness program proposed by President Kennedy by warning that both Hitler and Mussolini fostered comparable programs.

3. How can you disbelieve in miracles? The sunrise that occurs every day is a miracle.

4. All lemons are yellow. My girl friend's brother is a lemon. My girl friend's brother is yellow.

5. I'm from Milwaukee and I ought to know: Blatz is Milwaukee's finest beer.

6. "Well, I used to be bad when I was a kid, but ever since then I have gone straight, as I can prove by my record— thirty-three arrests and no convictions."—Big Jule, *Guys and Dolls*

7. I love you; therefore I am a lover. All the world loves a lover. You are all the world to me. Therefore you love me.

8. Both Catholics and Protestants are Christians. No one can be both Catholic and Protestant. Therefore no one can be Christian.

Intelligent Life Elsewhere

EDWARD U. CONDON

Whether there is intelligent life elsewhere (ILE) in the Universe is a question that has received a great deal of serious speculative attention in recent years. A good popular review of thinking on the subject is *We Are Not Alone* by Walter Sullivan (1964). More advanced discussions are *Interstellar Communication*, a collection of papers edited by A. G. W. Cameron (1963), and *Intelligent Life in the Universe* (Shklovskii and Sagan, 1966). Thus far we have no observational evidence whatever on the question, so therefore it remains open. An early unpublished discussion is a letter of 13 December 1948 of J. E. Lipp to Gen. Donald Putt (Appendix D). This letter is Appendix D of the Project Sign report dated February 1949 from Air Materiel Command Headquarters No. F-TR-2274-IA.

The ILE question has some relation to the ETH [Extra-terrestrial Hypothesis] or ETA [Extra-terrestrial Actuality] for UFOs as discussed in the preceding section. Clearly, if ETH is true, then ILE must also be true because some UFOs have then to come from some unearthly civilization. Conversely, if we could know conclusively that ILE does not exist, then ETH could not be true. But even if ILE exists, it does not follow that the ETH is true.

For it could be that the ILE, though existent, might not have reached a stage of development in which the beings have the technical capacity or the desire to visit the Earth's surface. Much speculative writing assumes implicitly that intelligent life progresses steadily both in intellectual and in its technological development. Life began on Earth more than a billion years ago, whereas the known geological age of the Earth is some five billion years, so that life in any form has only existed for the most recent one-fifth of the Earth's life as a solid ball orbiting the Sun. Man as an intelligent being has only lived on Earth for some 5,000 years, or about one-millionth of the Earth's age. Technological development is even more recent. Moreover

Reprinted from *Scientific Study of Unidentified Flying Objects* (New York: Bantam Books, 1968), pp. 26–33.

the greater part of what we think of as advanced technology has only been developed in the last 100 years. Even today we do not yet have a technology capable of putting men on other planets of the solar system. Travel of men over interstellar distances in the foreseeable future seems now to be quite out of the question. (Purcell, 1960; Markowitz, 1967.)

The dimensions of the universe are hard for the mind of man to conceive. A light-year is the distance light travels in one year of 31.56 million seconds, at the rate of 186,000 miles per second, that is, a distance of 5.88 million million miles. The nearest known star is at a distance of 4.2 light-years.

Fifteen stars are known to be within 11.5 light-years of the Sun. Our own galaxy, the Milky Way, is a vast flattened distribution of some 10^{11} stars about 80,000 light-years in diameter, with the Sun located about 26,000 light-years from the center. To gain a little perspective on the meaning of such distances relative to human affairs, we may observe that the news of Christ's life on Earth could not yet have reached as much as a tenth of the distance from the Earth to the center of our galaxy.

Other galaxies are inconceivably remote. The faintest observable galaxies are at a distance of some two billion light-years. There are some 100 million such galaxies within that distance, the average distance between galaxies being some eight million light-years.

Authors of UFO fantasy literature casually set all of the laws of physics aside in order to try to evade this conclusion, but serious consideration of their ideas hardly belongs in a report on the scientific study of UFOs.

Even assuming that difficulties of this sort could be overcome, we have no right to assume that in life communities everywhere there is a steady evolution in the directions of both greater intelligence and greater technological competence. Human beings now know enough to destroy all life on Earth, and they may lack the intelligence to work out social controls to keep themselves from doing so. If other civilizations have the same limitation then it might be that they develop to the point where they destroy themselves utterly before they have developed the technology needed to enable them to make long space voyages.

Another possibility is that the growth of intelligence precedes the growth of technology in such a way that by the time a society would be technically capable of interstellar space travel, it would have reached a level of intelligence at which it had not the slightest interest in interstellar travel. We must not assume that we are capable of imagining now the scope and extent of future technological development of our own or any other civilization, and so we must guard against assuming that we have any capacity to imagine what a more advanced society would regard as intelligent conduct.

In addition to the great distances involved, and the difficulties which they present to interstellar space travel, there is still another problem: If we assume that civilizations annihilate themselves in such a way that their effective intelligent life span is less than, say, 100,000 years, then such a short time span also works against the likelihood of successful interstellar communication. The different civilizations would probably reach the culmination of their development at different epochs in cosmic history. Moreover, according to present views, stars are being formed constantly by the condensation of interstellar dust and gases. They exist for perhaps 10 billion years, of which a civilization lasting 100,000 years is only 1/100,000 of the life span of the star. It follows that there is an extremely small likelihood that two nearby civilizations would be in a state of high development at the same epoch.

Astronomers now generally agree that a fairly large number of all main-sequence stars are probably accompanied by planets at the right distance from their Sun to provide for habitable conditions for life as we know it. That is, where stars are, there are probably habitable planets. This belief favors the possibility of interstellar communication, but it must be remembered that even this view is entirely speculation: we are quite unable directly to observe any planets associated with stars other than the Sun.

In view of the foregoing, we consider that it is safe to assume that no ILE outside of our solar system has any possibility of visiting Earth in the next 10,000 years.

This conclusion does not rule out the possibility of the existence of ILE, as contrasted with the ability of such civilizations to visit Earth. It is estimated that 10^{21} stars can be seen using the 200-inch Hale telescope on Mount Palomar. Astronomers surmise that possibly as few as one in a million or as many as one in ten of these have a planet in which physical and chemical conditions are such as to make them habitable by life based on the same kind of biochemistry as the life we know on Earth. Even if the lower figure is taken, this would mean there are 10^{15} stars in the visible universe which have planets suitable for an abode of life. In our own galaxy there are 10^{11} stars, so perhaps as many as 10^8 have habitable planets in orbit around them.

Biologists feel confident that wherever physical and chemical conditions are right, life will actually emerge. In short, astronomers tell us that there are a vast number of stars in the universe accompanied by planets where the physical and chemical conditions are suitable, and biologists tell us that habitable places are sure to become inhabited. (Rush, 1957.)

An important advance was made when Stanley L. Miller (1955) showed experimentally that electrical discharges such as those in natural lightning when passed through a mixture of methane and ammonia, such as may have been present in the Earth's primitive atmosphere, will initiate chemical reactions which yield various amino acids. These are the raw materials from which are constructed the proteins that are essential to life. Miller's work has been followed up and extended by many others, particularly P. H. Abelson of the Carnegie Institution of Washington.

The story is by no means fully worked out. The evidence in hand seems to convince biochemists that natural processes, such as lightning, or the absorption of solar ultraviolet light, could generate the necessary starting materials from which life could evolve. On this basis they generally hold the belief that where conditions make it possible that life could appear, there life actually will appear.

It is regarded by scientists today as essentially certain that ILE exists, but with essentially no possibility of contact between the communities on planets associated with different stars. We therefore conclude that there is no relation between ILE at other solar systems and the UFO phenomenon as observed on Earth.

There remains the question of ILE within our solar system. Here only the planets Venus and Mars need be given consideration as possible abodes of life.

Mercury, the planet nearest the Sun, is certainly too hot to support life. The side of Mercury that is turned toward the Sun has an average temperature of 660°F. Since the orbit is rather eccentric this temperature becomes as high as 770°F, hot enough to melt lead, when Mercury is closest to the Sun. The opposite side is extremely cold, its temperature not being known.* Gravity on Mercury is about one-fourth that on Earth. This fact combined with the high temperature makes it certain that Mercury has no atmosphere, which is consistent with observational data

---

*Mercury rotates in 59 days and the orbital period is 88 days, so there is a slow relative rotation.

on this point. It is quite impossible that life as found on Earth could exist on Mercury.

Jupiter, Saturn, Uranus, Neptune and Pluto are so far from the Sun that they are too cold for life to exist there.

Although it has long been thought that Venus might provide a suitable abode for life, it is now known that the surface of Venus is also too hot for advanced forms of life, although it is possible that sóme primitive forms may exist. Some uncertainty and controversy exists about the interpretation of observations of Venus because the planet is always enveloped in dense clouds so that the solid surface is never seen. The absorption spectrum of sunlight coming from Venus indicates that the principal constituent of the atmosphere is carbon dioxide. There is no evidence of oxygen or water vapor. With so little oxygen in the atmosphere there could not be animal life there resembling that on Earth.

Although it is safe to conclude that there is no intelligent life on Venus, the contrary idea is held quite tenaciously by certain groups in America. There are small religious groups who maintain that Jesus Christ now sojourns on Venus, and that some of their members have travelled there by flying saucers supplied by the Venusians and have been greatly refreshed spiritually by visiting Him. There is no observational evidence in support of this teaching.

In the fantasy literature of believers in ETH, some attention is given to a purely hypothetical planet named Clarion. Not only is there no direct evidence for its existence, but there is conclusive indirect evidence for its non-existence. Those UFO viewers who try not to be totally inconsistent with scientific findings, recognizing that Venus and Mars are unsuitable as abodes of life, have invented Clarion to meet the need for a home for the visitors who they believe come on some UFOs.

They postulate that Clarion moves in an orbit exactly like that of the Earth around the Sun, but with the orbit rotated through half a revolution in its plane so that the two orbits have the same line of apsides, but with Clarion's perihelion in the same direction from the Sun as the Earth's aphelion. The two planets, Earth and Clarion, are postulated to move in their orbits in such a way that they are always opposite each other, so that the line Earth-Sun-Clarion is a straight line. Thus persons on Earth would never see Clarion because it is permanently eclipsed by the Sun.

If the two orbits were exactly circular, the two planets would move along their common orbit at the same speed and so would

remain exactly opposite each other. But even if the orbits are
elliptical, so that the speed in the orbit is variable, the two
planets would vary in speed during the year in just such a way as
always to remain opposite each other and thus continue to be
permanently eclipsed.

However, this tidy arrangement would not occur in actuality
because the motion of each of these two planets would be per-
turbed by the gravitational attractions between them and the
other planets of the solar system, principally Venus and Mars.
It is a quite complicated and difficult problem to calculate the
way in which these perturbations would affect the motion of
Earth and Clarion.

At the request of the Colorado project, Dr. R. L. Duncombe,
director of the Nautical Almanac office at U.S. Naval Observatory in Washington, D. C., kindly arranged to calculate the
effect of the introduction of the hypothetical planet Clarion into
the solar system. The exact result depends to some extent on the
location of the Earth-Sun-Clarion line relative to the line of
apsides and the computations were carried out merely for one
case.

These calculations show that the effect of the perturbations
would be to make Clarion become visible from Earth beyond the
Sun's limb after about thirty years. In other words, Clarion would
long since have become visible from Earth if many years ago it
were started out in such a special way as has been postulated.

The computations revealed further that if Clarion were there
it would reveal its presence indirectly in a much shorter time.
Its attraction on Venus would cause Venus to move in a different
way than if Clarion were not there. Calculation shows that Venus
would pull away from its otherwise correct motion by about $1''$ of
arc in about three months time. Venus is routinely kept under
observation to this accuracy, and therefore if Clarion were there
it would reveal its presence by its effect on the motion of Venus.
No such effect is observed, that is, the motion of Venus as actually observed is accurately in accord with the absence of
Clarion, so therefore we may safely conclude that Clarion is
nonexistent.*

In his letter of transmittal Dr. Duncombe comments "I feel
this is definite proof that the presence of such a body could not
remain undetected for long. However, I am afraid it will not

*These calculations assume Clarion's mass roughly equal to that of the
Earth.

change the minds of those people who believe in the existence of Clarion."

We first heard about Clarion from a lady who is prominent in American political life who was intrigued with the idea that this is where UFOs come from. When the results of the Naval Observatory computations were told to her she exclaimed, "That's what I don't like about computers! They are always dealing death blows to our fondest notions!"

Mars has long been considered as a possible abode of life in the solar system. There is still no direct evidence that life exists there, but the question is being actively studied in the space research programs of both the United States and Soviet Russia, so it may well be clarified within the coming decade.

At present all indications are that Mars could not be the habitation of an advanced civilization capable of sending spacecraft to visit the Earth. Conditions for life there are so harsh that it is generally believed that at best Mars could only support the simpler forms of plant life.

An excellent recent survey of the rapidly increasing knowledge of Mars is *Handbook of the Physical Properties of the Planet Mars* compiled by C. M. Michaux (NASA publication SP-3030, 1967). A brief discussion of American research programs for study of life on Mars is given in *Biology and Exploration of Mars*, a 19-page pamphlet prepared by the Space Science Board of the National Academy of Sciences, published in April 1965.

The orbit of Mars is considerably more eccentric than that of the Earth. Consequently the distance of Mars from the Sun varies from 128 to 155 million miles during the year of 687 days. The synodic period, or mean time between successive oppositions, is 800 days.

The most favorable time for observation of Mars is at opposition, when Mars is opposite the Sun from Earth. These distances of closest approach of Mars and Earth vary from 35 to 60 million miles. The most recent favorable time of closest approach was the opposition of 10 September 1956, and the next favorable opposition will be that of 10 August 1971. At that time undoubtedly great efforts will be made to study Mars in the space programs of the U.S.S.R. and the United States.

Some of the UFO literature has contended that a larger than usual number of UFO reports occur at the times of Martian oppositions. The contention is that this indicates that some UFOs come from Mars at these particularly favorable times. The claimed correlation is quite unfounded; the idea is not supported by observational data. (Vallee and Vallee, 1966, p. 138.)

Mars is much smaller than Earth, having a diameter of 4,200 miles, in comparison with 8,000 miles. Mars' mass is about one-tenth the Earth's, and gravity at Mars' surface is about 0.38 that of Earth. The Martian escape velocity is 3.1 mile/sec.

At the favorable opposition of 1877, G. V. Schiaparelli, an Italian astronomer, observed and mapped some surface marking on Mars which he called "canali," meaning "channels" in Italian. The word was mistranslated as "canals" in English and the idea was put forward, particularly vigorously by Percival Lowell, founder of the Lowell Observatory of Flagstaff, Arizona, that the canals on Mars were evidence of a gigantic planetary irrigation scheme, developed by the supposed inhabitants of Mars (Lowell, 1908). These markings have been the subject of a great deal of study since their discovery. Astronomers generally now reject the idea that they afford any kind of indication that Mars is inhabited by intelligent beings.

Mars has two moons named Phobos and Deimos. These are exceedingly small, Phobos being estimated at ten miles in diameter and Deimos at five miles, based on their brightness, assuming the reflecting power of their material to be the same as that of the planet. The periods are $7^h 39^m$ for Phobos and $30^h 18^m$ for Deimos. They were discovered in August 1877 by Asaph Hall using the then new 26-inch refractor of the U.S. Naval Observatory in Washington. An unsuccessful search for moons of Mars was made with a 48-inch mirror during the opposition of 1862.

I. S. Shklovskii (1959) published a sensational suggestion in a Moscow newspaper that these moons were really artificial satellites which had been put up by supposed inhabitants of Mars as a place of refuge when the supposed oceans of several million years ago began to dry up (Sullivan, 1966, p. 169). There is no observational evidence to support this idea. Continuing the same line of speculation Salisbury (1962), after pointing out that the satellites were looked for in 1862 but not found until 1877, then asks, "Should we attribute the failure of 1862 to imperfections in existing telescopes, or may we imagine that the satellites were launched between 1862 and 1877?" This is a slender reed indeed with which to prop up so sensational an inference, and we reject it.

DISCUSSION QUESTIONS

1. "Thus far we have no observational evidence whatever on the question [of ILE], so therefore it remains open." Is an open question one for which one answer is just as likely as another?

2. For ETH to be true, the author submits, there must be not only ILE, but ILE which has both "the technical capacity [and] the desire to visit the Earth's surface." Trace and evaluate the syllogism built on this major premise.

3. "In short, astronomers tell us that there are a vast number of stars in the universe accompanied by planets where physical and chemical conditions are suitable, and biologists tell us that habitable places are sure to become inhabited." Reconstruct this as a valid syllogism. Discuss the reliability of the inductive evidence supporting the major and minor premises.

4. The discussion of ILE within our solar system is based on the implicit major premise: Where physical and chemical conditions are right, advanced forms of life may have developed. Trace the deductive argument.

5. Arrange the argument affirming Clarion in syllogistic form. Evaluate the major premise.

6. Arrange the argument denying Clarion in syllogistic form. Evaluate the minor premise.

7. How does the author attack this deduction:
   If a larger than usual number of UFO reports occur at the times of Martian oppositions, it is likely that UFO's come from Mars.
   A larger than usual number of UFO reports do occur at the times of Martian oppositions.
   Therefore, it is likely that UFO's come from Mars.

8. In an essay which is generally formal and scholarly in tone, why does the author mention the groups who believe that Christ now lives on Venus, the lady who introduced the subject of Clarion, and Shklovskii's and Salisbury's sensational thesis concerning the satellites of Mars?

Standard English:
Who(m) Does It Serve?
Who(m) Does It Hurt?

MARY TYLER KNOWLES and BETTY RESNIKOFF

Most English teachers can no longer be ridiculed as language purists jealously guarding the standard or prestige dialect from all change. They know that change is inevitable and not necessarily bad. However, despite the fact that modern English teachers have probably also heard from linguists that "there is no reason to think that any dialect of a language has intrinsic merit over the others,"[1] most teachers continue to devote a great deal of time to teaching Standard English as the most proper and socially desirable American dialect. They insist that all students be taught to *use* and not just *understand* Standard English in its most up-to-date form. The only problem that seems to bother these teachers and the many linguists ready to assist them is to find the most efficient method of helping everyone learn Standard English as a second, if not as a first, dialect.[2]

For students, however, efficient retraining is often experienced as cruel and unusual punishment which downgrades them as human beings. The message they receive is that their home communities are inferior groups of people from whom they should separate themselves as quickly as possible if they want to embrace the American Dream.

Standard English as it is taught today in elementary and high schools prescribes class-linked syntactical, lexical, and even

---

An essay distributed by the New University Conference at a meeting of the Modern Languages Association of America, Denver, Colorado, 1969.

[1] Ronald W. Langacker, *Language and Its Structure* (New York, 1967), p. 54. Also, see H. A. Gleason, Jr., *Linguistics and English Grammar* (New York, 1965), pp. 364–5.

[2] For example, see Charlotte K. Brooks, "Some Approaches to Teaching English as a Second Language," *Non-Standard Speech and the Teaching of English*, ed. William A. Stewart (Washington, D.C. Center for Applied Linguistics, 1964), pp. 24–32; reprinted in *The Disadvantaged Learner*, ed. Staten W. Webster (San Francisco, 1966), pp. 515–523. See G. Green, "Negro Dialect, the Last Barrier to Integration," *Journal of Negro Education* (1962), pp. 81–83. And also see L. Shearer, "Americans Who Can't Speak Their Own Language," *Parade* (June 11, 1967), pp. 6–7. Note also later references to Werner Cohn, Ellen Newman, and W. A. Stewart.

phonological rules under the guise of "levels of usage." The opening sentence of *Huckleberry Finn* is an example of a sentence which violates Standard syntactical (and some lexical) rules: "You don't know about me, without you have read a book by the name of *Adventures of Tom Sawyer*, but that ain't no matter."[3] *Without you have read* violates Standard parts-of-speech usage; an English teacher would correct it to *without having read* — the second person singular would become a present participle; the *you* would be deleted. *Ain't* might be cited as an example of lower-class, non-prestigious usage; Huck would be warned against saying it, at least in polite company, if he wanted to become upwardly mobile. A schoolteacher would probably patiently explain, "When we write we use formal Standard English. *Without you have read* might be all right on the football field but not in polite speech or in the classroom."

A second example from *Huckleberry Finn* which shows non-Standard phonological, lexical, and syntactic features is that of Jim, the black slave's, speech: "Say — who is you? Whar is you? Dog my cats ef I didn' hear sumf'n. Well, I knows what I's gwyne to do. I's gwyne to set down here and listen tell I hears it agin."[4] Jim's speech is characterized by his lowering the vowels [ɛ] and [ɪ] to [æ] and [a] (or [ɛ]), respectively. He drops terminal [ə]'s and elides *thing* into *f'n* where he transforms [ə] into [f]. This last characteristic could be a result of general syncopations; that is, all American speakers elide it (e.g., s⌄mp'm), but only when a lower-class person's speech is being transcribed is this trait especially marked by different spelling. (See comic strips for other examples of this.) Jim's speech is also characterized by several unusual lexical items such as: *Dog my cats.* He also makes one syntactical non-Standard usage when he uses the third person singular form of *to be* with both *I* and *you* rather than the second and third person plural forms (*am, are*) — he does not conjugate *to be* with its usual inflections but uses one inflection for each person.

Jim's underlying deep structure, however, is very much the same, if not identical to, Standard English. Note the inversion

---

[3]Mark Twain, *Adventures of Huckleberry Finn* (Indianapolis, 1965), p. 11. In his "Explanatory" Twain describes the precise nature of his dialect transcriptions: "In this book a number of dialects are used . . . The shadings have not been done in a hap-hazard fashion, or by guesswork but painstakingly and with trustworthy guidance and support of personal familiarity with these several forms of speech."

[4]Twain, p. 15.

of word order to form a question and the use of the negative
which follows the auxiliary but which precedes the main verb.
Because of this underlying syntactical similarity, it is relatively
easy for the reader (or listener) to understand Jim's speech even
though the surface manifestation is quite different from Standard
English.[5]

Whatever logical-sounding justification teachers may give
today for insisting that everyone master Standard English, the
real reasons are essentially no different from the nineteenth
century attitudes revealed in *Huckleberry Finn*. If you want to
have a substantial share of the American pie, you must prove
your recognition of the superiority of those who control the
distribution of the pie; you must, for example, learn the dialect
and manners of that class.

In *Huckleberry Finn*, the Widow Douglas and Miss Watson,
two of the town's leading citizens, speak prestigious Standard
Southern English and are the arbiters of Huck's manners and
speech: "Don't put your feet up there, Huckleberry," and "Don't
scrunch up like that, Huckleberry—set up straight."[6] Huck, on
the other hand, is from a dead-beat family and his speech shows
it, shows the reader immediately that here is a boy who won't
make good "materially" (except by the fluke of finding treasure)
or "socially." Jim's speech is even less Standard than Huck's
(in terms of the larger number of nonstandard lexical, syntactical,
and phonological items it contains) and this is a signal therefore
to the reader that his social position is even lower—the slave
(who has no opportunities at all to make "good").

Things have not drastically changed today, even though
slavery has been abolished, for what seems to be one's social
mobility still depends, in part, on how well he or she can use
Standard, prestigious English. (True social mobility is not occurring any more, according to many viewers of the contemporary
American scene; rather, college-educated operators of comput-

[5]However, see Deutsch (1967) and Deutsch, Katz, and Jensen (1968) who
maintain that the black dialect is incapable of expressing certain grammatical
and logical relations because of the culturally impoverished background from
which the speakers come. On the other hand, Baratz (1969) and Lavov (in press)
argue that the differences are only superficial ones, that these differences do not
prevent people using either dialect from expressing any logical or grammatical
relations possible in the other dialect nor do they reflect any difference in the
linguistic intelligence of the users. All the evidence for either point-of-view
is not in; nevertheless the Baratz work casts real doubt on the validity of Jensen's
conclusions.

[6]Twain, pp. 12–13.

erized inventory systems, who do essentially the same job as their fathers who may have been shipping clerks, think they have risen in the world.) LeRoi Jones, in his essays, *Home*, points to the demands of illusion: "The culture of the powerful is very infectious. . . .To be any kind of 'success' one must be fluent in this culture. Know the words of the users, the semantic rituals of power. This is a way into wherever it is you are not now, but wish, very desperately, to get into."[7] As Ronald Langacker comments in his *Language and Its Structure*, a text that is used to shape the attitudes of many prospective teachers at the University of Wisconsin: "There are practical reasons for getting school children to modify their speech in some of these ways—a person could well be handicapped socially and professionally by speech traits that run counter to those accepted as 'correct' by people he will have to deal with."[8]

Several studies have demonstrated that children from "deprived" backgrounds do poorly in school because the Standard English they are taught is like a foreign language to them.[9] In the Baratz study (1969), black and white children were asked to listen and repeat sentences in both their own and in the other's dialect; the black ghetto children were able to do both (although with less success in Standard English) whereas the white children could read Standard English but failed miserably to understand or to repeat the black dialect. This indicates that it is difficult for any person to do as well in a dialect other than his own, although the black ghetto child has been forced into constant contact with Standard English.

Since a student's achievements in school determine, to a great extent, what kind of job he can get when he finishes school, and as his speech from there on is partly responsible for his promotion or social "mobility," then language etiquette—the willingness to conform or not conform to Standard English, to break away from class backgrounds or not—is a kind of "tracking

[7] LeRoi Jones, *Home: Social Essays* (New York, 1966).

[8] Langacker, p. 51. Also see Ellen Newman, "An Experiment in Oral Language," A Ford Foundation Project (Jan. 1965) described in *The Disadvantaged Learner*, p. 510: "The language of the disadvantaged child is also unacceptable in the larger society. Prospective employers find a substandard language difficult to understand and indicative of a lack of intelligence. If the disadvantaged child is to have a fair chance in our mobile society, he must develop a new language pattern—a standard language."

[9] See W. A. Stewart, "Urban Negro Speech: Sociolinguistic Factors Affecting English Teaching," *Social Dialects and Language Learning*, ed. R. W. Shuy (Champaign-Urbana, 1965), pp. 10–18.

system." Only if a lower class person painstakingly learns to speak a new way is the *possibility* open for him or her to move into certain kinds of jobs with work that seems superior to repetitious factory tasks.

If, however, everyone were encouraged to use his or her own dialect in all situations (not just in the home or on the streets as several linguists have advocated) and, if no one dialect were given more prestige than another, one of the ideological props for the myth of upper-class intellectual superiority would be removed. The evidence of the above studies suggests that children would not have so much difficulty in school no matter what background they are from if they could only communicate in their *own* dialect. Then the truth about their unfettered intellectual potential might be discovered. Such a change would also remove a psychological irritation suffered by children whose dialect is "non-Standard." Teachers could no longer harp on "correctness" in word choice, pronunciation, and syntax, nor would they be able to make the child feel inferior by expressing their exasperation at what they consider the child's stupidity or intransigence.

A Dartmouth Afro-American student expressed his dissatisfaction with Americans who refuse to learn and understand his speech and who force him and other black college students to become fluent in Standard English. He feels separated from those brothers at home who communicate in a different way:

MY PEOPLE

My people
  Come to me
And ask
  My purpose,
My reason for being
  Here
And not there,
My people
  Distrust me
Because I am
  Around him
And influenced
  Though unwilling,
My people
  Don't dig

> My phonetics,
> They say why
>   Must we
> Talk like him
> If he doesn't understand
>   Why can't he
> Talk like us?[10]

If all dialects were given equal weight, this would also eliminate one way in which students are tracked in high-schools (not
to speak of other levels). For example, in a semi-rural New
Hampshire high school, students from a nearby college community
are invariably tracked in the upper college-prep levels whereas
the majority of students from small impoverished farming villages are put into special education or vocational tracks. Their
speech is enough to give away their class background. Those who
do the tracking are probably not conscious of how they are reinforcing the class structure. They only feel that somehow Sally
"won't profit from" college. Since she dresses and looks much
like the college-prep students, is it her speech which shows she
should be encouraged to be a beautician? After all, even her
teachers know she is sharp, though not always "grammatical."

Throwing the spotlight on language as one handle used to
track people is not likely to eliminate such class-biased teaching,
but it might help to bring it out in the open where the causes
of it can be attacked directly. This attack will, of course, have to
be concentrated on changing the society that discriminates
against various people and their dialects.

How, specifically, one may wonder, can linguists and English
teachers lay the groundwork for such an attack and an eventual
multi-dialect acceptability?

1. We can point out how language works as a way of dividing
workers from workers (white from black, "normal" Appalachians
from "hillbillies"), reinforcing racist, xenophobic attitudes by
allowing the myth to be perpetuated that one man is inferior
to another because he "talks different." And one must point out
how these divisions between workers are beneficial to the
employers, who can differentiate on pay scales between workers.
And workers being divided by prejudice—also based, in part, on
their reaction to another's peculiar dialect—will not support
other workers paid less.

[10] Herschell Johnson, "My People," *Blackout*, I, no. 2 (Spring, 1968), p. 13.
Permission to use granted by the author.

We should also point out how the speech differences of working class and middle class Americans are cited as supposedly objective proof that middle-class people deserve higher wages and more prestigious responsibilities. After all, the thinking goes, someone who speaks a lower class dialect obviously does not think straight.

2. We can work at changing teachers' attitudes, for many are full of the same prejudices as employers. For years the great number of public school teachers have been recruited from the ranks of desperately mobile lower or lower-middle class families. To become a teacher meant to make it into the solid middle class and to feel relief and gratitude for the escape from the lower depths.

This experience of struggle did not leave the new member of the middle class at ease. Such a teacher was anxious to prove that he or she really had the credentials, had not achieved the new status under false pretenses, did share the values of the "best" people, and was ready to try hard to please them by spreading their standards. Such a teacher had paid the price of entry and was only too willing to urge that his or her students also get rid of their debasing language and culture as quickly as possible.

The task of making lower class children feel inferior was usually taken on voluntarily with the zeal of the convert, who, in his eagerness to remake himself, becomes a caricature of those he wants to join. Thus did old Miss Jones get her students to practice answering: "It is I" in the false belief that upper class usage is totally regular and rational. And thus have English teachers become figures of fun in their obsequious subservience to what they imagined the upper class was saying. Given such a background many teachers will undoubtedly resist a change until the power structure is changed for, until then, their own mark of having "made it" – Standard prestigious English – would be inconsequential.[11]

3. Perhaps playing tapes of various dialects for teachers in education courses and showing how quickly they can understand unfamiliar dialects if they try to do so would be helpful in breaking down their language prejudices. One study asked teachers to listen to various tapes and to classify the speaker according to intelligence. Invariably, the most pronounced "dialect speakers"

[11]Also see Werner Cohn, "On the Language of Lower Class Children," *The Disadvantaged Learner*, p. 332.

were classified as the dumbest—an indication of our deep-seated prejudices.[12]

4. Also, teachers could encourage the reading of books by authors such as Twain, Faulkner, and Hemingway, focusing discussion on the lack of connection between the preferred dialect and good character. For example, in the midst of the panorama of cupidity and hypocrisy in *Huckleberry Finn*, Huck and Jim stand out as the only characters who put human values first. One can argue that their superior humanity is ironically related to their disapproved language. The point is not to wax sentimental about noble ignorance. Instead it is to note that Jim and Huck with their "inferior" dialects are people somewhat outside the American system. They have not been as successfully socialized into its racist values as Tom Sawyer, a middle-class character, has been. The slave and the son of the ne'er-do-well know that the society considers property rights sacred, but they have not really internalized the idea that slaves are property first and human beings second, if at all. But *Tom* can, without compunction, treat Jim as an object at the end of the novel. After all, that is what he will be expected to do as an adult solid citizen with vested interests in a slave society. It should be no surprise that both his attitudes and his dialect differ from Huck's.[13]

5. In first grade classes with more than one dialect represented a teacher might transcribe each child's dialect as an early part of the experience of learning to read and write. Each child would first read what he or she actually hears or says rather than be asked to struggle with an unknown dialect. Reading would thus be experienced as an activity directly related to speaking and writing rather than as an incomprehensible puzzle with little clear connection to real life. A classroom where a blackboard is filled with the different things (in different dialects) children actually say when they do not want to go to bed, is a classroom where no child is made to feel that his dialect is not worthy of transcription and where difference is not immediately criticized

[12] L. S. Harms, "Listener Judgments of Status Cues in Speech," *Quarterly Journal of Speech*, 47 (1961), pp. 164–168.

[13] One example of blatant racial and class bigotry that makes specious connections between morality and Standard English comes in an article by the well-known linguist, L. Bloomfield, "Literate and Illiterate Speech," *American Speech*, II (1927), pp. 432–439: "by a cumulation of obvious superiorities, both of character and standing, as well as of language, some persons are felt to be better models of conduct and speech than others." Recent writings are more subtle about the "necessity" of having all children learn Standard English. For example, see page 61 for a quote from Langacker.

as sub-standard.

6. It should be noted that some of the most significant attitude teaching can be done in classrooms (especially on the secondary and college levels) where Standard English is the native dialect. These students almost invariably come from families who make discriminatory decisions about people with different dialects. The teacher willing to tell the truth about dialect equality is in a good position to expose the real meaning of such discrimination by removing academic support for class bias.

7. And finally, in the classroom the teacher should explain what reservations he or she has about Standard English, what the implications of teaching it would be. He or she should thoroughly discuss and debate this with the students, for days perhaps, playing tapes of different dialects — Standard speech, white working class speech, and black ghetto speech — giving students books written in dialect — some contemporary black poetry, for example, or Charles Waddell Chestnut's "The Gooper'd Grapevine." He or she should thoroughly discuss the socio-eco-political implications of Standard vs. non-Standard speech and the pros and cons of learning or not learning Standard. And, after all sides and their implications are understood, *and only after this*, let the students decide to what extent they wish to learn Standard English.

We realize that it is mistakenly idealistic to believe that re-forming the teaching of English is a basic change in the American system of privilege for some and oppression for others. Yet isn't it time for English teachers and linguists to change their role from the prissy policemen of "good" usage to the forthright spokesmen for the truth about the traditional class bias in language "preference"? Isn't it time for us not only to express our dissatisfaction but to begin to work actively both in the class-room and in the wider political arena to do away with the ar-rangements that allow a small class of people to use and oppress the rest?

DISCUSSION QUESTIONS

1. How do the authors challenge this syllogism?

    People who wish to advance socially and professionally in American society ("to have a substantial share of the American pie") must use standard English.

> Most young people wish to advance socially and profes-
> sionally in American society.
>
> Therefore, most young people must be taught to use
> standard English.

2. Central to this essay is the contention that no relationship
exists between a person's dialect and his intelligence. Is
any evidence offered for or against this contention? Is this
an open question?

3. The authors offer a syllogism:

> Any teaching goal which cruelly downgrades particular
> students, which perpetuates the myth of class inferi-
> ority, and which reinforces racist, xenophobic at-
> titudes, should be discouraged.
>
> Teaching the exclusive value of standard English does
> these things.
>
> Teaching the exclusive value of standard English should
> be discouraged.

Discuss the reliability of this deductive argument.

4. "Only if a lower class person painstakingly learns to speak
a new way is the *possibility* open for him or her to move
into certain kinds of jobs . . . " In the present state of
things, are there any jobs which a person who lacks standard English cannot perform? Assuming a new state of
things in which all language dialects are equally acceptable,
might there be any jobs which a person who lacks standard
English could not perform?

5. The authors recommend that the teacher first discuss standard vs. dialectical speech and the socio-eco-political impli-
tions involved and then "let the students decide to what
extent they wish to learn Standard English." Should the
same latitude be applied to classes in mathematics? (Or is
this a false analogy?)

Love Is the Only Measure

JOSEPH FLETCHER

The new morality, so called, is taking a long, hard second look at some of our assumptions. It does not oversimplify the issues at stake, even though some of its professed advocates do, yet it most certainly poses the essential questions. It might be said to be a revolt against what Henry Miller, the paper tiger of the sex rebels, calls "the immorality of morality."

Any serious discussion of the new morality should begin with philosophical candor. Let it be understood, then, that the new morality is a form of ethical relativism. A *locus classicus* might be Paul Tillich's blunt statement, "The truth of ethical relativism lies in the moral law's inability to give commandments which are unambiguous both in their general form and in their concrete applications. Every moral law is abstract in relation to the unique and totally concrete situation. This is true of what has been called natural law and of what has been called revealed law."

An old joke can serve to pose the problem. When a rich old man asked a lovely young woman if she would sleep the night with him she said, indignantly, "No." He then asked if she would do it for $100,000? She said "Yes!" She even agreed to $10,000, but when he came down to $500 she exclaimed, "What do you think I am?" He replied, "We have already established that. Now we are haggling over the price." Is any girl who has "relations" (a debased way to use the word) outside marriage *ipso facto* a prostitute or loose woman, guilty of sin or wrong? Or, as the new moralist would say, does it all depend upon the situation?

There are at bottom just three lines of approach to moral decision-making. One of them, perhaps the least followed but having at least some following, is the antinomian or law-less (non-principled) method. It operates with spontaneous decisions. Christian antinomians or extemporists, such as those St. Paul opposed in Corinth, often claim to be above any moral law (since they are "saved" or guided directly by the Holy Spirit). In any case they repudiate not only all rules of morality but even

Reprinted from *Commonweal* (14 January 1966), pp. 428–432. This essay presented one side of a debate.

general principles. Non-Christian antinomians, such as Jean-Paul Sartre, make their moral decisions with "autonomy" and "instantaneity," i.e., without help from general maxims, unpredictably, wholly within the situation, in the belief that one "moment" of existence is entirely discontinuous from others — so that we cannot generalize about our decision-making.

For example, even if you described in the most complete detail all of the facts involved and all of the considerations *pro* and *con* joining a labor union where the antinomian works, or whether he should respond to a plea for a loan from a good family man or from a hopeless wastrel, he could not possibly say how he might decide until he was there, then, led by God's spirit or his own. Spontaneity is the key to his method.

At the opposite end of the spectrum of approaches is legalism. In this ethical strategy the "situational variables" are taken into consideration, but the circumstances are always subordinated to predetermined general "laws" of morality. Legalistic ethics treats many of its rules idolatrously by making them into absolutes. Classical Christian ethics and moral theology ("seminary" or "manualistic" ethics and casuistry), like the conventional wisdom, has been mainly of this kind. Not all legalism is cruelly rigid or callous about sticking to the letter even if the spirit is ignored but too much of it is guilty on that score. The scriptural law of Protestant morality and the natural law of Catholic morality, each in its own way, have treated principles as rules rather than maxims. In this kind of morality, properly labeled as legalism or law ethics, obedience to prefabricated "rules of conduct" is more important than freedom to make responsible decisions.

For example, if you were a Roman Catholic husband and found that, for whatever reason, the only method of family limitation which worked was contraception, you would either have to go on begetting unwanted children beyond a responsible number or cease the unitive lovemaking which is a vital part of a good marriage. This would be because contraception is declared (at least as of this writing) by your Church to be always "against nature." If you were a Jehovah's Witness you would refuse a blood transfusion to save your life, or even your child's, because "the Bible says we must abstain from blood" (which it does, however differently you might exegete the "texts" cited).

The third method of approach is that of the "new" morality. This is situation ethics. In this moral strategy the governing consideration is the situation, with all of its contingencies and exigencies. The situationist enters into every decision-making situation armed with principles, just as the legalist does. But the all-important difference is that his moral principles are *maxims* of general or frequent validity; their validity always depends upon the situation. The situationist is prepared in any concrete case to suspend, ignore or violate any principle if by doing so he can effect more good than by following it. As Dietrich Bonhoeffer said in his prison-written *Ethics*, after conspiring to assassinate Hitler, "Principles are only tools in the hand of God, soon to be thrown away as unserviceable."

Adultery, for instance, is ordinarily wrong, not in itself but because the emotional, legal and spiritual entailments are such that the over-all effects are evil and hurtful rather than helpful — at least in our present-day Western society. But there is always the outside case, the unusual situation, what Karl Barth calls the *ultima ratio*, in which adultery could be the right and good thing. This writer knows of such a case, in which committing adultery foreseeably brought about the release of a whole family from a very unjust but entirely legal exploitation of their labor on a small farm which was both their pride and their prison. Still another situation could be cited in which a German mother gained her release from a Soviet prison-farm and reunion with her family by means of an adulterous pregnancy. These actions would have the situationist's solemn but ready approval.

With these three ethical perspectives in mind, how are we to "judge" the Puerto Rican woman in Bruce Kendrick's story about the East Harlem Protestant Parish, *Come Out the Wilderness*? She was proud of her son and told the minister how she had "made friends" with a married man, praying God she'd have a son, and eventually she bore one. The minister, dear silly man that he is, told her it was okay if she was repentant, and she replied, "Repent? I ain't repentin'. I asked the Lord for my boy. He's a gift from God." She is *right* (which, by the way, does *not* mean a situationist approves in the abstract of the absence of any husband in so many disadvantaged Negro and Puerto Rican families).

It is necessary and important to note this: that situation ethics or the "new morality" is *not* the existentialists' or antinomians' method. Unfortunately the waters of debate have been badly muddied since the second world war because some observers, both Catholic and Protestant, have got the two all mixed

up and confused. Future historians of modern ethics may fix the
start of this confusion in the advice of Roman Catholic moral
theologians which led to an allocution by Pope Pius XII on April
18, 1952. He used the terms "existential" and "situational" as
synonymous. On February 2, 1956, situation ethics in another
papal utterance was called "the new morality," and ever since
then the debate has been at sixes and sevens. The *situationism*
of the "new" morality is definitely *not* existential, in the sense
that secular and atheist exponents of it use the term.

There are three, not just two, alternatives open to honest
people who want to choose their moral course, whether they
happen to be Christians or not. We don't have to be either
legalists who absolutize ethical principles, or extemporists who
make decisions without any principles at all. We can choose
(and I would urge it) to be situationists, acknowledging our
heritage of canonical and civil principles of right and wrong but
remaining free to decide for ourselves responsibly in all situations which principles are to be followed, or in some cases to decide that the "relevant" principles are to be rejected because
they would result in more evil than good.

What, then, is good? Asking this question drives home the
basic fact that the "new" morality, situationism, is a moral
strategy or procedural doctrine which has to be seen in tandem
or partnership with a substantive companion-doctrine — personalism. And "personalism" here means the ethical view that the
highest good, the *summum bonum* or first-order value, is human
welfare and happiness (but not, necessarily, pleasure). Good is
first and foremost the good of *people*. Christians call it "love,"
meaning neighbor-concern or *agape*. This love means, of course,
a social attitude, not the romantic emotion that the word has
come to connote in popular literature. The Great Commandment
orders Christians to love, i.e., to seek the well-being of people —
not to love principles. Non-Christians may call it something
else, for example, "justice" or "altruism" or "humanism" or the
like, but whatever label they use, it is a personalist devotion to
people, not to things or abstractions such as "laws" or general
principles. Personal interests come first, before the natural or
scriptural or theoretical or general or logical or anything else.

When we think about the conflict between the old or classical
morality, the law ethic, and the new morality, the love ethic,
we can see that the nub of it is the choice between the notion that
a thing is right or wrong inherently and intrinsically, given in

the nature of the thing (maybe because God created it "to be what it is"), as legalists or absolutizers would say, or only contingently and extrinsically right or wrong, depending on the circumstances, as situationists or relativists would say. It goes back, in intellectual history, to such controversies as the realist-nominalist debate. The intrinsic idea of moral quality is Thomist, the extrinsic idea is Occamist. The situation ethic is extrinsicalist; it claims that moral quality is nominal, not real. Practical men may not recognize that this kind of philosophical issue is at stake, but it is.

It all depends on the situation, say the extrinsicalists. In some situations unmarried love could be infinitely more moral than married unlove. Lying could be more Christian than telling the truth. Stealing could be better than respecting private property. No action is good or right in itself. It depends on whether it hurts or helps people, whether or not it serves love's purpose — understanding love to be personal concern — *in the situation*.

The situational-personal ethic, in short, subordinates principles to circumstances and the general to the particular, as well as making the "natural" and the biblical and the theoretical give way to the personal and the actual.

For the sake of a clear and striking illustration we might turn to sex relations and the ethics of reproduction. And, furthermore, let us address the subject in terms of the *Christian* version of situation ethics. (We could use truth telling, or buying and selling, or diplomacy and national defense, or something else. The same considerations would come into play whatever the area or "field" of decision-making might be.)

Alas, the very word "morals" in popular use means sex conduct, as we can see in newspaper headlines about a "morals charge." (This ridiculous reduction of morality to sexuality probably got its start in English translations of references in the Bible to fornication, as when I Thess. 4.3 is rendered "abstain from immorality." The Greek and Latin texts without pruriency or evasion say *fornication*.) Actually, the "new morality" is a wide-ranging ethical theory of far more varied bearing than sex, but that is what it is focussed upon in the street debates. So be it. Suppose we look at sex, to give our discussion a specific of operational terms.

Sexual intercourse may or may not be an act of love. Love, as understood in the Christian situation ethic, is an attitude of

concern and not an emotion of desire. A *Playboy* cartoon went to
the heart of the matter by showing a rumpled young male saying
to a rumpled young female in his arms, "Why speak of love at
a time like this?" The point is that, Christianly speaking, sex
which does not have love as its partner, its *senior* partner, is
wrong. If there is no responsible concern for the *other* one, for
the partner as a subject rather than a mere object, as a person
and not a *thing*, the act is immoral.

The new morality, therefore, requires its practitioners to be
who-askers (who will be helped or hurt?)—not, as with legalistic
morality, what-askers (what does the law prescribe?). Immanuel
Kant, even though he was a legalist himself, was nevertheless
right about his maxim: treat persons as ends, never as means.
This is essentially the personalism of the Summary of the Law
in the gospels: love God and neighbor, with nothing about following a code of law or a set of abstract, before-the-fact rules.

It comes down to this: people are to be loved and things are to
be used. "Things" include material objects and general principles. Immorality occurs when things are loved and people are
used. When anybody "sticks to the rules," even though people
suffer as a consequence, that is immoral. Even if we grant, for
example, that generally or commonly it is wrong or bad or un-
desirable to interrupt a pregnancy, it would nevertheless be
right to do so to a conceptus following rape or incest, at least
if the victim wanted an abortion. (Legalism of the Protestant,
"scriptural law" variety has no biblical prohibition of abortion,
and like Jewish opinion approves of therapeutic abortions and is
divided over the morality of non-therapeutic reasons for it.)

The Christian situationist says to all men, to all who care
about others, whether they are Christians or not: "Your love is
like mine, like everybody's. It is the Holy Spirit. Love is not the
work of the Holy Spirit, it *is* the Holy Spirit—working in us.
God *is* love, he doesn't merely 'have' it or 'give' it; he gives himself, to all men of all sorts and conditions: to believers and non-
believers, high degree and low, dark and pale, learned and
ignorant, Marxists and Christians and Hottentots."

Long ago, St. Chrysostom said the essence of sin is in the substitution of means for ends. Modern social analysts are saying
the same thing when they speak of "the error of substituting
instrumental for terminal values!" Chrysostom meant that sin
treats means as if they were ends in themselves. But in the
Christian ethic (at least in its situational version) things are

means only, and only persons are ends. We could restate it by the assertion that sin is the exploitation or use of persons. This is precisely what prostitution is. Therefore in a familiar phrase, the prostitute is far more sinned against than sinning. She is infinitely closer to righteousness than are her customers. In the same way, on the same logical base, we can say that the classical capitalist commodity theory of labor, largely a dead letter now due to trade unionism's struggles, is or was a sinful, evil principle.

In teenage social life if a boy seduces a girl in order to appear in his own eyes or his friends' as a Big Man, he is using her; he is guilty of sin or "moral evil." If a girl seduces a boy out of curiosity or some such motive, she is committing the same wrong; if she seduces him in order to lure him into marriage she is committing a far greater sin than simple fornication every could possibly be, even if they are married to make it legal. Such married sex is legal prostitution and a case of sinning not only formally and materially but also with malice! Even if she lured him into marriage *without* fornication the guilt lies just the same. What is more despicable than a technical virgin, male or female? The new morality weighs motive heavily in its scales, along with means and ends. The new morality is not *soft* morality.

As we have noted, Karl Barth, the Swiss theologian, who speaks of "law" a great deal, nevertheless allows for what he calls the *ultima ratio*, the outside chance that in a particular situation what the law forbids can be excused. In this way Barth, like many Catholic moral theologians, is prepared out of mercy and compassion to excuse an act of fornication or a loveless marriage *in the situation*, in the rare case. But it would be a matter of excusing an evil (because unlawful) act. For Barth and Catholic metaphysics, the evil is "real"—objectively given *de rerum natura* in such categories as fornication, adultery, homosexual acts, contraception, abortion, sterilization, and the like.

This is not the situationist's view. For him nothing is inherently good or evil, except love (personal concern) and its opposite, indifference or actual malice. Anything else, no matter what it is, may be good or evil, right or wrong, according to the situation. Goodness is what *happens* to a human act, it is not *in* the act itself. This is, in a way, a "nominalistic" doctrine. Like the situationists, Emil Brunner, another Swiss theologian, is more plainly in the camp of such a morality. To use language not his own but in keeping with his thought, he sees that *goodness*

or rightness is a predicate of actions, not a property of them!
A clarion statement of this position is William Temple's:

> The rightness of an act, then, nearly always and perhaps always, depends on the way in which the act is related to circumstances; this is what is meant by calling it relatively right; but this does not in the least imply that it is only doubtfully right. It may be, in the circumstances, certainly and absolutely right.

That is, the action even if unlawful, even if it violates a moral maxim or rule, will be positively right; not merely an excusable wrong!

Bishop Pike of California, following the situational method in large part, has turned in his ethical treatise (*Doing the Truth*) to the story of how Judith used her sex to save Israel from Holofernes' army. The Bible obviously approves and applauds her action, her deliberate sexual seduction. (They wrote the story in such a way as to leave her technically chaste by getting away before Holofernes got her into bed with him, thus illustrating the ethical dishonesty of legalism, as well as its willingness to accept the lesser of evils. But this is what the notion of intrinsic evil always degenerates into!) A situationist would also applaud Judith's action, but wouldn't be driven by the theory to extricate her from the logic of her seduction. In any case, the Biblical Judith is a model for governments which use a woman's sex to entrap enemy espionage agents in blackmail, to inactivate them. Is the girl who gives her chastity for her country's sake any less approvable than the boy who gives his leg or his life? No!

True chastity is a matter of personal integrity, of sincerity and purity of heart. It is not sexual. Righteousness or virtue is willing the good of the neighbor. Von Hügel said that "caring is the greatest thing, caring matters most." Not all legalists and not all relativists are agreed about sexual promiscuity, of course, but the chances are that the Christians among them look upon promiscuity as irresponsible, care-less, insincere, even as indifference. They (we) believe that promiscuity ignores and flouts the value and integrity of persons, turning casual sexual partners from true subjects into what some psychologists significantly call "love *objects*." It turns them into things. In the same way that sex is right or wrong according to its treatment of persons, so with the so-called "obscene." Frankness about sex is not wrong. As somebody said recently, obscenity is the word "nigger" on the lips of a Bull Connor type cop.

Even a transient sex liaison, if it has the elements of caring, of tenderness and selfless concern, of mutual offering, is better than a mechanical, egocentric exercise of conjugal "rights" between two uncaring or possibly antagonistic marriage partners. Sexual intercourse is not right or good just because it is legal (by civil or canonical law), nor is it wrong just because it is outside the law. So-called common-law marriages recognize this.

The personal commitment, not the county clerk, sanctifies sex. A man or wife who hates the partner is living in sin. A couple who cannot marry legally or permanently but live together faithfully and honorably and responsibly, are living in virtue—in Christian love. In this kind of Christian sex ethic the essential ingredients are caring and commitment. Given these factors, the only reason for disapproving sexual relations would be situational, not legal or principled. It would because the circumstances, realistically and imaginatively weighed, with a responsible eye on remote as well as immediate consequences, balance out against the liaison rather than for it. There is nothing against extramarital sex as such, in this ethic, and in *some* cases it is good.

As an example of the fact-weighing problem (situationism is *very* data conscious) we can cite a recent proposal by a Unitarian-Universalist minister in Michigan. He recommends that teenagers be prepared for sexual maturity in temporary trial marriages of limited duration and with parental consent. From a Christian perspective, most situationists (if not all) would hold that the teenagers would simply be practicing on each other, and the mere fact that their using each other would be *mutual* would only compound the evil, not justify it. The scheme seems unbelievably naïve on the score of emotional and cultural risks.

Advocates of Hugh Heffner's *Playboy* doctrine of promiscuity, arguing that sex is just "fun," are backing a naturalistic hedonism which is poles apart from the Christian ethic. Their argument is that anything sexual is all right if it does not hurt anybody. A lot hangs on that big word "hurt." But Christians say that nothing is right unless it *helps* somebody. Here lies the true issue of sex ethics—not moral maxims nor sentimentality nor romanticism nor antisexual fears. We do not praise a technical virgin whose petting practices are sexually unrestrained, nor do we condemn a loving transgressor of the law who is emotionally honest although technically unchaste.

If a defensive maneuver can be forgiven here, suppose we hear Msgr. Pietro Palazzini, a Catholic moralist and Secretary of the Sacred Congregation of the Council, in his article about situation ethics in the *Dictionary of Moral Theology*. He says that situation ethics "must not be understood as an escape from the heavy burden of moral integrity. For, though its advocates truly deny the absolute value of universal norms, some are motivated by the belief that in this manner they are better safeguarding the eminent sovereignty of God."

One last word. The *Christian* criteria for sex relations are positive: sex is a matter of certain ideals of relationship. These ideals are based upon a certain faith: about God, Christ, the Church, who man is, and his destiny. Therefore, if people do not embrace that faith (and most don't), there is no reason why they should live by it. And most do not! It is time we faced up to this. Nowadays in the "secular city" it is easier and easier to see who are committed Christians and who are not. On any serious view of the matter, sex is not the decisive thing. Character shapes sex, sex does not shape character. Virtue never goes out of style but styles change. If true chastity means a marital monopoly, then let those who believe in it recommend it by reason and example. Nothing is gained by condemning the unbeliever. Indeed, to condemn him is more unjust (immoral) than a sexual escapade!

The fact is that all along churchmen have relied on *prudential* arguments against sexual freedom—the triple terrors of conception, infection and detection—not upon Christian sanctions. But modern medicine and urban anonymity have made sex relatively safe. The danger-argument is almost old hat. It is true, of course, that coital adventures may bring on delayed emotional reactions, but the same is true of petting. And in any case, these feelings are largely guilt feelings which changing cultural norms are making archaic or even antediluvian. The guilt is going. If Christians honestly and seriously believe that there are matters of *principle* at stake, as distinct from situational factors, they had better make them clear. And whatever they come up with, they aren't going to make a good case for absolute, universal, and unexceptionable ethical negatives. Or positives. The new morality is a better morality than that—than the old morality.

DISCUSSION QUESTIONS

1. How would the author respond to this syllogism:
   Practices outlawed by the Roman Catholic Church are
   immoral.

Artificial birth control has been outlawed by the Roman
Catholic Church.
Therefore, artificial birth control is immoral.

2. Consider the author's deductive argument:
   Any action which — in a defined situation — expresses love
   for (i.e., personal concern for the well-being of) persons, is morally right.
   Adultery, stealing, homosexuality, etc. — in a defined
   situation — can express such love.
   Therefore, these actions can be morally right.
   Is the major premise here any less vulnerable to criticism
   than the one in the preceding syllogism? Why this emphasis
   on love?

3. The author refers to the words and ideas of a number of
   authorities: Paul Tillich, Jean-Paul Sartre, Dietrich Bonhoeffer, Karl Barth, Bruce Kendrick, William of Occam, the
   Bible, Immanuel Kant, "Jewish opinion," St. Chrysostom,
   Emil Brunner, Bishop Pike, and Msgr. Pietro Pallazzini.
   Why does he present such a mass of authorities to support
   his argument for situational ethics?

4. The author illustrates his argument by mentioning a
   variety of practices. Discuss occasions — using the situational
   ethic of love — when each might be moral or might be
   immoral.

birth control	exploitive capitalism
abortion	obscenity
lying	trial marriages
seduction	homosexuality
marital entrapment	sterilization
blood transfusions	condemnation of the unbeliever
prostitution	stealing

   Are there any events which must always be immoral? Are
   there any events (perhaps, Dietrich Bonhoeffer's conspiring
   to assassinate Hitler) which might be too complex for
   moralist to make a purely situational judgment?

5. With legalistic ethics, the author says "obedience to
   prefabricated 'rules of conduct' is more important than
   freedom to make responsible decisions." Is this a perfectly clear distinction? What are the criteria which
   determine responsible decisions — as opposed to irresponsible ones?

6. "Love is not the work of the Holy Spirit, it *is* the Holy Spirit—working in us. God *is* love . . . " Does this ethic have any need of a god who is more than an expression of human love?

7. The reference to Judith's saving Israel by an act of "deliberate sexual seduction" illustrates certain problems which attend Biblical argument. Consult *The Book of Judith* (in *The Apocrypha*) and comment on the validity of the argument.

How About Him?

"A thing isn't a sin unless it harms somebody."

The SITUATIONAL THEOLOGIANS

Reprinted from *The Catholic Week* (25 July 1969), p. 6.

DISCUSSION QUESTIONS

1. The cartoon responds to the situational theologians who argue that "A thing isn't a sin unless it harms somebody." Does this group include Joseph Fletcher?

2. The argument (which appeared in *The Catholic Week*) can be resolved into two syllogisms and made to comment on, say, homosexuality.

    The major premise of the first grants that "A thing is a sin if it harms somebody."

    The major premise of the second is identical with the conclusion of the first.

    Construct the syllogisms and comment on their reliability.

4

Argument by Authority

Everyone knows Kennedy stole the 1960 election.
Trust John R. Brinkley, MD., C.M., Dr. P.H. . . .
Washington Post assails Nixon administration.
Musical is ". . . a delight" — *New Yorker*
Scientist offers new book affirming Atlantis.

Many of the things a person believes (or is asked to believe) must be accepted simply on the authority of an expert. His doctor says he has high blood pressure. His mechanic says the car needs a new clutch-plate. His newspaper reviews a new book and calls it dreadful. Scientific authorities say that his universe is expanding. In such instances, one is asked to accept a view on the basis of someone's testimony.

It is reasonable to credit such testimony if it fulfills two conditions: (1) The speaker must be a genuine authority on the subject at hand. (2) There must exist no reasonable probability of his being biased. When Doctor Benjamin Spock, for example, turns from his distinguished career as a pediatrician to criticize American involvement in Vietnam, one can justly question his expertness in the area. And when Debbie Reynolds appears on television proclaiming the excellence of Lustre-Creme shampoo, one knows she is being paid for doing the commercial and infers a degree of bias.

It must be remembered, of course, that these unreliable arguments are not necessarily false. Doctor Spock may be expressing a profound truth about Vietnam, and Debbie Reynolds may be giving her honest opinion of Lustre-Creme shampoo. Nonetheless, it would be unreasonable to accept the arguments *solely* on the authority of these speakers. One should relate their views to other evidence and to the word of other authorities.

Many arguments raise the question of genuine expertness. The authority cited may be unnamed. (An advertisement for *The Illustrated Encyclopedia of Sex* includes glowing recom-

mendations from "a teacher," "a judge," and "a minister.") He
may be unfamiliar. ("*Future Profile* is an important book—
readable, provocative, and profoundly informed"—Dr. Winston
X. Reynolds.) He may be known largely by his degrees. (A
Kansas medico, in recommending goat-gland surgery to restore
virility, signed himself "John R. Brinkley, M.D., C.M., Dr. P.H.,
ScD. . . . ") Or he may appear with magnified credentials. (A
temperance circular quoting William Gladstone's on "the ravages
of drink," described him as "the greatest prime minister in
English history.")

Sometimes speakers of unquestioned authority (like William
Gladstone) express themselves in areas outside their competence.
One hears physicists talking politics, priests discussing demog-
raphy, and movie stars recommending floor wax. An advertisement describes a star third-baseman, then adds, "His good
judgment on the ball field holds true with his selection of wearing
apparel. That's why he picks Munsingwear all the way." A religious newspaper headlines an article by L. Nelson Bell, M.D.,
"A Physician Looks at the Virgin Birth," then prints his Biblical
argument based on a reading of Isaiah, Matthew, and Luke.
Dr. Bell makes no medical references at all. Such spokesmen
must be judged on the quality of their evidence, not on their
word as experts.

Equally questionable as authorities in argument are "God"
and "everyone." Because the claim is not subject to hard evidence,
one can maintain almost any conclusion by saying it conforms to
the divine will. A Bermuda woman once explained to James
Thurber: "I hoped that my sister would be married before the
baby came, but God had other plans for her." At a California
Democratic rally in 1956, a clergyman announced that Adlai
Stevenson was God's choice for President of the United States.
And a correspondent to the *Mobile Press*, in 1969, expressed
confidence that the tragedies falling on the Kennedy family
were divine justice answering their misdeeds.

Christian spokesmen often quote passages from the Bible to
declare the will of God, and thus open up a complex area of
argument. As mentioned earlier, religious questions often do not
lend themselves to meaningful discussion because disputants
cannot agree on necessary definitions. Clearly, an argument
involving Biblical authority can be persuasive only when addressed to someone who already accepts the validity of Scripture
and who interprets it in the same sense as the speaker. (Large

differences exist, for example, between those who claim the Bible *is* the word of God, those who believe it *contains* the word of God, those who accept it as a literary expression of human truths, and those who reject it altogether.) And even where preliminary accord exists, problems remain. Because the Biblical texts were written over some 1300 years and represent a wide variety of authors, occasions, opinions, literary types, and translations, a spokesman can find a passage or two to support any argument he chooses to make. Bishop James Pike illustrated this by asking ironically: "How many persons have been reborn from meditating on the last line of Psalm 137: 'Blessed shall be he that taketh and dasheth the little ones against the stones'?" Consequently, the reader facing a Scriptural argument should take time to trace the references. He will find that authors often quote passages out of context and that, not uncommonly, they quote from an inaccurate memory and refer to lines scarcely related to the issue at hand.

The authority of "everyone" is cited in statements beginning "they say," "everyone knows," "all fair-minded people agree," etc. Such argument can be convincing in instances where "they" (i.e., some notable majority) have demonstrably committed themselves in an area they are competent to judge. Advertisements announcing "More women choose Simplicity than any other pattern" and "Budweiser — Largest Selling Beer in the World" tend to be impressive because, in these areas, a mass authority is superior to that of any particular expert. It is important to remember that America's democratic procedures and its jury system both rely on the expertness of "everyone."

But mass authority can be distorted in a number of ways. It can be claimed arbitrarily. ("Everyone knows that John Kennedy stole the 1960 election.") It can be coupled with ambiguous language. ("More men get more pleasure out of Roi-Tan than any other cigar at its price.") And it can be invoked in areas which call for technical expertness. (A recent Gallup Poll revealed that 48 percent of Americans believe that flying saucers are real.) In such instances, "everyone" is a dubious authority.

The word of a genuine expert will not, of course, settle all questions. Many issues are notably complex, and on these authorities differ. Legal authorities disagree whether particular eavesdropping measures violate constitutional safeguards. Scientists differ in arguing whether certain insecticides are hazardous. Sociologists cannot agree whether pornography contributes to criminal acts. Which opinions should the layman accept? In such cases, it is probably wise to credit the larger body of expert opinion or to withhold judgment and await further pronouncements in the area.

It must be noted that some authorities have a more established reputation than others. Many periodicals carry reviews of books, plays, and movies, for example, but those of some of the New York newspapers, *The Christian Science Monitor*, and such national magazines as *Time, Harper's, Saturday Review,* and *The New Yorker* are generally deemed most critically reliable.

If a book, movie, or play wins praise from these critics, the reviews may be quoted in magazine advertisements and on book jackets. If an advertisement quotes reviews from other sources, it strongly suggests that the work was *not* praised by the major critics. The advertisement for Ian Fleming's *On Her Majesty's Secret Service*, for example, boasted these reviews:

> "Packed with danger, mystery, crime and wild pursuit . . . I can recommend it with confidence to readers who sat up late nights to finish the preceding 10." — Vincent Starret, *Chicago Tribune*
>
> "Hair raiser." — *Boston Herald*
>
> "Astonishing . . . ingenious." — *Diner's Club Magazine*
>
> "The hottest sleuth in the suspense field, James Bond, really tops himself in this new Ian Fleming thriller." — *St. Paul Dispatch*
>
> "More fun than Tarzan and Superman combined." — *Denver Post*
>
> "Taut, instructive and artfully told." — *Chicago Daily News*
>
> "You can't argue with success." — Anthony Boucher, *New York Times Book Review*
>
> "A fine surge of adrenalin in our veins." — *Columbus Dispatch*
>
> "Solid Fleming." — *New York Herald Tribune Books*

Though it appears at first glance that authorities were unanimous in acclaiming this novel, such is scarcely the case. Only two of the quoted reviews were from major critics, and these were notably less enthusiastic than the others. *The New York Times* declared it will not argue with general taste. And *The New York Herald Tribune* said that the novel is a good example of the kind Fleming writes.

This is not to suggest that a reader should not enjoy Ian Fleming novels. He should, however, recognize the varying standards of critical authorities and not misread such advertisements as expressions of universal acclaim.

Even when a spokesman is an admitted expert in the field under discussion, his argument should be examined for the possibility of bias. An argument is said to have a probable bias if the authority profits from the view he expresses or if he reflects the predictable loyalty or routine antagonism of a group. To dismiss the testimony of such a person is not to call him a liar or even to say he is wrong; it means that a condition exists which makes it unreasonable to accept a conclusion solely on his authority.

An authority profits from making an argument when it enhances his financial position, his prestige, or both. The money factor is easy to recognize when Lorne Green recommends Chevrolet automobiles, when the Tobacco Institute denies evidence that cigarettes cause lung cancer, and when spokesmen for outdoor movies protest the unnaturalness of daylight savings time. However, the effects of prestige on an expert are more difficult to determine. Few genuine scientific authorities have affirmed the existence of the Loch Ness monster or of abominable snowmen, for example; but these few have won a level of recognition—along with television appearances, speaking engagements, book contracts, etc.—which they could never gain voicing more orthodox opinions. This acclaim must be taken into consideration when assessing their testimony.

Similarly, argument by authority is presumed biased if it reflects the traditional loyalty or antagonism of a particular group. An example is this criticism of the movie *Martin Luther*:

> Although technically well produced and acted, I detected in it the writing and directing techniques of "emphasis and omission" often employed by communist film propagandists.

The reviewer is William H. Mooring of *The Catholic Herald*. Equally unreliable authorities would be *Pravda* picturing the plight of blacks in the United States, or a Ku Klux Klan leader describing the condition of blacks in Louisiana.

This presumption of bias appears most notably in political argument. When any Democrat is nominated for president, the man and his platform will be lauded in Democratic periodicals (*Washington Post, St. Louis Post-Dispatch, Commonweal*) and condemned by Republican publications (*Chicago Tribune, Los Angeles Times, National Review, U.S. News & World Report*). When any president finishes a State of the Union message, opposition spokesmen will call his program inadequate, wrong-headed, and potentially dangerous. These claims must be judged on specific evidence; such predictable views carry little authority.

Besides a doubtful expert and a biased opinion, other misleading features attend argument by authority. Statements are sometimes abridged. (The advertisement for Kyle Onstott's *Mandingo* offers the review: ". . . like no other book ever written about the South . . . "—*Dallas News*) Assertions may be irrelevant to the present issue. (The paperback edition of *Nightmare in Pink* carries Richard Condon's opinion that "John D. MacDonald is the great American storyteller.") Quotations appear without source. (See *Hand in Hand*—"The Most Widely Praised Motion Picture of Them All!") Undated statements can be impressive. (During the 1968 presidential campaign, Nixon spokesmen gave wide circulation to a statement about federal spending which Vice President Humphrey had made twenty years earlier.) And exact quotations can be presented in distorting context. (Under the heading "HOW L. B. J. WOULD REMAKE AMERICA," *Common Sense* printed a sentence from the President's 1964 State of the Union message: "We are going to try to take all the money that we think is unnecessarily being spent and take it from the 'haves' and give it to the 'have nots' that need it so much." As the context of his speech made clear, Johnson did not advocate taking from the rich to give to the poor. He proposed taking money from the more heavily funded federal programs and putting it in those with smaller appropriations.)

Expert testimony can lend itself to bald misstatement of fact, either on the part of an authority or of those who quote him. A national columnist attacked Quentin Reynolds as a communist, a voluptuary, and a war-profiteer. A U.S. Senator called newsman Drew Pearson a child-molester. Many have circulated the story that three Pennsylvania students on LSD became blind from staring at the sun for several hours, and that a Michigan teacher took off all of her clothes to demonstrate female anatomy to her co-ed sex-education class. These claims were total fabrications.

Similarly, fictional quotations appear as evidence. For many years, the statement "We shall force the United States to spend itself to destruction" has been attributed to Nikolai Lenin and used to ground American political argument. More recently, spokesmen have circulated a statement protesting the communist threat and concluding "We need law and order"; they ascribe this to Adolph Hitler. Both quotations are fictional. A recent news story arguing that marijuana may cure cancer quoted Dr. James H.

Kostinger, director of research for the Pittsburgh Academy of Forensic Medicine, who had been conducting studies in this area for four years. Investigation revealed that the Academy did not exist and that no medical school in Pittsburgh had ever heard of Dr. James H. Kostinger.

HOW RELIABLE ARE THESE ARGUMENTS FROM AUTHORITY?

1. *"Miracle of Saint Therese* is a film of unusual spiritual worth." — *Messenger of the Sacred Heart*

2. In the Song of Solomon, 6:10, God describes a pure woman as being "fair as the moon, clear as the sun." I do not believe that our Lord will permit the fairness and beauty of the moon to be corrupted by sinful men seeking to establish bases from which they can spread military death and destruction.

3. *Shakespeare of London* by Marchette Chute. "The best biography of Shakespeare" — Bernadine Kielty, *Book-of-the-Month Club News*

4. From 1958 to 1963, the rate of forcible rape in this country decreased by 1 percent. But from 1964 to 1969 it jumped 67 percent. A survey conducted by Hollywood Social Studies polled police chiefs, vice squad commanders, and juvenile division commanders from the nation's 56 largest cities, plus 72 others ranging down to 10,000 population. Over 91 percent of these authorities thought that revealingly short skirts were part of the cause of this rise in rape statistics. Only 5 percent said they were not.

5. Winston is America's largest-selling cigarette.

6. In 1968, Pope Paul VI said that bones found beneath St. Peter's Basilica eighteen years earlier, had been identified "in a manner we can think of as convincing" as those of the apostle St. Peter.

7. Sirhan B. Sirhan insists that in killing Senator Robert Kennedy, he was a cool and rational assassin, a martyr nobly seeking to save his people, the Arabs.

Pot: A Rational Approach

JOEL FORT, M.D.

There are an estimated 10,000,000 Americans who smoke
marijuana either regularly or occasionally, and they have very
obvious reasons for wishing that pot were treated more sensibly
by the law. As one of the 190,000,000 who have never smoked
marijuana, I also favor the removal of grass from the criminal
laws, but for less personal reasons. It is my considered opinion,
after studying drug use and drug laws in 30 nations and dealing
with drug-abuse problems professionally for 15 years, that the
present marijuana statutes in America not only are bad laws for
the offending minority but are bad for the vast majority of us
who never have lit a marijuana cigarette and never will.

That some changes in these laws are coming in the near future
is virtually certain, but it is not at all sure that the changes will
be improvements.

On May 19, 1969, the U.S. Supreme Court, in an 8–0 vote,
declared that the Marijuana Tax Act of 1937 was unconstitutional. This decision delighted the defendant, Timothy Leary,
and was no surprise at all to lawyers who specialize in the fine
points of constitutional law. It had long been recognized that
the Marijuana Tax Act was "vulnerable" – a polite term meaning
that the law had been hastily drawn, rashly considered and rail-
roaded through Congress in a mood of old-maidish terror that
spent no time on the niceties of the Bill of Rights, scientific fact
or common sense.

Celebrations by marijuanaphiles and lamentations by mari-
juanaphobes, however, are both premature. The Court, while
throwing out this one inept piece of legislation, specifically declared that Congress has the right to pass laws governing the
use, sale and possession of this drug (provided these laws stay
within the perimeter of the Constitution). And, of course, state
laws against pot, which are often far harsher than the Federal
law, still remain in effect.

There were two defects found by the Supreme Court in the
Federal anti-marijuana law – a section that requires the suspect
to pay a tax on the drug, thus incriminating himself, in violation
of the Fifth Amendment; and a section that assumes (rather than
requiring proof) that a person with foreign-grown marijuana in

---

Abridged from *Playboy* (October 1969), pp. 131, 154, 216–218.

his possession knows it is smuggled. These provisions were per-
versions of traditional American jurisprudence, no less than the
remaining parts of the law that are bound to fall when challenged
before the Supreme Court. These forthcoming decisions will,
inevitably, affect the anti-marijuana laws of the individual
states as well. However, the striking down of the old laws does
not guarantee that the new ones will be more enlightened; it
merely invites more carefully drawn statutes that are less vulnerable to judicial review. In fact, in a message to Congress,
President Nixon specifically demanded harsher penalties for
marijuana convictions. But every sane and fair-minded person
must be seriously concerned that the new laws are more just and
more in harmony with known fact than the old ones. In my
opinion, such new laws must treat marijuana no more harshly
than alcohol is presently treated.

It is ironic that our present pot laws are upheld chiefly by the
older generation, and flouted and condemned by the young; for
it is the senior generation that should understand the issue most
clearly, having lived through the era of alcohol prohibition.
They saw with their own eyes that the entire nation—not just
the drinkers and the sellers of liquor—suffered violent moral
and mental harm from that particular outbreak of armed and
rampant puritanism. They should certainly remember that attempts to legislate morality result only in widespread disrespect
for law, new markets and new profits for gangsters, increased
violence and such wholesale bribery and corruption that the
Government itself becomes a greater object of contempt than
the criminal class. Above all, they should be able to see the
parallel between the lawless Twenties and the anarchic Sixties
and realize that both were produced by bad laws—laws that had
no right to exist in the first place.

"Bad law," it has been said, "is the worst form of tyranny."
An open tyranny breeds open rebellion, and the issues are clear-
cut; bad law, in an otherwise democratic nation, provokes a kind
of cultural nihilism in which good and evil become hopelessly
confused and the rebel, instead of formulating a single precise
program, takes a perverse delight in anything and everything
that will shock, startle, perplex, anger, baffle and offend the
establishment. Thus it was during alcohol prohibition and thus it
is under marijuana prohibition. The parallel is not obvious only
because there were already millions of whiskey drinkers when
the Volstead Act became law in 1919, leading to immediate

flouting of "law and order" by vast hordes—whereas the use of marijuana did not become extensive until the early 1950s, more than 13 years after the Government banned pot in 1937. But the results, despite the delay, are the same: We have bred a generation of psychological rebels.

Banning marijuana not only perpetuates the rebelliousness of the young but it also establishes a frightening precedent, under which puritanical bias is more important to our legislators than experimentally determined fact—something every scientist must dread. Dr. Philip Handler, board chairman of the National Science Foundation, bluntly told a House subcommittee investigating drug laws, "It is our puritan ethics . . . rather than science" that say we should not smoke marijuana.

Consider the most recent study of the effects of marijuana, conducted under careful laboratory conditions and reported in *Science*. This is the research performed by Drs. Norman E. Zinberg and Andrew T. Weil at Boston University in 1968. This study was "double-blind": that is, neither the subjects nor the researchers knew, during a given session, whether the product being smoked was real marijuana (from the female Cannabis plant) or an inactive placebo (from the male Cannabis plant). Thus, both suggestibility by the subjects and bias by the experimenters were kept to the scientific minimum. The results were:

1. Marijuana causes a moderate increase in heartbeat rate, some redness of the eyes and virtually no other physical effects. Contrary to the belief of both users and policemen, pot does not dilate the pupils—this myth apparently derives from the tradition of smoking Cannabis in a darkened room; it is the darkness that dilates the pupils.

2. Pot does not affect the blood-sugar level, as alcohol does, nor cause abnormal reactions of the involuntary muscles, as LSD often does, nor produce any effects likely to be somatically damaging. In the words of Zinberg and Weil, "The significance of this near absence of physical effects is twofold. First, it demonstrates once again the uniqueness of hemp among psychoactive drugs, most of which strongly affect the body as well as the mind. . . . Second, it makes it unlikely that marijuana has any seriously detrimental physical effects in either short-term or long-term usage."

3. As sociologist Howard Becker pointed out long ago, on the basis of interviews with users, the marijuana "high" is a learned

experience. Subjects who had never had Cannabis before simply did not get a "buzz" and reported very minimal subjective reactions, even while physically "loaded" with very high doses, while experienced users were easily turned on.

4. The hypothesis about "set and setting" strongly influencing drug reactions was confirmed. The pharmacological properties of a psychoactive drug are only one factor in a subject's response: equally important—perhaps more important—are the set (his expectations and personality type) and the setting (the total emotional mood of the environment and persons in it).

5. Both inexperienced subjects and longtime users did equally well on some tests for concentration and mental stability, even while they were on very high doses. On tests requiring a higher ability to focus attention, the inexperienced users did show some temporary mental impairment, but the veterans sailed right on, as if they were not high at all. In short, experienced potheads do not have even a *temporary* lowering of the intelligence while they are high, much less a permanent mental impairment.

6. On some tests, the experienced users scored even higher while stoned than they did when tested without any drug.

7. Not only alcohol but even tobacco has more adverse effects on the body than marijuana does.

As Zinberg and Weil noted sardonically in a later article in *The New York Times Magazine*, there is a vicious circle operating in relation to marijuana: "Administrators of scientific and Government institutions feel that marijuana is dangerous. Because it is dangerous, they are reluctant to allow [research] to be done on it. Because no work is done, people continue to think of it as dangerous. We hope that our own study has significantly weakened this trend."

One slight sign that the trend may have been weakened was the appearance last June of a study by the Bureau of Motor Vehicles in the state of Washington concerning the effects of Cannabis on driving ability. Using driving-traffic simulators, not only did the study find that marijuana has less adverse effect on driving ability than alcohol—which many investigators have long suspected—but also, as in the Boston study, the evidence indicated that the only detrimental effect is on inexperienced users. Veteran potheads behave behind the wheel as if they were not drugged at all.

In short, we seem to have a drug here that makes many users very euphoric and happy — high — without doing any of the damage done by alcohol, narcotics, barbiturates, amphetamines or even tobacco.

But we didn't have to wait until 1968 to learn that pot is relatively harmless. Some research has been done in the past, in spite of the vicious circle mentioned by Zinberg and Weil. As far back as 1942, the mayor of New York City, Fiorello La Guardia, alarmed by sensational press stories about "the killer drug, marijuana" that was allegedly driving people to rape and murder, appointed a commission to investigate the pot problem in his city. The commission was made up of 31 eminent physicians, psychiatrists, psychologists, etc., and six officers from the city's narcotics bureau. If there was any bias in that study, it must have been directed against marijuana, considering the presence of the narcotics officers, not to mention psychiatrists and M.D.s, who were then, as now, rather conservative groups. Nevertheless, after two years of hard study, including psychological and medical examinations of users, electroencephalograms to examine for brain damage, sociological digging into the behavior patterns associated with marijuana use and intelligence tests on confirmed potheads, the commission concluded:

Those who have been smoking marijuana for a period of years showed no mental or physical deterioration which may be attributed to the drug. . . . Marijuana is not a drug of addiction, comparable to morphine. . . . Marijuana does not lead to morphine or heroin or cocaine addiction. . . . Marijuana is not the determining factor in the commission of major crimes. . . . The publicity concerning the catastrophic effects of marijuana smoking in New York City is unfounded.

Even earlier, a study of marijuana use in the Panama Canal Zone was undertaken by a notably conservative body, the United States Army. Published in 1925, the study concluded, "There is no evidence that marijuana as grown here is a habit-forming drug" and that "Delinquencies due to marijuana smoking which result in trial by military court are negligible in number when compared with delinquencies resulting from the use of alcoholic drinks which also may be classed as stimulants or intoxicants."

What may be the classic study in the whole field goes back further: to the 1893–1894 report of the seven-member Indian Hemp Drug Commission that received evidence from 1193 witnesses from all regions of the country (then including Burma and Pakistan), professionals and laymen, Indians and British, most of whom were required to answer in writing seven comprehensive questions covering most aspects of the subject. The commission found that there was no connection between the use of marijuana and "social and moral evils" such as crime, violence or bad character. It also concluded that occasional and moderate use may be beneficial; that moderate use is attended by no injurious physical, mental or other effects; and that moderate use is the rule: "It has been the most striking feature of this inquiry to find how little the effects of hemp drugs have intruded themselves on observation. The large numbers of witnesses of all classes who profess never to have seen them, the very few witnesses who could so recall a case to give any definite account of it and the manner in which a large proportion of these cases broke down on the first attempt to examine them are facts which combine to show most clearly how little injury society has hitherto sustained from hemp drugs." This conclusion is all the more remarkable when one realizes that the pattern of use in India included far more potent forms and doses of Cannabis than are presently used in the United States. The commission, in its conclusion, stated:

Total prohibition of the hemp drugs is neither necessary nor expedient in consideration of their ascertained effects, of the prevalence of the habit of using them, of the social or religious feelings on the subject and of the possibility of its driving the consumers to have recourse to other stimulants [alcohol] or narcotics which may be more deleterious.

Ever since there have been attempts to study marijuana scientifically, every major investigation has arrived at, substantially, the same conclusions, and these directly contradict the mythology of the Federal Bureau of Narcotics. In contrast with the above facts, consider the following advertisement, circulated before the passage of the 1937 Federal anti-marijuana law:

Beware! Young and Old—People in All Walks of Life! This [picture of a marijuana cigarette] may be handed you by the *friendly stranger*. It contains the Killer Drug "Marijuana"—a powerful narcotic in which lurks *Murder! Insanity! Death!*

Such propaganda was widely disseminated in the mid-1930s, and it was responsible for stampeding Congress into the passage of a law unique in all American history in the extent to which it is based on sheer ignorance and misinformation.

Few people realize how recent anti-marijuana legislation is. Pot was widely used as a folk medicine in the 19th Century. Its recreational use in this country began in the early 1900s with Mexican laborers in the Southwest, spread to Mexican Americans and Negroes in the South and then the North, and then moved from rural to urban areas. In terms of public reaction and social policy, little attention was paid to pot until the mid-1930s (although some generally unenforced state laws existed before then). At that time, a group of former alcohol-prohibition agents headed by Harry J. Anslinger, who became head of the Federal Bureau of Narcotics, began issuing statements to the public (via a cooperative press) claiming that marijuana caused crime, violence, assassination, insanity, release of anti-social inhibitions, mental deterioration and numerous other onerous activities.

In what became a model for future Federal and state legislative action on marijuana, Congressional hearings were held in 1937 on the Marijuana Tax Act. No medical, scientific or sociological evidence was sought or heard; no alternatives to criminalizing users and sellers were considered; and the major attention was given to the oilseed, birdseed and paint industries' need for unrestrained access to the hemp plant from which marijuana comes. A U.S. Treasury Department witness began his testimony by stating flatly that "Marijuana is being used extensively by high school children in cigarettes with deadly effect," and went on to introduce as further "evidence" an editorial from a Washington newspaper supposedly quoting the American Medical Association as having stated in its journal that marijuana use was one of the problems of greatest menace in the United States. Fortunately for historical analysis, a Dr. Woodward, serving as legislative counsel for the American Medical Association, was present to point out that the statement in question was by Anslinger and had only been reported in the A.M.A. journal.

Dr. Woodward deserves a posthumous accolade for his single-handed heroic efforts to introduce reason and sanity to the hearing. Most importantly, the doctor (who was also a lawyer) criticized the Congressmen for proposing a law that would interfere with future medical uses of Cannabis and pointed out that no one from the Bureau of Prisons had been produced to show the number of prisoners "addicted" to marijuana, no one from the Children's Bureau or Office of Education to show the nature and extent of the "habit" among children and no one from the Division of Mental Hygiene or the Division of Pharmacology of the Public Health Service to give "direct and primary evidence rather than indirect and hearsay evidence." Saying that he assumed it was true that a certain amount of "narcotic addiction" existed, since "the newspapers have called attention to it so prominently that there must be some grounds for their statements," he concluded that the particular type of statute under consideration was neither necessary nor desirable. The Congressmen totally ignored the content of Dr. Woodward's testimony and attacked his character, qualifications, experience and relationship to the American Medical Association, all of which were impeccable. He was then forced to admit that he could not say with certainty that no problem existed. Finally, his testimony was brought to a halt with the warning, "You are not cooperative in this. If you want to advise us on legislation, you ought to come here with some constructive proposals rather than criticism, rather than trying to throw obstacles in the way of something that the Federal Government is trying to do."

A similar but shorter hearing was held in the Senate, where Anslinger presented anecdotal "evidence" that marijuana caused murder, rape and insanity.

Thus, the Marijuana Tax Act of 1937 was passed—and out of it grew a welter of state laws that were, in many cases, even more hastily ill conceived.

DISCUSSION QUESTIONS

1. Since the essay says little about specific features of the experimental tests with marijuana, the reader must base his judgment on the word of cited authorities. Compare and evaluate the following:
   (a) Joel Fort, M.D.
   (b) 10,000,000 Americans who smoke marijuana
   (c) the U.S. Supreme Court
   (d) the Bill of Rights
   (e) common sense
   (f) President Nixon [who later changed his mind about this matter]
   (g) every sane and fair-minded person

    (h) the person who said "Bad law is the worst form of
          tyranny"
    (i) Dr. Philip Handler, board chairman of the National
          Science Foundation
    (j) Drs. Norman E. Zinberg and Andrew T. Weil
    (k) Boston University
    (l) *Science*
    (m) sociologist Howard Becker
    (n) the Bureau of Motor Vehicles in the state of Washington
    (o) the New York City commission made up of thirty-one
          eminent physicians, psychiatrists, psychologists,
          etc., and six officers from the City's narcotics bureau
    (p) the United States Army
    (q) the Indian Hemp Drug Commission that received
          evidence from 1193 witnesses
    (r) the Federal Bureau of Narcotics
    (s) Harry J. Anslinger
    (t) Congress
    (u) a U.S. Treasury Department witness
    (v) the A.M.A. journal
    (w) Dr. Woodward (who was also a lawyer)
    (x) various state legislatures
    (y) *Playboy*

2. What conclusions can one draw from the author's definition of the word "vulnerable"?

3. The author bases his central conclusions on the Zinberg-Weil experiments ("the most recent study of the effects of marijuana"), on a study by the Bureau of Motor Vehicles in the state of Washington, on the report of the New York City commission, on the U.S. Army study in the Panama Canal Zone, and on the conclusions of the Indian Hemp Drug Commission. Are these equally impressive as evidence?

4. Do these seem to be the only marijuana tests conducted to date? Is there any reason to infer that there were other studies which did not reach the same conclusion?

5. If it is true—as many of these studies suggest—that marijuana is no more harmful than alcohol or tobacco, is this persuasive evidence that the use of marijuana should be fully legalized?

6. The New York City commission reported that "Marijuana is not a drug of addiction, comparable to morphine. . . . Marijuana does not lead to morphine or heroin or cocaine addiction. . . . Marijuana is not the determining factor in the commission of major crimes." Discuss these as statements which need careful definition before they can be argued at all.

Heroin, Marijuana, and LSD

DAVID A. NOEBEL

Narcotics, of course, are dangerous even when administered under the care of a physician. Both heroin and marijuana are exceedingly dangerous. Heroin is the strongest and most addictive opium derivative and is either sniffed into the nasal passages through the nose or mixed in water and heated to form a solution and injected intravenously with a hypodermic directly into the bloodstream. Marijuana is a derivative from the hemp weed, which affects the nervous system and the brain of the user, causing mental unbalance for varying periods of time and in which a sufficient dose of the active substance — tetrahydrocannabianol — is capable of producing all the hallucinatory and psychotic effects relative to LSD (which is conceded to be one of the most powerful drugs known).

Repeated use of heroin produces psychological and physical dependence in which the user has an overwhelming compulsion to continue using the drug. Under heroin the body develops a tolerance for it in the bloodstream and virtually all bodily functions are attuned to that presence. Of course, once the victim has the habit, he stops at nothing to satisfy it, and since heroin is considered incurably addictive, when the narcotic is no longer in the body, death can result even during the withdrawal process.

Marijuana, on the other hand, is no less to be desired. In a timely article on narcotics, Dr. Susan Huck, in a personal interview with the noted geneticist, Dr. Louis Diaz de Souza (who has spent 18 years investigating the effects of marijuana on the human body) found that "even one smoke of marijuana does calamitous damage to the chromosomes." The doctor told her that damage to one chromosome, "may mean that the child will be hemophilian, or mongoloid, or afflicted with leukemia. The chromosome may pass on from one generation to another. The child of the marijuana user may show this damage or his child may show it."[1]

Unfortunately, a semantical argument has developed over the usage of the word "addictive" and "dependent." Some argue the

Reprinted from *The Beatles: A Study in Drugs, Sex and Revolution* (Tulsa: Christian Crusade Publications, 1969), pp. 13–17.

[1]*American Opinion*, May, 1969, p. 58.

drug is not addictive, but rather the user only becomes dependent
on it. Others, e.g., Dr. Hardin Jones, of the Donner Laboratory
at the University of California (Berkeley), maintains that
marijuana is habit-forming and with continued use it is addictive.
Naturally, the argument makes little difference since (1) few are
so sophisticated as to see any difference between "addictive"
and "dependent" and (2) since it takes the user away from reality
and removes his normal inhibitions, marijuana is harmful
apart from either word. Smith, Kline & French Laboratories,
in a special report prepared primarily for educators, found marijuana not only impairing the user's ability to drive an automobile,
but producing such physical effects as dizziness, dry mouth,
dilated pupils and burning eyes, urinary frequency, diarrhea,
nausea and vomiting.[2]

Dr. Hardin Jones in his research found marijuana not only
habit-forming and addictive with continued use, but also reported
(1) that although it does not lead to the use of harder narcotics
through chemical addiction, it promotes a curiosity about the
harder drugs; (2) that its effect is cumulative, witness that a
neophyte needs several joints to "turn on," whereas a professional can get high on one; (3) that it interferes with normal
perceptions; (4) that its cumulative impact brings repeated
hallucinations that disturb the reference memory, causing
(5) wholesale abandonment of goals and ambitions.

Jones goes on to say that marijuana and other drugs are in
a very real sense sexual stimulants. Marijuana is a mild aphro-
disiac. "It enhances sensitivity and makes a person more receptive to sensual stimuli," he says, "but this condition only lasts
a short period of time and chronic marijuana users find that sex
activities without the drug are difficult and confusing."[3]

And the world-famous authority on marijuana, Dr. Constandinos J. Miras, of the University of Athens, who has been
studying man and marijuana for over twenty-five years, found
marijuana users to have abnormal brain wave readings and
marked behavioral changes. Longtime users, for example,
revealed chrónic lethargy and loss of inhibitions for two years
after their last usage. Many of his subjects were slipping into
less demanding jobs as the habit got a firmer grip on them and
were variously depressed and exalted, not always sure when
they were having hallucinations. Others went through a rapid

[2] *Tulsa Daily World*, May 5, 1967, p. 8.
[3] *Tulsa Daily World*, September 25, 1969, p. 16A.

succession of physical changes—crying, laughing, sluggishness, hunger for sugar, hallucinating. The idea of the so-called harmless use of marijuana is either ignorance or deception. And one State official in Maryland remarked that marijuana not only induces a lethargy in most people, but a dangerous attitude toward the community.

The hallucinogens which are popularly known as psychedelics (since they produce sensations distorting time, space, sound and color) include LSD, STP and DMT. All hallucinogens create hallucinations which lessen the user's ability to discriminate between fact and fancy, and studies indicate that LSD may cause chromosome damage which could result in mental deficiencies and blood diseases in children born to users. One of the foremost authorities in the United States on LSD is Dr. J. Thomas Ungerleider. He states that, "LSD has been called a conscious-expanding drug. In fact, it is quite the reverse. It decreases one's ability to select and pay attention. Therefore, it decreases conscious functions. Sensations do become intensified. Perception, however, is not enhanced, and visual and auditory acuteness are not revolutionized, but rather are distorted." Since LSD dulls the user's objective judgment, which is replaced by purely subjective values, Dr. Ungerleider says, "LSD seems to affect a person's value system."[4]

Then, too, both the amphetamines and barbiturates are danger drugs. Amphetamines, often called pep pills, produce a feeling of excitation which usually manifests itself in appetite loss with an increasing ability to go without sleep for long periods of time. The most common amphetamines are Benzedrine (called Bennies), Dexedrine (called Dexies) and Methadrine (referred to as crystal or speed). The danger, of course, with amphetamines as well as barbiturates is the psychological desire to continue using the drugs. The most common barbiturates are Amytal (referred to as Blue Heavens), Nembutal (or Yellow Jackets) and Seconal (called Red Devils or Red Birds). In the jargon of drug addicts, barbiturates in general are referred to as "goofballs" and affect the central nervous system and the brain by slowly depressing the mental and physical functions of the body. A person under the influence of a barbiturate will be disoriented to time, place and person and may experience delusions and hallucinations.

Obviously, such drugs cannot be equated with apple pie and

[4]*Tulsa Tribune*, February 24, 1967, p. 14.

vanilla ice cream. And any drug—marijuana, for example, which at one moment makes a person feel so tiny he is not able to step off an eight-inch curb, and yet an hour later makes him feel so huge he could step off a ten-story building—is dangerous. Any individual, who under the influence of marijuana can barrel down the highway at 80 mph and assume he is only traveling 20 mph, or drive through a red light which appears to be green and smash into a row of cars which appeared to be a mile away, is dangerous. And, any drug—LSD, for example, which makes a person feel he can fly like a bird and so take off from a four-story building only to discover he is flying to his death—is not safe.

DISCUSSION QUESTIONS

1. Because no experimental studies are described in the essay, the reader must base his judgment on the testimony of a number of authorities. Compare and evaluate them:
   (a) David A. Noebel
   (b) Dr. Susan Huck
   (c) Dr. Louis Diaz de Souza
   (d) *American Opinion*
   (e) some [who] argue the drug is not addictive
   (f) others
   (g) Dr. Hardin Jones
   (h) the Donner Laboratory at the University of California (Berkeley)
   (i) Smith, Kline & French Laboratories
   (j) a special report prepared primarily for educators
   (k) *Tulsa Daily World*
   (l) Dr. Constandinos J. Miras
   (m) the University of Athens
   (n) one State official in Maryland
   (o) Dr. J. Thomas Ungerleider
   (p) *Tulsa Tribune*
   (q) Christian Crusade Publications

2. The author writes that "Narcotics, of course, are dangerous even when . . . ," that "The danger, of course, with amphetamines as well as barbituates is . . . ," that LSD "is conceded to be one of the most powerful drugs known," that "heroin is considered incurably addictive,"

that "such drugs cannot be equated with apple pie," etc.
Comment on the value of this argumentative technique.

3. In the statements taken directly from *American Opinion*, who is being quoted?

4. Compare these statements about the effects of marijuana smoking with those cited by Dr. Fort in the preceding essay. Which seem more credible? How can one account for the massive difference of opinion?

The Womanly Image:
Character assassination through the ages

PAULA STERN

I had a job interview several weeks ago. Friends warned me not to be too aggressive. During the interview, I tried to present myself as a competent candidate, able to "think like a man" and yet not to be a "masculine" female. After fielding several questions relevant to the job, I suddenly heard, "Miss Stern, are you in love?"

Do you think they asked my competition—seven men—the same question? No, for a cultureful of reasons. Jacqueline Kennedy Onassis was quoted once as saying, "There are two kinds of women: those who want power in the world and those who want power in bed." And the majority seem to agree with Jackie that the latter is socially more acceptable. That's how many women in America have been taught to think. And that's how many men think women ought to think.

Children are taught sexual stereotypes early, as well as the appropriate behavior for a sex-determined role in life. Asking a little boy, "What do you want to be when you grow up?" implies to him unlimited possibilities in his future. But most often we ask a little girl, "Where did you get that pretty dress?" suggesting she has only one real option open to her. If we do ask her what she wants to be, she's likely to give the conditioned female response—"A mother." Why? So she can replace her dolls with real babies.

The inspiration for teaching girls to expect less than boys comes from a range of cultural sources, religious, literary, psychiatric, and pop. Even in the Bible, exceptional, independent women like Rebecca, Sarah, Deborah, or Ruth are practically "unknowns" compared with infamous Eve or Delilah.

Eve was made from one of Adam's spare parts, almost as an afterthought, to help him out on earth: "And the Lord God said: 'It is not good that the man should be alone; I will make him a helpmeet for him.'"

There is a contrary legend of the first female, Lilith, who was created equal to man.

Reprinted from *Atlantic Monthly* (March 1970), pp. 87–90.

When the Lord created the world and the first man, he saw that man was alone, and quickly created a woman for him, made like him from the earth, and her name was Lilith. Right away, they began to quarrel. He would say "You sleep on the bottom," and she would say "No, you sleep on the bottom, since we are equals and both formed from the earth. . . ." When Lilith saw what the situation was, she pronounced the Ineffable Name and disappeared into thin air.

But Eve, not Lilith, is the prototypal woman — man's little helper, and his temptress.

Today the heirs to the Bible in America — Jews and Christians — have formalized biblical biases in laws and ceremonies and thereby elevated folklore to religious truths. Among the Orthodox Jews, for example, discrimination against women is so blatant that they are forced to sit segregated behind a curtain or in a balcony. The rationale is that women will distract men from their prayers. It is no wonder that men thank God every morning in their ritual prayer "that Thou has not made me a woman."

The majority of Jews have modified most traditional formalities, but independent female expression is still discouraged if outside the confines of the home or not channeled through husband and children.

A Jewish wife is less subservient to her husband than a gentile wife; so say comparative studies on the subject. That's somewhat understandable since Christianity owes much to a prominent classical heritage, that held the second sex in even lower esteem. Utopia for the male chauvinist is Demosthenes' description of Hellenic male-female arrangements: "We have hetairae for the pleasure of the spirit, concubines for sensual pleasure, and wives to bear our sons."

Aristotle's definition of femininity was "a certain lack of qualities; we should regard the female nature as afflicted with a natural defectiveness." And his disciple Saint Thomas Aquinas echoed him religiously: ". . . a female is something deficient and by chance."

Contempt for women helps explain why they can't become Catholic priests, and why theologians, religious education courses, and Catholic marriage manuals highlight the supposedly inferior and passive qualities of women, who "naturally" subordinate themselves to men.

Traditional Protestant marriage services also perpetuate the attitude that the female is a second-class human being. Like a piece of property, the bride is "given" by her father to the groom, whom she promises to "obey." (Although formally removed from the liturgy, this vow still persists in the popular image of the wedding ceremony.) The clergyman reminds her of her proper place when he says, "I pronounce that they are man and wife." Not husband and wife. Not man and woman. The man keeps his status, while she takes on a new one. Her identity vanishes when she sheds her maiden name for his identification. (Blackstone's *Commentaries* on the law strips a married woman of her rights altogether as she legally dies on her wedding day and becomes "incorporated and consolidate with her husband." Accordingly, "A man cannot grant anything to his wife for the grant would be to suppose her separate existence.")

Although reputedly "progressing" beyond the attitudes of antiquity and the Middle Ages, our enlightened European ancestors continued furnishing us some not too enlightened guidelines on a woman's place — or lack of it — in the world.

High school English students learn from Shakespeare that "Frailty, thy name is woman." Rousseau's contribution to the ideas of man's equality and natural goodness makes one exception: "Woman was made to yield to man and put up with his injustice."

Samuel Johnson's word to the wise woman is that "a man is in general better pleased when he has a good dinner upon his table, than when his wife talks Greek." Honoré de Balzac adds, "A woman who is guided by the head and not the heart is a social pestilence: she has all the defects of a passionate and affectionate woman with none of her compensations: she is without pity, without love, without virtue, without sex."

When in 1776 in America, Abigail Adams asked her husband, John Adams, to "be more generous and favorable to them [women] than your ancestors" and to see to it that the new government not "put such unlimited power into the hands of the husbands," John reportedly chuckled. The Continental Congress ignored her. Two hundred years later Spiro Agnew said: "Three things have been difficult to tame — the ocean, fools, and women. We may soon be able to tame the ocean; fools and women will take a little longer."

America's twentieth-century gospel is the work of Freud. Although Freud supposedly has altered the entire course of Western intellectual history, many of his ideas about women are simply male chauvinism. Letters he wrote his fiancée reveal that he, too, wanted his woman kept relatively docile and ignorant so she couldn't compete with him.

His theories have given scientific status to prejudice. The Freudians—psychiatrists, clinical psychologists, psychiatric social workers, marriage counselors, pastoral counselors, educators, writers, literary critics, historians, anthropologists, sociologists, criminologists, and just plain subway psychiatrists in the newspapers, magazines, and on TV—all subscribe to the belief that "anatomy is destiny." In other words, biological differences between the sexes determine personality differences; standards of mental health depend on the sex of the sick.

How? Dr. Judd Marmor, clinical professor of psychiatry at UCLA, has summarized Freud's views on feminine psychology:

> The most significant of the biological factors . . . is the lack of the penis, which inevitably leads to "penis envy" in the woman. Freud considered penis envy to be a dominant theme in all feminine life, and one that inevitably causes women to feel inferior to men. These deep seated feelings of inadequacy can be compensated for only partially by giving birth to a male child. . . .
>
> Masochism and passivity . . . are natural aspects of normal femininity and whenever a woman behaves in non-passive or aggressive ways or competes with men, she is being neurotically unfeminine. . . .
>
> The most complicated sequence of personality development that women are subject to . . . leads inevitably . . . to less adequate superego formation than in men. This presumably is reflected in women having a poorer sense of justice and weaker social interests than men have.

The myths of marriage counselor G. C. Payetter (from his book *How to Get and Hold a Woman*) have been praised by a number of psychiatrists, and he is consulted in earnest by troubled people. Payetter counsels:

> Feelings, moods, and attitude . . . rule a woman, not facts, reason, nor logic.
>
> By herself woman is all mixed-up but superb as an auxiliary (Genesis: helper).
>
> Woman is inanimate or on the defensive until you create a feeling such as a praise. Then she goes all out.
>
> Never scold or explain when she is angry, remember she is feeling not thinking. . . .
>
> Stop bossing; just manipulate her in her feelings. . . .
>
> The acquisition of knowledge or responsibilities does not lessen women's need for support, guidance, and control. Quite the contrary.
>
> Why ask women when they only need to be told? Why ask women when they hope to be taken?

Any resemblance between women and pet dogs or mute concubines is purely coincidental. No doubt, Payetter's model woman is the runner-up to this year's Miss America, who said women

shouldn't try to run things "because they are more emotional
and men can overcome their emotions with logic."

Even more objectionable are psychiatrist-authors who pronounce final judgment on the mental health of thousands of
women reading books like *The Power of Sexual Surrender*.
Featured in the book, which has had at least ten paperback
printings and been excerpted in *Pageant* magazine, is "The
Masculine Woman." (Doctor, how can a woman be a female and
be masculine simultaneously?) She's "frigid"—"a driving,
competitive woman who was very successful in the business
world, having graduated from a leading woman's college."
"Clear thinking and logical mind, her emotionless almost masculine forthrightness in expressing herself belied her softly
feminine appearance." Surrendering to her "real nature," the
doctor's cure, is the only way she can be mentally healthy.
Then miraculously

. . . those details of life that once seemed so difficult become simple.
And because they are feminine tasks, household work, planning and
getting dinners, keeping the children busy or in line—whatever life
demands—soon lose their irksome and irritating quality and become
easy, even joyful. . . . At this juncture, or closely following on it, a
woman begins to feel her full power, the power that comes to her for
her surrender to her destiny.

The spuriously Freudian vision of a truly "feminine" female
serves the purposes of admen who woo women to spend millions
on clothes and cosmetics in vain pursuit of their "real nature."
To sell a new product, industry need only simultaneously make
the product and manufacture anxiety in gals, pressing them to
consume or be consumed in a female identity crisis. For example,
featured in every women's magazine, including those for teen-
agers, are the latest advertising campaigns for vaginal deo-
dorants, a "female necessity." One called Cupid's Quiver comes
in four flavors—Orange Blossom, Raspberry, Champagne, or
Jasmine. Madison Avenue courts the female, even seducing
minors. Teenform, Inc., manufacturers of bras for teen-agers,
estimates that nine-year-olds spend $2 million on bras annually.

Ingenue magazine pushes teen-agers into adult posturing.
The format is peppered with advertisements for engagement
rings, pictures of desirable adolescent boys, and occasionally a
plan of attack such as dinners for two. The ads for cosmetics
and clothes are practically identical to those in magazines designed for their mothers. Typical of women's magazines, *Ingenue*

includes at least one psychologically centered article. Recently,
it explained in "The Hardest Thing About Growing Up" that "inevitably, relationships with boys affect relationships with girls."
It condoned the statement, "I don't trust other girls in the same
way anymore. They become rivals." This is how girls learn the
platitudes: women can't work with other women when men are
around, and never work for a woman.

If a girl manages to survive *Ingenue* without succumbing to
marriage, *Glamour* picks her up. ("How Five Groovy Men Would
Make You Over into Their Dream Girls") Where the boys are is
where it's at for the reader who is shunted from high school to
college to career to marriage to motherhood—"Find Your New
Look. College Into Career Make-over. Job Into Mother Make-
over."

The lucky gal who's made the grade by landing a man is
promoted to *Modern Bride*, which induces her to buy "utterly
feminine" wedding gowns, bride-and-groom matching wedding
rings, silver, china, furniture, ad nauseam. The wedding itself
is big business; Wediquette International, Inc., offers total
planning—the place, time, invitations, gown, caterers, florist,
photographer . . .

Ah, then conjugal bliss—and of course, a magazine for mothers.
Redbook boasts its biggest year because it knows "Young Mamas
Spend More Than Big Daddies" and so talks "to that 18–34
year old the way she wants to be talked to," which means in
baby talk or kitchen chatter.

McCall's claims 16 million matrons who "buy more than the
readers of any other woman's service magazine." Its reader
"buys more cosmetics and toiletries, more prepared foods, owns
more life insurance, more automobiles . . ."

Although *Cosmopolitan* says its reader is the career woman
who desires success in her own right, it is pitched to the gal
who missed the marriage boat the first time around. Female
passivity is still the accepted mode of behavior. She can be
assertive in the office, but when man-hunting after five, she
must be seductively submissive. Who knows? She might hook
a divorced man or married man looking for an affair.

Cosmo repeats an old tip from Jackie and Delilah—sex is a
woman's hidden arsenal. Under a pseudonym, "a well-known
American gynecologist" instructs readers "How to Love Like
A Real Woman." "If your man bawls at you and you know you
are in the right, what should you do?" "You should take your

clothes off. Sex is a woman's strongest weapon. It is her proper weapon."

Taking a cue from *The Power of Sexual Surrender*, the expert explains, "Women must give and give and give again because it is their one and only way to obtain happiness for themselves." Further, "To argue is a male activity. To fight is a male activity. I say to women: 'Don't become a man in skirts. Don't fight. Don't argue. . . .'" Any female who would practice this advice must be masochistic — typical of a "normal" female, according to Freudian thought.

A popular misconception is that in time education will erase all the ill effects of thinking in stereotypes. But the educational system takes over where cultural myths, Freudian folklore and the media leave off in depressing a girl's aspirations and motivations. All along, she's taught to accept a double standard for success and self-esteem: It's marriage and motherhood for girls, while it's education and career for boys. She's pushed to be popular, date, and marry young (more than half of all American women are married before the age of twenty-one). Success in school only inhibits her social life. Intellectual striving, a necessity for academic success, is considered competitively aggressive; that is unnatural and unladylike behavior, since the essence of femininity, she has learned, is repressing aggressiveness. Telling her she thinks like a man is a backhanded compliment, which is discouraging if she has tried to be a woman using her brains, not sex, in the classroom and office.

While girls outperform boys intellectually in prepuberty, attrition in IQ sets in during adolescence when they learn from new, extracurricular lessons that looks, not brains, are what counts. After high school, achievement in terms of productivity and accomplishment drops off even more. More than 75 percent (some say as high as 95 percent) of all qualified high-schoolers not entering college are girls. Those who go attend more for husband-hunting than for educational self-advancement; one study at a Midwestern university revealed 70 percent of the freshmen women were there for an MRS. Women BA's are less than half as likely to try for a graduate degree as equally qualified men.

Women should not be given an even break in education and careers, says a clichéd argument, because they will get married and quit anyway. But that's because they are given an arbitrary, unfair option which men aren't forced to accept — either career

or marriage. Career opportunities and salary levels for women
are so poor that a calculating female would figure marriage is
a better bargain. Once married, she can stop fighting the stereotypes and start teaching them to her children.

DISCUSSION QUESTIONS

1. Both the conclusion of the argument and the author's
   attitude concerning it are somewhat implicit. Find the passages which come closest to expressing her view.

2. "The inspiration for teaching girls to expect less than boys
   comes from a range of cultural sources, religious, literary,
   psychiatric, and pop." Compare and evaluate the authorities cited by the author. Which more clearly lead to the implicit conclusion of the article?
   (a) Paula Stern
   (b) Jacqueline Kennedy Onassis
   (c) the Bible
   (d) the legend of Lilith
   (e) Orthodox Jews
   (f) Demosthenes
   (g) Aristotle
   (h) Saint Thomas Aquinas
   (i) the Catholic Church
   (j) the Protestant marriage services
   (k) Blackstone's *Commentaries*
   (l) Shakespeare
   (m) Rousseau
   (n) Samuel Johnson
   (o) Honoré de Balzac
   (p) John Adams
   (q) the Continental Congress
   (r) Spiro Agnew
   (s) G. C. Payetter, author of *How to Get and Hold a
        Woman*
   (t) Freud
   (u) Freudians
   (v) Dr. Judd Marmor
   (w) UCLA
   (x) the runner-up to this year's Miss America
   (y) psychiatrist-authors
   (z) books like *The Power of Sexual Surrender*

(aa)   *Pageant*
(bb)   admen who woo women to spend millions on clothes
         and cosmetics
(cc)   Teenform, Inc.
(dd)   *Ingenue*
(ee)   *Glamour*
(ff)   *Modern Bride*
(gg)   *Redbook*
(hh)   *McCall's*
(ii)   *Cosmopolitan*
(jj)   "a well-known American gynecologist"
(kk)   IQ tests
(ll)   one study at a Midwestern university
(mm) *Atlantic*

3. In this kind of argument which cites a mass of authorities, does it seem that the whole is greater than the sum of its parts? Would the argument have been stronger if it mentioned more authorities? If it mentioned fewer?

4. Discuss how the author uses detail to characterize the various women's magazines. Is her argument effective?

5. Do the ellipsis marks in some of the quotations seem to indicate distortions of what the authors really said?

6. Why does the author conclude her essay with reference to women's success in IQ tests and to their high school achievement?

7. Is the concluding paragraph effective? Why or why not?

"Pope Denounces Birth Control . . ."

Pope denounces birth control as millions starve

"Every marriage act must remain open to the transmission of life," said Pope Paul in his recent encyclical. He ruled out every action which proposes "to render procreation impossible."

The Pope denounced artificial contraception—the only practical means of controlling population. He held that it is not reasonable "to have recourse to artificial birth control" even though "we secure the harmony and peace of the family, and better conditions for the education of the children already born."

By his edict the Pope has struck a crushing blow against current efforts to reduce the flood of people now engulfing the earth.

In the advanced countries most couples—Catholics as well as Protestants—already practice birth control.

But in the underdeveloped countries, such as in Latin America, the Pope's teaching may result in the birth of hordes of children who will not have enough to eat.

Famine already stalks the earth. Half of humanity goes to bed hungry every night. Ten thousand or more people are dying of starvation every day. This means that more than three and a half million starve to death every year. (The present tragic Biafra toll is *in addition* to these figures.)

As recently as 1953 there were 2½ billion people on earth. Today only 15 years later there are *3½ billion.* A generation from now that number will approximately double at the present rate of increase.

The Pope dismissed the population explosion with a few brief words, merely saying that it should be met by greater social and economic progress, rather than to resort to "utterly materialistic" measures to limit births.

The encyclical appears to millions of Catholics and Protestants as a rather incredible document, considering the eminence of the author and his access to the world's leading demographic, agricultural and other authorities. It is viewed by many as one of the most fateful blunders of modern times.

For there can be no doubt that unless population is brought under control at an early date the resulting human misery and social tensions will inevitably lead to chaos and strife—to revolutions and wars, the dimensions of which it would be hard to predict.

Nothing less than the survival of civilization is at stake.

CAMPAIGN TO CHECK THE POPULATION EXPLOSION
EMERSON FOOTE, CHAIRMAN

THE POPULATION BOMB KEEPS TICKING

DISCUSSION QUESTIONS

1. Here is the complete version of the passages from *Humanae Vitae* (29 July 1968) which are quoted in this advertisement:

   "Nonetheless, the Church, calling men back to the observance of the norms of the natural law, as interpreted by their constant doctrine, teaches that each and every marriage act must remain open to the transmission of life."

   "Similarly excluded is every action which either in anticipation of the conjugal act, or in its accomplishment, or in the development of its natural consequences, proposes, whether as an end or as a means, to render procreation impossible."

   "Now, some may ask: in the present case, is it not reasonable in many circumstances to have recourse to artificial birth control if, thereby, we secure the harmony and peace of the family, and better conditions for the education of the children already born? To this question it is necessary to reply with clarity: the Church is the first to praise and recommend the intervention of intelligence in a function which so closely associates the rational creature with his Creator; but she affirms that this must be done with respect for the order established by God."

   "We are well aware of the serious difficulties experienced by public authorities in this regard [the demographic problem], especially in the developing countries. To their legitimate preoccupations we devoted our encyclical letter *Populorum Progressio*. But with our predecessor Pope John XXIII, we repeat: no solution to these difficulties is acceptable 'which does violence to man's essential dignity' and is based only on an utterly materialistic conception of man himself and of his life. The only possible solution to this question is one which envisages the social and economic progress both of individuals and of the whole of human society, and which respects and promotes of true human values."

   Did the author make a fair abridgment of the papal encyclical? Would there have been value in his including longer or additional quotations?

2. "Pope Denounces Birth Control . . . " Do any of the passages quoted in the advertisement carry the tone of denunciation?

3. The author describes the population and hunger problems of the earth, both now in prospect, then refers to the Pope's encyclical as "one of the most fateful blunders of modern times." Is there a suggestion that an encyclical affirming birth control would notably alleviate the population and hunger problems? Is there evidence that such is the case?

4. Discuss the variety of authorities who are either directly or indirectly referred to in the advertisement. Compare and evaluate them.
    (a) Pope Paul VI
    (b) the Roman Catholic Church
    (c) the natural law
    (d) the author of the advertisement
    (e) the many who view the Encyclical as one of the fateful blunders of modern times
    (f) the named members of the Campaign to Check the Population Explosion
    (g) the institutions they serve or represent

5. Is it possible for those signing the statement to do so only "in their personal and individual capacity"?

6. Who is Rockefeller Prentice?

5

Semantic Argument

Federal spending is irresponsible and dangerous.
Drive a Buick Wildcat.
Oil heat is SAFE.
Support right-to-work laws.
Arguments hypostatize the bigoted renitency . . .

The importance of individual words in argument has already been mentioned. It was noted that meaningful discussion is impossible unless disputants agree on the definition of key terms and that deductive argument is unreliable if it employs ambiguous words. Yet to be considered is the kind of argument which makes its point, not by presenting or arranging evidence, but by using impressive language.

Semantic argument should convince no one. It is simply a conclusion offered without evidence. Its effectiveness derives from the nature of words. A word can have two levels of meaning. It has a denotative meaning, i.e., some specific thing or condition to which it refers (*mailman, swim, brown*). And it can have a connotative meaning, i.e., certain emotional responses which it arouses. Connotations can be negative (*politician, deal, filibuster*) or affirmative (*statesman, negotiation, right of unlimited debate*). Semantic argument consists in using connotative words to characterize an issue or to enhance the tone of a discussion.

Connotative words (sometimes called "purr words" and "snarl words") do not prove anything. Commonly they simply label a thing as good or bad. American politicians of both parties regularly run for office, for example, on a program of obedience to God, family, and country; adherence to law and order; separation of powers; peace with honor; and unlimited economic progress. They oppose absenteeism, wasteful spending, communism, flag-burning, anarchy, and stagnation. The essence of such persuasion is that key terms are not defined. In the given list, only "flag-burning" has an unequivocally clear meaning.

Such argument can praise any entity (a party platform, a current novel, a union demand) as *authentic, reasonable, just,*

118

natural, and *realistic* or condemn it as *irresponsible, asinine, phony, dangerous,* and *superficial.* It can laud any citizen as a *Samaritan,* a *patriot,* and an *independent thinker* or reject him as a *do-gooder,* a *comsymp,* and a *pseudo-intellectual.* (One man's *academic freedom* is another man's *brain-washing.*) These terms have little specific meaning. Their nature was illustrated when actress Jayne Mansfield told interviewer Mike Wallace that her career was "based on womanliness, not sex." Asked to spell out the difference, she responded, "One is a ruder word than the other."

Such language depends on its emotional associations. An automobile is more appealing when named *Thunderbird,* an actor when renamed *Rock Hudson,* and a bill when called a *right-to-work* law. A hair preparation can be discredited as *greasy kid-stuff,* a business practice as *payola,* and a senator as part of the *military-industrial complex.* Advertisers can call up an impressive range of associations in offering *Blue Cross, Buick Riviera, Cashmere Bouquet, Viceroy,* and *Old Grand-Dad* — plus *Lark, GL-70, Hai Karate,* and *Brut by Fabergé.* Though denotatively vague, such terms are effective as argument. No vermouth advertisement was needed to persuade the public that "a dry martini is not a hooker of gin."

Semantic argument can work both directly and indirectly, i.e., in particular contexts, a purr word expressed is also a snarl word implied. To call Camels "a *real* cigarette," for example, is also to suggest that filtered products are frivolous and artificial. To advertise that "Oil heat is SAFE" is to imply that gas and electric heat are dangerous. Again, politics offers rich examples. When a senator says he is not a candidate for the presidency, commonly he is making the crucial announcement. If his opponent is divorced, he will describe himself as a devoted family man. If it is revealed that his opponent once spoke to a communist leader (say, in 1937), he will grant that this does "not necessarily" mean the man is a Russian agent. In such instances, one is expected to recognize the implications of the surface argument.

Often, however, semantic claims are not meant to be penetrated. This is especially true when impressive language is used to mask a negative admission. For example, when government spokesmen announce that a particular recession is *leveling off,* they wish to communicate optimistic reassurance rather than denotative meaning of the phrase, i.e., that the economy is still sick and is getting sicker. When manufacturers label a garment *shrink-resistant*, they want to suggest that it will not shrink, not what the term literally says, that the garment will resist shrinking and thus that shrinking will certainly occur. Advertisements for an inexpensive portable radio wish to imply that it is powerful and can pull in signals from distant stations, but what they say is "You can take it anywhere."

This attempt to communicate more than is literally said also occurs when a spokesman uses impressive language to add character to his argument. Couching his views in religious allusions, folksy talk, or esoteric jargon, he argues more with this manner than his substance. In a letter to *The Saturday Review*, for example, Gelett Burgess maintains that Shakespeare of Stratford did not write the plays attributed to him and begins his argument thus:

> Sir: My recent communication relative to Oxford-is-Shakespeare elicited responses which evince and hypostatize the bigoted renitency usual in orthodox addicts. For the Stratfordian mythology has engendered a strange nympholepsy like a fanatical religion which is not amenable to reason or logic, and abrogates all scientific method.

Here the writer does more than say that his earlier letter received much silly comment. He uses pedantic language to make it clear that this response and his whole Shakespeare argument derive from a profoundly learned individual.

One should, of course, judge an argument solely on the evidence brought forward to support a conclusion, not on the effect of connotative language used to describe the issue or to elevate the tone of the discussion.

Connotative language defies meaningful analysis. Is it true that "Education without God produces a nation without freedom," that NATO is "the devil in disguise," that Fleischmann's Gin is "Clean . . . Clean . . . Clean"? Who can say? Until the claims are clarified and documented, such vague language can produce only empty and repetitive argument. Fleischmann advertisements, it should be noted, once offered to explain "What do they mean   CLEAN . . . CLEAN . . . CLEAN?"   The   answer:

> They mean that the crispest, brightest drinks under the sun are made with clean-tasting Fleischmann's Gin.

This is about as meaningful as semantic argument gets.

HOW EFFECTIVE ARE THESE SEMANTIC ARGUMENTS?

1. Look morning-lovely all day long. Use Revlon "Love-Pat."

2. Advertisement for *Valley of the Dolls*: "Any similarity between any person living or dead, and the characters portrayed in this film is purely coincidental and not intended."

3. The Russian purges of the 30s have been too emotionally depicted. What really occurred was a transfer of population, a rectification of frontiers, and an elimination of unreliable elements.

4. Concerned about Foreign Aid Give-a-ways, and Communist Infiltration? *Beat the Washington Crowd!* Vote for JIM ALLEN — Alabama's Candidate for the U.S. Senate.

5. The human organism is a homeostatic mechanism, i.e., all behavior is an attempt to preserve organismic integrity by homeostatic restoration of equilibrium, as that equilibrium is disturbed by biologically significant organizations of energies in the external or internal environments of the organism.

6. Wisconsin Congressman Henry Reuss said on the death of Senator Joseph McCarthy: "His sudden death at forty-eight is a staggering loss to his wife, to his family in Wisconsin, and to his many friends."

7. Prudent People Smoke King Sano — the Purposeful Cigarette.

8. "ABORTION ON DEMAND IS MURDER BY REQUEST" — A *New York Times* advertisement sponsored by William Crist, Jr.

9. When a correspondent wrote *Personality Parade* asking whether Elvis Presley had learned to act, columnist Walter Scott responded, "Mr. Presley has always been good to his mother."

The Nonsense of Liberal Catholics

JAMES P. DEGNAN

At a Catholic university recently I listened to a discussion between a liberal Catholic theologian and an atheist. "Tell me," said the atheist, "what is a Catholic? What must one believe if he is to consider himself a good Catholic? Must he believe in heaven and hell and in the immortality of the soul? In papal infallibility? Must he believe that premarital sex and artificial birth control and remarriage after divorce are all morally wrong, seriously sinful?"

"Most of that is mere legalism, mere negativism," the liberal Catholic theologian quickly responded.

"Well," the atheist persisted, "if people needn't believe any of these things to consider themselves good Catholics, what must they believe? What *isn't* mere legalism? Just what do you people mean when you say you are *in* the church? What does being a Catholic really mean?"

The theologian clearly did not like this line of thought. Such questions are considered "unecumenical" and "devisive" by the contemporary Catholic liberal. They stress "differences rather than similarities" and belong to the old, the "closed," the "defensive," and "medieval" church, to the world of "mere apologetics." They are "irrelevant" to the new, the "open and authentic" church; and it is considered bad form to raise such questions these days. Nevertheless, after careful thought the liberal theologian attempted an answer: "Being a Catholic means awareness of community—awareness of human unity related to Christ."

Bemused, the atheist replied: "That's interesting, because by your definition *I* am a Catholic." And, of course, he was right; by the liberal's "definition" practically anyone qualifies as a Catholic.

I cite this theologian's remarks because they typify what, in honesty, I can only call the nonsense flourishing in liberal Catholic circles today (a nonsense particularly repugnant to me because my sympathies have always been far more with the liberal than with the conservative wing of the church). And one need not attend theological seminars or lectures or read esoteric theological journals to discover this sort of thing in all its plenti-

---

Reprinted from *Christianity Today* (21 November 1969), pp. 3–6.

tude, for it has become a favorite subject of the popular press. Consider, for instance, the following answers to the question, "What is a Catholic?"—answers given by prominent liberal Catholic theologians, the Rev. Robert Adolfs and the Rev. Leo Alting Von Geusau, and prominently displayed, not in *Cross Currents*, but in *Look* magazine (January, 1968). Being a Catholic, says Father Adolfs, is "the experience of human unity related in one way or another toward the person of Jesus of Nazareth." Father Van Geusau says that "belonging [to the Catholic Church] is *not* determined by sociological or sacramental criteria but by one's *awareness of community*" (my italics). By such answers, by such "definitions," Baptists and Methodists and Quakers, Hindus and Buddhists and Jews, Holy Rollers and Satanists and members of the YMCA and of the Ku Klux Klan are all Catholics. This kind of writing is typical of many liberal Catholic thinkers today. Read any of a number of prominent liberal Catholic theologians, philosophers, and journalists—among them, Leslie Dewart, Father Gregory Baum, Michael Novak, Daniel Callahan—or any of a number of the various popular liberal Catholic publications, such as *Commonweal* or the *National Catholic Reporter*, and you will find example after example of the same kind of thing.

And when today's liberals aren't producing the terribly vague— indeed, quite meaningless—assertions mentioned above, they seem to be engaged in saying things that are either clear but wrong, or vague and wrong. For example, consider the following statements—also in *Look*—by prominent liberal Catholic theologians, clerics, and laymen: (1) It is meaningless to talk about heaven and hell, since we can know nothing about the hereafter; (2) of course remarriage after divorce is permissible for Catholics; (3) Catholics not only *may* practice artificial birth control but have a moral duty to do so (because of the population problem); (4) papal infallibility is not a valid dogma but only a medieval, outmoded notion; (5) premarital sex (either hetero-sexual or homosexual) is not sinful if it is "humanly integrated" or "directed toward a total human relationship."

Now anyone—Catholic or non-Catholic—knowing anything about Catholic moral teaching should recognize that for persons to hold these beliefs and still regard themselves as good Catholics is wrongheadedness of the most obvious kind. And anyone who respects the integrity of language should be able to see the vagueness of such statements as number five. Phrases like "humanly integrated" and "directed toward a total human re-lationship" are as meaningless as the following definition of God given by the well-known Catholic theologian Leslie Dewart: "that which lies in the openness of the transcendence which we grasp in consciousness as constituting the spiritual substance of man."

The prevalence of this sort of thing is in large part, I think, what has motivated Pope Paul to reaffirm strongly and clearly in recent months many of the church's basic teachings, not only on birth control but on such teachings as Christ's divinity and the immortality of the soul. What the Pope seems to realize is that while de-emphasizing the differences between Catholics and non-Catholics (the major goal of the "ecumenical," the "relevant," the "liberal" church) is thoroughly laudable, *denying* these differences, as do many liberals today (by, for example, defining a Catholic as anyone with "an awareness of community"), is nonsense; for when these differences are denied, definition becomes impossible, and the identity of the church is destroyed. No matter how much we may favor the liberal's goals of "ecu-menism" and "relevance" (and I strongly sympathize with both), and no matter how unsympathetic we may be to particular pro-nouncements of the Pope (such as the birth-control statement), I think it only fair that we recognize what seems to me to be the Pope's *general* concern with liberals and liberal reforms. He is obviously concerned that, in the name of "ecumenism" and "relevance," the church may become little more than an organiza-tion of social workers. And obviously he realizes that when ques-tions like "What is a Catholic? Why be a Catholic?" are considered irrelevant, immature, inauthentic; when concern over eternal life, over heaven and hell, is thought to be, in Leslie Dewart's words, "mere childishness"; when, in short, the Catholic Church becomes nothing more than an international (and probably not very efficient) welfare agency, then people of common sense are going to demand in quite justified disgust: Who needs Catholicism? Why don't we simply beef up UNESCO?

Increasingly, Catholic liberals of the sort I've been discussing are coming under attack, not by church conservatives, but by liberals who have left the Catholic Church. If, these former Catholics contend, today's Catholic liberals were really intel-lectually honest and morally courageous, they would state their heresies clearly instead of obscurely, and, much more important, would have the courage to follow their heresies to their logical end—that is, to leave the Catholic Church. An example is an exchange between David Perkins, a former Catholic, and the Editors of the *National Catholic Reporter* (August 14, 1968), the most widely circulated of the American liberal Catholic publications.

Responding to the confused thinking of the many liberal Catholics, including the *NCR* editors, who have denied the morally binding nature of the Pope's encyclical on birth control and other key Catholic teachings, Mr. Perkins reminds the liberals that the Catholic Church is (1) authoritarian and (2) voluntary. "Rational men and women," he says, "do not remain in an authoritarian structure when they no longer accept the authority." He points out that, beyond the bad reasons of "ceremony and nostalgia," liberals like the *NCR* editors have no reasons for staying in the church. The editors' answer to his question, "Why do you stay in the Church?," is typical of the sort of thing I've been talking about.

Although Perkins makes it absolutely clear that, as an intellectually honest man, he has left the church because he no longer believes in essential church teachings, the editors begin by saying that Perkins's trouble is that he insists on regarding the church as "an institution rather than a movement." In other words, if he would only think of the church as a "movement," incredible teachings would somehow become credible. Then— though Perkins makes it clear that he has left the church, that, indeed, he is hostile to the church, whether it be thought of as institution *or* movement—the editors go on to declare that Perkins stands "to our left performing for us the same useful service Rap Brown performed for Martin Luther King, Jr." Obviously, it would make more sense to say that Perkins stands to the *NCR*, not as Rap Brown stood to Martin King, but as Rap Brown stands to Jim Eastland. But the editors, I fear, don't do a very good job of making sense. Consider the remainder of their answer:

> You stay because of the Eucharist, because of its connection with the Last Supper, because of the connection with men you think it gives. You stay to be taught; the magisterium can be misused, unused, or abused, but it has things to say. You stay because of people like Martin Luther King (Baptist), Martin Marty (Lutheran), William Coffin (Episcopal), Dorothy Day and the Fathers Berrigan, who supply something not so often found in the secular saints. You stay because outside the community you probably won't pay much attention to Christ—and even though you know the structure of the community sometimes denies him.

One stays in the church "because of the Eucharist, because of its connection with the Last Supper, because of the connection with men" one thinks it gives. What does this mean? What do the editors mean by "Eucharist"? Do they mean the traditional Real Presence, the presence that distinguishes the Catholic Eucharist from the Eucharists of other groups? If this is what they mean (and as a regular reader of the *NCR*, I'm sure it is not), why don't they say so? The truth, I fear, is that the editors, like so many Catholic liberals today, while they regularly use the term, can provide no sensible definition of it. (Asked what he meant by "Eucharist," the liberal Catholic theologian I mentioned at the beginning, a priest sympathetic with the Delano, California, grapestrikers, replied: "Having dinner with Cesar Chavez and the grapepickers at the Filipino mess hall in Delano.") For the clear (if, from the point of view of most non-Catholics, incredible) traditional meaning of the Eucharist, today's liberal Catholics have substituted what amounts to little more than a pretentious vagary. Father Adolfs calls the Eucharist a "coming together to pray and break bread." But who needs the Catholic Church to do this? One can "pray and break bread" in any number of "movements." What the *NCR* editors mean by the term "connection" and why one can only *think* — that is, why a Catholic can't, assured by doctrine, *know* — that the Eucharist can give him this "connection," are other questions they leave unanswered.

One stays in the Church, the editors next tell us, "to be taught" (taught *what*?); "the magisterium can be misused, unused, or abused, but it has things to say." That the magisterium has "things to say" seems rather obvious. The question that should be answered is *What* things? And, more important in answering Perkins's question, *Must* Catholics believe these things if they wish to call themselves legitimate Catholics?

The editors next tell us that one stays in the church because of "people like William Coffin (Episcopal), Martin Luther King (Baptist), Martin Marty (Lutheran), Dorothy Day and the Fathers Berrigan, who supply something not so often found in the secular saints." I find the logic of this hard to follow. Why should a Catholic stay in the Catholic Church because he admires any of the well-known Protestants the editors mention? Wouldn't it make more sense for such a Catholic to become an Episcopalian or a Baptist or a Lutheran? Who, one wonders, are the "secular saints"? What is the "something" the secular saints, whoever they may be, cannot supply, at least "not so often" as can these persons whom the editors apparently regard as "religious saints"?

Next, we are told that one stays in the church because "outside the community you probably won't pay much attention to Christ—and even though you know the structure of the community sometimes denies him" What do they mean by "paying attention to Christ?" And why must one stay in the Catholic Church to do this? Many scholars dedicated to proving Christ a charlatan have spent their lives "paying attention to Christ"; Ernest Renan undoubtedly paid more attention to him than most Catholics ever have or ever will.

Wrapping up their answer, the editors conclude:

> There are other reasons for staying *including inertia and the nostalgia* [my italics] Mr. Perkins mentions. For some people who would rather fight than switch, the reason may be that the Church supplies an effective filter against too harsh realities. The good reasons and the bad reasons aren't coercive. Thank God you no longer feel obliged to prove your case. . . .

What this implies is that there are no good reasons for staying in the Catholic Church. Yet the intention of this full-page editorial essay was to answer the question, "Why stay in the church?" I find this all rather confusing, and in charity toward the editors I would like to write it off as mere clumsiness. But the editors apparently regard lack of clarity as a virtue. At one point, in fact, they actually condemn Perkins for being "too utterly clear." "One's idea of the Church," they admonish him, "ought to be fuzzy at the moment, not for the sake of fuzziness but to be true to the reality." To *what* reality? That is another of the many questions the editors apparently feel no obligation to answer.

After reading this editorial, one might suspect that perhaps truth itself is one of those "too harsh realities" the editors claim the church protects Catholics from. For refusal to face the truth, the desire (conscious or unconscious) to conceal the truth (not only from others, but often from ourselves) rather than to reveal it, is, in George Orwell's words, "the great enemy of clear language."

I refuse to believe, however, as Mr. Perkins believes, that the rhetoric of liberal Catholics reveals wide scale, willful intellectual dishonesty and moral cowardice; and in dwelling on that rhetoric I have not intended a broadside attack on either the *National Catholic Report* or the institution of liberal Catholicism. I have long admired and championed many of the *NCR* causes, and, as I said previously, my sympathies have always been far more with the liberal than with the conservative wing of the church. Many of the liberals Perkins attacks, liberals who stay in the church for no good reason, do so, I am sure, because they wish to use the weight and moral authority, the tradition of the Church, to achieve good ends in civil rights and similar causes — to achieve, for instance, fair wages for the grapestrikers by reminding grapeowners (many of whom are Catholic) that the encyclicals bind them to paying a just wage. (The problem with these liberals is that they invoke and abide by only the encyclicals they agree with, thus making a farce of the "authority" they claim the grapeowners must abide by.) And though I cannot intellectually sympathize with these liberals, I certainly think their intentions are good. I also share their openness to dissent, to the idea of an open church, to dialogue with non-Catholics; but I wonder how we can have either real dissent or real dialogue unless we first have a rigorous respect for the integrity of language and logic, unless we recognize that clear definitions and distinctions are as indispensable to genuine dissent and dialogue as is recognition of the principle of contradiction. And I firmly believe that, while the tone and some of the conclusions of some critics of liberal Catholicism may be rabid, there is certainly much truth in what they are saying.

What they are saying, at its most charitable and valuable, seems to be something like this: Perhaps it is time for Catholic liberal intellectuals to quit dismissing the rational discussion of religious matters as "mere apologetics." Perhaps, indeed, it is time for these liberals to present a new apologetic in place of the old one they have so thoroughly abandoned. Perhaps it is time for them to stop declaring smugly that Catholics need "no longer prove their case," and to start, if not proving, at least clearly presenting that case. Behind the harsh voice of these critics there seems a much gentler voice; and what, finally, that voice seems to be saying to the Catholic liberals is simply this: You have demonstrated your ability to love God with your hearts; is it not time to demonstrate your ability to love him with your minds as well?

DISCUSSION QUESTIONS

1. The opening paragraph offers dialogue quoted from "a liberal Catholic theologian" and "an atheist" at a Catholic university. Would this argument have been stronger if the author had named real people at a real place?

2. The author rejects particular definitions:

(a) "Being a Catholic means awareness of community—awareness of human unity related to Christ."

(b) Leslie Dewart's concept of God as "that which lies in the openness of the transcendence which we grasp in consciousness as constituting the spiritual substance of man."

(c) The liberal Catholic theologian's definition of *Eucharist* as "Having dinner with Cesar Chavez and the grape-pickers at the Filipino mess hall in Delano."

Is it self-evident that these are "nonsense"? Compare and evaluate them.

3. Implicit in all the author's statements—particularly those discussing heaven, hell, sin, and the Eucharist—is a definition of what the Catholic Church is and what it stands for. Articulate this as clearly and specifically as possible. Must everyone who has respect for "the integrity of language and logic" accept this definition?

4. The author complains that Catholic liberals are producing "terribly vague—indeed, quite meaningless—assertions." He rejects terms like these:

mere legalism	the open and authentic church
mere negativism	humanly integrated
unecumenical	mere apologetics
the medieval church	paying attention to Christ

And he responds with this kind of language:

vague
meaningless
liberal theologian
nonsense
wrongheadedness
pretentious vagary
an intellectually honest man
legitimate Catholics
rigorous respect for the integrity of language and logic
genuine dissent

Consider all these terms in context. How many carry a clear, definable meaning? How many are little more than snarl and purr words?

5. The *National Catholic Reporter* editorial suggested that some liberals remain Catholic because "the Church supplies an effective filter against too harsh realities." What does this mean?

SDS: an Introduction

The Emergence of the New Left

In the spring of 1968, thousands of students in New York's Columbia University erected barricades and battled police following a successful four-week strike against University complicity in the Vietnam War and racist expansion programs in nearby Harlem. At the same time, hundreds of thousands of French workers and students—after seizing factories, schools, and streets—nearly toppled the deGaulle government. Significantly, the mass revolt grew out of student protests against the policies of the first French "multiversity" at Nanterre. In West Germany student strikes and demonstrations involving thousands were directed against the Government's passage of "emergency laws" giving near-dictatorial powers to itself. In Japan, Italy, and the Scandinavian countries, similar actions have been occurring as well.

The identifiable thread running through these internationally dramatic events is an assortment of radical student organizations. These groups make up the core of what has come to be known as the New Left. Although they have only been visible to the general public for the past two or three years, most of these organizations first formed in the late 1950s and early 1960s. Generally, they are made up of students and unaffiliated young people within those advanced capitalist countries with highly developed technological societies.

The post-World War II rapid transformation of these economies had a similar effect on their systems of higher education—the growth of the "knowledge factories" or multiversities. With the dominant social themes of this period being affluence, consumption, and adjustment, the young men and women were expressing their cultural oppression and personal alienation with growing intensity. Out of apathy and the gray flannel suit emerged James Dean, Marlon Brando, and the Angry Young Man—the Beat Generation. Also, following the Hungarian Revolt crushed by the Soviets in 1956, hundreds of young intellectuals left the European and US Communist Parties in disgust over the crimes of Stalin.

All this, to be sure, was only an undercurrent, a minor key. In the mainstream was the Cold War, Joe McCarthy, the silent

Reprint of a pamphlet published by the Students for a Democratic Society, 1608 West Madison, Chicago, Illinois. No date.

generation filing into heavily-mortgaged Ozzie and Harriet suburbia, the prototypes of Carl Oglesby's man of those times— slim-waisted, swivel-hipped, bullet-headed make-out artists. While many young activists of today may find these images rather alien, this is where the history of the New Left begins. These were the conditions giving birth to our present movement.

THE GROWTH OF SDS

The central force of the New Left in the United States has been Students for a Democratic Society or SDS. We are a young, rapidly growing movement: only sixty-odd people attended our founding convention at Port Huron, Michigan in 1961. Even by early 1965, SDS had fewer than twenty-five hundred members with chapters on less than forty campuses. However, with its April 17th, 1965 March on Washington to End the War in Vietnam, SDS grew in national prominence. Presently, there are over forty thousand national and local SDS activists in more than three hundred chapters in universities across the country.

In the early years, SDS was a coalition of liberals and radicals, working from a multi-issue perspective on the questions of peace and disarmament, civil rights, poverty, and university reform. We supported reform Democratic electoral campaigns, and in 1964 even put out a button saying "Part of the Way with LBJ."

Our bitter yet powerful experience with American politics in the 1960s has moved us considerably away from our original Left-liberal stance. Today SDS is a mass radical and anti-imperialist student movement. The critique we are developing of American corporate capitalism has brought us to advocate the necessity of an activist and revolutionary politics for the New Left.

WHERE DO WE STAND?

ON VIETNAM AND US FOREIGN POLICY: SDS completely opposes the US Government's immoral, illegal, and genocidal war against the people of Vietnam. We insist on the immediate withdrawal of all US personnel from that country. Moreover, we see the US policy in Vietnam as part of a global strategy for containing revolutionary change in the "Third World" nations of Asia, Africa, and Latin America. Rather than the result of an essentially good government's mistaken decisions, we see the world-wide exploitation and oppression of those insurgent peoples as the logical conclusion of the giant US corporations' expanding and necessary search for higher profits and strategic resources. That system is most properly named imperialism, and we stand by and support all those who struggle against its onslaught. They are our brothers and sisters, not our enemies.

ON THE DRAFT AND THE MILITARY: SDS demands the abolition of the Selective Service System. We see the Draft as racist and anti-democratic, procuring manpower for aggressive wars abroad. Moreover, through the "deferment" system, the primary coercive function of the Draft is "channeling" the lives of millions of young people outside the Military into lifelong vocations deemed "essential" by corporate military elites rather than freely chosen by themselves. We urge and will organize all young men to wage a collective struggle in resistance to the Draft by refusing to serve in the Military. We also seek to break the barriers placed between us and our brothers in uniform. When forced by threat of imprisonment or exile, some of us will organize within the Armed Forces, advocating desertion and other forms of resistance to US foreign policy.

ON THE BLACK LIBERATION MOVEMENT: SDS has long and actively supported the struggle of black Americans for freedom and self-determination. Racism and exploitation confront black people as a group, together as a people. From this given condition of their daily lives, black people must act as a group in establishing their common identity, and in planning a strategy to challenge their oppression. We do not simply "tolerate" the growth of black consciousness, we encourage it. Criticizing "black power" as "racism in reverse" is as mistaken as denouncing the American Revolution of 1776 as "colonialism in reverse." In addition to confronting all aspects of institutionalized racism in American life, we strongly believe that the strongest support we can afford the black movement comes from our efforts to engage exploited whites in the struggles and values of radical politics.

ON LABOR AND THE STRUGGLES OF WORKING PEOPLE: From its beginnings, SDS has recognized the crucial role that the working class has to fulfill in any movement for radical social change. More recently, we have rejected the false notion that most Americans are "middle-class." Considering professional, service, white-collar, and university-trained technical workers as a "class" separate from blue-collar industrial workers serves only to confuse and divide millions of workers and students and prevent them from realizing the corporate capitalist source of their exploitation and their common interest in uniting against its oppression. To further the unity and radical consciousness of the working class as a whole we support the rank-and-file insurgencies of working people against their employers, the Government, and corrupt union leadership. Our concern is not only the improvement of wages and working conditions for our brothers and sisters in the shops, but for a transformation of all labor issues growing out of alienation and lack of control into a movement against the capitalist system itself.

ON THE STUDENT REVOLT: SDS views the multiversity as a knowledge factory, a kind of service station producing skilled manpower and intelligence for integration with the marketable needs of the major corporate, government, and military institutions. Neither the content of the educational process, nor the ends to which our learning and resources are directed, further the fulfillment of humane social needs. Rather, the "knowledge commodity" (ourselves and the results of our work) is shaped to further the production of waste, social oppression, and military destruction. The recognition of this process has been the driving force in our work to transform student "alienation" into a radical force reaching out and uniting with constituencies beyond the campus in struggles against oppressive university administrations.

FROM MORAL OUTRAGE TO RADICAL VISION

The New Left has not been noted for the completeness or coherence of its analysis or strategy for change. Within the ranks of SDS exists a variety of political positions: socialists, anarchists, communists, and humanist liberals. Nonetheless, the interplay of these ideas with a common commitment to action has produced a rich and powerful shared political experience emerging from an on-going struggle. We have looked primarily to that experience as the source and test of political truth, rather than to this or that dogmatic catechism. While not shunning analytical work, we have always seen this focus as a basis of our strength and authenticity.

Whatever the degree of the New Left's diversity, however, we have always asserted a common clarity in our values. Within our vision, all authentically revolutionary movements are seen as first, last, and always movements for human freedom, whatever form their demands may take in a given historic period. The New Left radical consciousness began with the perception of a gap between the actual reality of our daily lives and the accessible potentiality for human fulfillment already in existence. This tension—the contradiction between what is and what can be—first futilely sought its resolution in a quest for personal salvation.

When the interests of the dominant social order denied the realization of that potential, we discovered our powerlessness, our unfreedom. Moreover, the social character of our oppression revealed the need of a collective struggle for liberation. We discovered our deepest personal hopes and desires were the widely held aspirations of many. That discovery has led to our affirmation of a common humanity with all of the oppressed.

At present, the contradiction between the brutal and dehumanized reality of advanced corporate capitalism and the liberating potential of its technology and productive organization has never been greater. Planned obsolescence and waste production increase in the midst of growing scarcity. Fragmented job specialization and meaningless toil expand; while cybernation and automation contain the possibility of total job integration, the abolition of alienated labor, and the vast expansion of free and creative activity. From this viewpoint, all the world's people have never been more oppressed. At this moment of history, on the other hand, the potential of the struggle for human fulfillment has never been greater. The New Left will be at the center of that struggle. Our humanity is at stake. Join us.

DISCUSSION QUESTIONS

1. A survey of the language of the essay indicates that the SDS opposes the following:

    Columbia's "complicity in the Vietnam War"

    West Germany's "emergency laws"

    Post-World War II "affluence, consumption, and adjustment"

    "cultural oppression and personal alienation"

    American "imperialism"

    the "racism and exploitation" confronting black people

"the capitalistic system itself"
"the multiversity as a knowledge factory"
"waste, social oppression, and military destruction"
It affirms:
"young activists"
"activist and revolutionary politics"
"freedom and self-determination" for Black Americans
"black power"
the "radical consciousness of the working class"
"all authentically revolutionary movements"
"human freedom"
"human fulfillment"
"a collective struggle for liberation"
"the vast expansion of free and creative activity"
Considering such terms in context, discuss the kind and degree of definition necessary before meaningful argument can occur. Which terms carry a specific meaning? Which seem simply snarl and purr words?

2. The essay complains that universities work to produce skills useful to corporate, government, and military institutions, rather than those which "further the fulfillment of humane social needs." What specifically is the author opposing here? What would he like to see the universities doing?

3. Consider the references to particular groups:

citizens characterized by "apathy and the gray flannel suit"

James Dean, Marlon Brando, and the Angry Young Man — the Beat Generation

the silent generation filing into heavily-mortgaged Ozzie and Harriet suburbia

the prototypes of Carl Oglesby's man of those times — slim-waisted, swivel-hipped, bullet-headed make-out artists

the rank-and-file insurgencies of working people against their employers, the government, and corrupt union leadership

constituencies beyond the campus [united] in struggles against oppressive university administrations

Is there more here than oversimplified stereotyping? If so, whom is the author talking about?

4. The United States' involvement in Vietnam is described as an "immoral, illegal, and genocidal war." Are these adjectives equally accessible to argument and evidence?

5. The last three paragraphs of the essay form a cohesive unit. Discuss the evidence which leads to the conclusion "Our humanity is at stake. Join us."

Is This Your University?

AL CAPP
[*Delivered to the graduating class at Franklin Pierce College, Rindge, New Hampshire, April 27, 1969*]

I live in Cambridge, Mass., a stone's throw from Harvard—but if you duck you aren't hurt much—and I know you'll believe me when I tell you I'd rather be speaking here today. It's safer, and it's at your sort of college that I can use the commencement speaker's traditional phrase. I can say you're the hope of the future without bursting out laughing, as I would if I said it at a Harvard commencement—assuming, of course, that there will be a commencement there this year. They haven't heard from the Afros or the SDS yet.

Three or four of the Afros may decide that commencements are racist institutions, and then five or six SDSers may decide that commencements are a CIA plot, and then of course the entire faculty, administration and student body of Harvard, with the courage that has made them a legend, will replace its commencement by some sort of ceremony more acceptable—something they know the boys will approve of—say, a book burning; they loved that at Columbia, or a dean killing; they never quite accomplished that at University Hall. Dean Ford let them down by having recuperative powers they didn't count on.

But the fact that you can have a commencement here without getting down on your knees to a student wrecking crew, or without calling up the riot squad, is mainly luck. You enjoy advantages Harvard doesn't.

For one thing, you have the advantage of not being so revered for the wisdom and courage of past generations of administrators that you haven't noticed the moral flabbiness and intellectual flatulence of the majority of your present generation of administrators and faculty. You show me any institution with such a glorious past that anyone presently employed by it is regarded as retroactively infallible, and I'll show you a collection of sanctimonious fatheads.

But the greatest advantage Franklin Pierce has over Harvard is that you are not rich enough to hire three such famous professors as Rosovsky, Galbraith and Handlin and not extravagant

Reprinted from *Vital Speeches of the Day* (1 August 1969), pp. 188–190.

enough to waste the wisdom of the only one of them with guts and sense—Handlin. All three are world-renowned historians. All three this week have helped make history.

Prof. Henry Rosovsky was born in Danzig. When the young Nazis invaded the University of Danzig in the '30's and beat up its professors and disrupted its classes, Rosovsky's family gave up their citizenship and fled to the United States. In the 60's, Rosovsky was teaching at Berkeley. When the young Nazis invaded there, Rosovsky gave up his professorship and fled to Harvard. When the young Nazis invaded there the other day, Rosovsky gave up the chairmanship of his department and started packing.

Prof. Galbraith, as national chairman of the ADA, was the intellectual leader of the Democratic Party in the last election and one of the Nation's few political thinkers over 19 who mistook Sen. McCarthy's menopausal capriciousness for high-principled statesmanship.

Prof. Handlin has won the Pulitzer Prize and other honors for his histories of those groups who, so far, have risen from their ghettos by sweating blood instead of shedding it, by shaping up instead of burning down.

Although Harvard is the home of these three wise men and hundreds more, it was the only bunch in town that was dumfounded at what happened there. Everybody else in the community expected it. We had all watched Harvard for the last few years educate its young in the rewards of criminality. We had watched Harvard become an ivy-covered Fagin.

We saw it begin a couple of years ago when Secretary of Defense McNamara was invited to speak at Harvard. Now, it is true that McNamara was a member of a despised minority group, the President's Cabinet, but under the law, he had the same rights as Mark Rudd. Harvard's Students for a Democratic Society howled obscenities at McNamara until he could not be heard.

He attempted to leave the campus. The SDS stopped his car, milled around it, tried to tip it over. McNamara left the car. The SDS began to club him on the head with the poles on which their peace posters were nailed. If it hadn't been for the arrival of the Cambridge police, who formed a protective cordon around McNamara and escorted him through a series of interconnecting cellars of university buildings to safety, he might have been killed.

The next morning, Dean Monroe was asked if he would punish the SDS. And he said—and if you want to know where the malignancy started that has made a basket case of Harvard, it started with this—Dean Monroe said that he saw no reason to punish students for what was purely a political activity. Now, if depriving a man of his freedom to speak, if depriving him of his freedom to move, if damn nearly depriving him of his life—if that's political activity, then rape is a social event and sticking up a gas station is a financial transaction.

Now, there's nothing unusual about a pack of young criminals ganging up on a stranger on their turf as the SDS ganged up on McNamara; it's called mugging. And there's nothing unusual about a respected citizen, even a dean, babbling imbecilities in an emotional crisis; it's called a breakdown.

Both are curable by the proper treatment but there was something unusual, and chilling, too, about seeing the responsible authority, Harvard, treat a plain case of mugging as democracy in action and a plain case of hysterics as a dean in his right mind.

Well, after Harvard taught its young that the way to settle a difference of opinion is to mug anyone who differed with them, it was no surprise that they'd soon learn that shoving a banana into an instructor's mouth is the way to win a debate and bringing a meat cleaver to a conference is the way to win a concession. Because that's what happened at Harvard in the last month.

When its militants stormed into the opening class in a new course on the causes of urban unrest and stopped it because they found it ideologically offensive, the instructor attempted to discuss it with them. So one of the militants shoved a banana into his mouth. This stopped the instructor, of course, he stopped the class and then Harvard dropped the entire course.

This week, the Crimson published a photograph of a black militant leaving an historic conference with the administration—historic because it was here that the administration granted black students, and only black students, hiring, firing and tenure powers equal to that of any dean. The militant was holding a meat cleaver. The next day President Pusey said that Harvard would never yield to threats. Shows how silly a man can look when he doesn't read his local paper.

President Pusey said that, by the way, at a televised mass meeting advertised as one in which all sides of the question would be fairly represented. The Harvard student body was represented by a member of the SDS (numerically, they are less than

1 per cent). The average resident of the Cambridge community
was represented by a black militant graduate student who lives
in Roxbury and commutes in a new Cadillac. And anyone who'd
call that unfair representation would have been mean enough
to say the same thing about the Chief Rabbi of Berlin being
represented by Adolf Eichmann.

And so when Harvard was raped last week, it had as much
cause to be surprised as any tart who continued to flounce around
the fellas after they'd unbuttoned her bodice and pulled down
her panties.

What surprised the world was Harvard's response. Nowhere in
the world was Mayor Daley's response to precisely the same sort
of attack by precisely the same sort of mob more loftily denounced
than at Harvard. Yet in its moment of truth, Harvard responded
in precisely the same way Daley did.

Pusey called for the cops just as Daley did, and the cops treated
the criminals at Harvard just as firmly as they treated the
criminals in Chicago. The Harvard administration applauded
President Pusey's action to a man. There is no record that they
ever applauded Daley.

That either proves that the Harvard administration believes
in the divine right of kings to act in a fashion that, in a peasant,
is considered pushy. Or it may prove that President Pusey is
just as Neanderthal as Mayor Daley. Or it may prove that
President Pusey learned how to handle Neanderthals from Mayor
Daley. At any rate, if they're looking for a new president of
Harvard, I suggest they teach Mayor Daley to read and write
and offer him the job.

Let's forgive the president of Harvard for not having the grace
to thank the Mayor of Chicago for teaching him how to protect
his turf; they aren't strong on graciousness at Harvard this year.
But as a member of the Cambridge community, what alarms me
is that Harvard doesn't have the brains to protect itself, and the
community, from further, more savage and inevitably wider-
ranging attacks. And I feel that I have the right to speak for
some in the Cambridge community, possibly equal to that of any
resident of Roxbury who parks his car there for a few hours a
few days a week.

I've lived in Cambridge over 30 years. My children and grand-
children were born and raised in Cambridge. I help pay the taxes
that support Harvard. I help provide Harvard with the police
that it will increasingly need to protect it from the once-decent

kids it has corrupted into thugs and thieves, and the worse kind of thugs and thieves — the sanctimonious kind.

I ask, and my neighbors in the Cambridge community are asking: If a horde of howling, half-educated, half-grown and totally dependent half-humans can attack visitors in their cars, and deans in their offices, and get away with it, how long before they'll widen their horizons a block or two and attack us in our homes?

If they can use clubs and meat cleavers on the Harvard community today and get away with it, who stops them from using clubs and meat cleavers on the Cambridge community tomorrow? Certainly not the Harvard community. If it was necessary last week for Harvard to organize a round-the-clock guard to prevent the untoilet-trained pups they've made into mad dogs from blowing up the Widener Library and the Fogg Museum, must we of the Cambridge community prepare to defend ourselves from the pack Harvard has loosed among us? Or should we all pull a Rosovsky and take off to safe, sane Saigon where it's legal to shoot back at your enemy?

When the president of Harvard proved that, in a crisis, he was the intellectual equal to the Mayor of Chicago and called the cops, it was his finest hour. Although it was true that he had presided over the experimental laboratory that created the Frankenstein's monster that stomped mindlessly into University Hall, fouling everything in its path, he did, at long last, recognize what he had wrought and took the steps to rid his university and our community of the filthy thing.

After throwing the SDS out physically, the next sane move was obviously to keep them out officially, and expel them. And leave them to the criminal courts to educate, or to the Army, or to the gutters of Toronto, or to the rehabilitation centers and public charity of Stockholm. Their few score places at Harvard, and those of their sympathizers, could have been instantly filled by any of the tens of thousands of fine youngsters, black and white, they had been chosen instead of.

And Harvard could have gone on with pride and strength as an institution of learning, as an example of the vigor of the democratic process to other universities, instead of degenerating into the pigpen and playpen it is today. But after the president of Harvard made the one move that might have saved Harvard, the Harvard faculty, in the words of San Francisco State President Hayakawa, betrayed him.

And that brings us back to Rosovsky and Galbraith. And to Handlin.

Rosovsky, whose family had given up and fled when the German Nazis invaded the University of Danzig, who gave up and fled when the California Nazis invaded Berkeley, gave up the chairmanship of his course and started packing when the Cambridge Nazis invaded University Hall. And all over this country—at Cornell, in New York—other professors are using the Rosovsky solution: giving up and running away. The only trouble with it is that, sooner or later, you run out of places to run away to.

Now, the Galbraith solution is one that is bound to be popular with his fellow puberty-worshipers: those who have just achieved puberty, and those who worship those who have just achieved it as sources of infinite wisdom and quite a few votes. But I'm not criticizing Galbraith's religious convictions. What I say is, in this country, any professor who is panting to get back into public life is free to worship the SDS chapter of his choice.

Galbraith's solution is to promptly restructure our universities—and Harvard more promptly than any other, because, in Galbraith's opinion, those who administer Harvard have "little comprehension of the vast and complex scientific and scholarly life they presume to govern." Well, now, who does Galbraith presume to replace them with?

If those who created Harvard, and made it into the vast and complex scientific and scholarly structure it became, must be restructured out of it because they have too little comprehension, who has enough? The only ones who claim they have, and who will shove a banana into the mouth of anyone who denies it, are the student militants.

And so the Galbraith solution is a forth-right one: Let the lunatics run the asylum.

Well, I'm going to tell Galbraith the news: they've already tried your sort of restructuring, Ken. They tried it at Berkeley; they tried it at Cornell; they tried it at Harvard all last week, and the result was that on Friday, a mob of militant students, of a Harvard frenziedly restructured to suit their wildest whims, marched into the Harvard planning offices.

They shouted obscene charges at Planner Goyette. When he attempted to answer, they shouted him down with obscenities. They demolished the architectural model of Harvard's building plans, they kicked over files, they hurled telephones to the floor. And while Goyette cowered and his secretaries screamed, they marched out, uninterfered with by the six policemen who were summoned there presumably to see that they remained uninterfered with, unrebuked and, of course, unsatisfied.

And they won't be satisfied until Harvard is restructured the way they restructured Hiroshima. They'll be back, on another day, to another office. Possibly Galbraith's.

Well, those were the voices that prevailed at Harvard, the resigners like Rosovsky, the restructurers like Galbraith. There was another voice, however, the voice of Oscar Handlin.

Prof. Handlin said he was appalled at the argument that the students' takeover of University Hall, their attack on the deans, their destruction of private property and their thefts from personal files were unwise but not criminal. It *was* criminal, said Handlin, by every decent standard.

If Harvard had not chickened out, said Handlin, if it had had the courage to recognize the criminality on its campus over the last few years, beginning with the beating up and silencing of McNamara and continuing through innumerable other incidents of the brutal deprivation by its mad-dog students of the rights of those who dared to dissent with them, it "would not be in the position it is in today—following the road that Berkeley has followed, following the road that has destroyed other universities."

Oscar Handlin urged Harvard not to go down that road. That was last week. This week, Harvard has gone so far down the road that it can never turn back. In this last frantic, fatal, foolish week, Harvard has reversed the civil rights advances of the last 20 years.

Today at Harvard, any student with the currently fashionable color of skin is given rights denied to students of the currently unfashionable color. Harvard, which educated the President who brought America into the war that defeated fascism, today honors and encourages and rewards its fascists. Harvard, which once turned out scholars and gentlemen, now turns out thugs and thieves—or let me put it this way: now, if you are a thug and thief, Harvard won't turn you out.

Once people were attracted to the Cambridge community because Harvard was there. Today, because Harvard is there, people are fleeing the Cambridge community, even Harvard's own.

Harvard's tragedy was that it was too arrogant to consider that it too might be vulnerable to the cancer that is killing other universities. And when Oscar Handlin diagnosed it as malignant,

Harvard was too cowardly to endure the radical surgery that could save its life.

And that's why I can say that colleges like yours, as yet too unproven to have become arrogant, and too determined to prove yourself to be anything but courageous, are the hope of the future. Because I believe that America has a future.

It has become unfashionable to say this; it may be embarrassing to hear it; but I believe that America is the most lovely and liveable of all nations. I believe that Americans are the kindest and most generous of all people.

I believe there are no underprivileged Americans; that even the humblest of us are born with a privilege that places us ahead of anyone else, anywhere else: the privilege of living and working in America, of repairing and renewing America; and one more privilege that no one seems to get much fun out of lately—the privilege of loving America.

DISCUSSION QUESTIONS

1. The essay is an impressive example of the effect that can be produced by snarl words (e.g., "half-humans" "raped" "the pigpen and playpen" where "sanctimonious fatheads" "presided over the experimental laboratory that created the Frankenstein's monster," etc.). Trace such words through the article and indicate which more nearly approach a specific meaning that is subject to evidence.

2. Dean Ford is described as the man whose recuperative powers kept the students from enjoying "a dean killing." What is one led to infer from this? Actually Dean Ford was in no way harmed during the student uprising; a few days later he was hospitalized with a mild stroke caused by his working long hours to resolve the conflict on campus. Does the author grossly misstate the situation?

3. Discuss the inductive evidence which contributes to the conclusion that Professor Rosovsky lacks "guts." Is the sample known, sufficient, and representative?

4. The author says that Senator Eugene McCarthy's "menopausal capriciousness [was mistaken] for high-principled statesmanship." Does this charge characterize McCarthy more than any of the other candidates in the 1968 presi-

dential primaries: i.e., Humphrey, Nixon, Rockefeller, Reagan, Wallace, Robert Kennedy, etc.?

5. The "malignancy . . . that has made a basket case of Harvard" is said to begin with Dean Monroe's refusal to punish students for their treatment of Robert McNamara. Does this seem an effective charge and a reliable conclusion? Is it less effective when one learns that McNamara did in fact give the speech he was invited to Harvard to deliver, that thereafter his car was stopped and he was shouted down, but that he was not clubbed or struck in any way, and that—after Dean Monroe wrote apologizing for the event—he responded "No apology was necessary"? Does the author make any false claims about this incident?

6. The author notes that Chicago's Mayor Daley responded with force when faced with "precisely the same sort of attack by precisely the same sort of mob" and that President Pusey finally "responded in precisely the same way Daley did." Were the two situations precisely the same?

7. President Pusey is said to have "presided over the experimental laboratory that created the Frankenstein's monster that stomped mindlessly into University Hall, fouling everything in its path." Discuss the argument by analogy here. Can it be said that Pusey *created* the monster?

Why we're dropping The New York Times

Last week the Times said it would accept cigarette ads only if they contain (1) a health caution notice, and (2) "tar" and nicotine figures.

We don't go along with this.

We offered to take our ads off TV and radio because of the claim that those media unavoidably reach large numbers of children.

We did not take that action because we agree with anticigarette crusaders (including The New York Times) who would like to blame cigarettes for the thousand and one ills that flesh is heir to.

Sure there are statistics associating lung cancer and cigarettes. There are statistics associating lung cancer with divorce, and even with lack of sleep. But no scientist has produced clinical or biological proof that cigarettes cause the diseases they are accused of causing. After fifteen years of trying, nobody has induced lung cancer in animals with cigarette smoke.

We believe the anticigarette theory is a bum rap. And each time the Congress of the United States has held Hearings on the cigarette controversy, distinguished, independent scientists have gone to Washington to say so.

Therefore, we are not going to knuckle under to the Times or anybody else who tries to force us to accept a theory which, in the opinion of men who should know, is half-baked.

In 1884, the New York Times said:

"The decadence of Spain began when the Spaniards adopted cigarettes and if this pernicious practice obtains among adult Americans the ruin of the Republic is close at hand..."

We think the New York Times was wrong in 1884. We think it is wrong in 1969.

The American Tobacco Company
A DIVISION OF AMERICAN BRANDS, INC.

DISCUSSION QUESTIONS

1. This advertisement expressed the judgment of a major American corporation responding to evidence produced by government agencies and medical societies and answering a respected newspaper. How can one account for the colloquial tone?

2. The advertisement rejects the view of "anticigarette crusaders . . . who would like to blame cigarettes for the thousand and one ills that flesh is heir to." Name some of the crusaders and some of the ills referred to. Why did the author choose to be general rather than specific here?

3. Go through the paragraphs identifying examples of snarl words and purr words. Which of these are furthest from specific meaning? Which are more subject to evidence?

4. How relevant is the final reference to the *Times*' attitude toward Spain in 1884?

5. Read William L. Laurence's report of the findings of the American Cancer Society (p. 187). Does it flatly contradict this statement—written several years later—that "no scientist has produced clinical or biological proof that cigarettes cause the diseases they are accused of causing"?

6

Fallacies

Where there's smoke, there's fire.
Luther left the priesthood to get married.
Is it true blondes have more fun?
If guns are outlawed, only outlaws will have guns.
Rockefeller is divorced; he'd make a poor president.

Certain forms of misleading argument occur so commonly that they have been specifically isolated and labeled. Though most could be analyzed as faulty induction, deduction, and so on, they are treated separately here because the terms describing them are frequently encountered. They are part of the language of argument.

FALSE ANALOGY

To argue by analogy is to compare two things known to be alike in some features and to suggest they will be alike in other features as well. This method constitutes reasonable argument if the compared features are genuinely similar. (Sam Jensen is an *outstanding player-coach*; he will make a fine *manager*.) It is fallacious if the features are essentially dissimilar. (You have *fruit* for breakfast; why not try *Jell-O* for breakfast?)

One tests an analogy by asking if the assumed statement is true and if the elements compared in the argument are sufficiently alike. The assumed assertion is particularly questionable when it exists as an adage. Re-election campaigns regularly submit, for example, that "You wouldn't change horses in the middle of a stream." But the smallest consideration will remind one of instances in which he would be glad to change horses. Equally vulnerable are arguments insisting "You can lead a horse to water but you can't make him drink," "Where there's smoke, there's fire," and "There's no use locking the barn after the horse is stolen."

More commonly, one challenges an analogy by showing the fundamental dissimilarity of the things compared. Facing the

148

standard argument "Old enough to fight is old enough to vote," one can ask if the qualities which make a good soldier (courage, quick reflexes, promptness in obeying orders) are those which make a good voter (intelligence, deliberation, independence). Recalling a super-patriot senator's justification of his rough treatment of suspected communists — "You don't chase tigers with a silk handkerchief" — one can question the comparison of tigers and *suspected* communists.

Some analogies are more complex. An instance is this argument which appears in most temperance campaigns:

> There are 10,000 deaths from alcohol poisoning to 1 from mad-dog bites in this country. In spite of this, we license liquor but shoot the dogs.

Since it is desirable to get rid of any dogs or any liquor which proves deadly, this analogy seems reasonable. But the argument hinges on the implicit recommendation that *all* liquor be outlawed. And this action is reasonable only if one is willing to pursue the comparison and get rid of certain diseased examples by shooting all dogs. Similarly one should appraise popular arguments comparing censorship with pure food laws, federal deficit spending with a family budget, and independent Asian nations with dominoes.

In argument, an analogy is valuable for illustrating a point or for speculating on an event. But, simply by itself, it can do little more than that. As the Yiddish proverb says, "'For example' is no proof."

Presumed Cause-Effect

Relating an event to its cause can lead to three different fallacies.

Argument in a Circle occurs when a spokesman offers a restatement of his argument as a reason for accepting it. He offers his conclusion, adds "because," then repeats the conclusion in different words. ("Smoking is injurious because it harms the human body" or "One phone's not enough in the modern home because modern homes have plenty of phones.") Sometimes the expression is more oblique, with the "because" implied rather than stated. (William Jennings Bryan once declared, "There is only one argument that can be made to one who rejects the authority of the Bible, namely, that the Bible is true.") It is

pointless to argue that a thing is true because it is true. Para-
phrase is not evidence.

Post Hoc Ergo Propter Hoc ("after this, therefore because of
this"; often shortened to *post hoc*) occurs when someone cites
two past events and insists that because one occurred first, it
necessarily caused the second. On such evidence, he can argue
that President Hoover caused the depression, that Democratic
presidents promote war, and that Martin Luther left the Catholic
priesthood in order to get married. This logic can make much of
trivial events: in 1964, an anti-Jewish newspaper found sinister
implications in the fact that President Johnson had breakfast
with Supreme Court Justice Arthur Goldberg shortly before he
announced Hubert Humphrey as his running mate.

Post-hoc reasoning is fallacious because it ignores the more
complex factors which contribute to an event. A successful
advertisement announced, for example, that students who type-
write their schoolwork get 30 percent higher grades than those
who do not, then suggested that buying one's child a typewriter
would improve his grades. The fallacy here is in the implication
that simply owning a typewriter caused the higher grades. Other
factors seem more accountable: the parents who would buy their
child a typewriter were those concerned with his education,
those who took pains to see he learned his lessons, those who
could give him other cultural advantages, and so on. It is this
range of "other factors" which one must consider in judging a
post-hoc argument.

Non Sequitur ("it does not follow") occurs when one submits
that a particular fact must have certain future consequences.
He can take a present fact. (Ted Kennedy was involved in an
auto accident which killed a young girl) and project a conclusion
(He would make a poor president). Or he can take an anticipated
fact (If sex education is offered in American schools . . .) and
spell out the consequences (Student morals will suffer). The response, of course, is that the conclusion does not necessarily
follow from the cited cause.

The term *non sequitur* is widely used, and it lends itself to
describe a multiple-cause argument. ("The more you know . . .
the more you do . . . the more you tax your nerves . . . the
more important it is to relax tired nerves. Try safe, nonhabit-
forming Sedquilin.") But it has little value in defining general
argument; almost any kind of fallacious reasoning is a non
sequitur.

BEGGING THE QUESTION

One begs the question by assuming what it is his responsibility to prove; he builds his argument on an undemonstrated claim. Generally this takes the form of a question. ("Have you stopped beating your wife?" or "Is it true blondes have more fun?") But it can appear as a declaration. ("Integration is no more the law of the land than is any other Communist doctrine.")

Another form of begging the question is to make a charge and then insist that someone else disprove it. ("How do you know that flying saucers haven't been visiting the earth for centuries?") In all argument, the burden of proof is on the individual making the assertion. It is foolish to try to disprove a conclusion which was never proven in the first place.

IGNORING THE QUESTION

One can ignore the question in two ways: he can leave the subject to attack his opponent, or he can leave the subject to discuss a different topic.

Argumentum ad Hominem is attacking the man, not the question at issue. ("You favor extension of the draft because you're too old to have to serve" or "So you think Bobby Seale deserved the contempt citation which sent him to jail; you fascist pig!") The speaker says nothing of the facts; he ignores the question by attacking the man. To avoid confusion, it should be added that an argument criticizing a particular individual — a governmental official, a candidate, etc. — is probably not *argumentum ad hominem*; in such cases, the man *is* the issue.

Extension has the same effect. Here one "extends" the question until he is arguing a different subject altogether. ("I know Spiro Agnew has his faults, but nobody's perfect, you know.") Invariably the new subject is one the speaker finds easier to maintain. Currently, opponents of gun *registration* begin their argument, "If guns are outlawed. . . ."

Either-Or is a form of extension. Here, a spokesman distorts the question by insisting that only two alternatives exist, his position and something much worse. He will describe a temperance resolution as a decision between Christianity and debauchery, and a fluoridation referendum as an option between pure water and poison. Should one question the wisdom of America's military involvement in Viet Nam, he can challenge, "Which side are you on, anyway?"

This technique is common in presidential elections where political statements regularly pit a favored candidate against a vulnerable figure who can be associated with his opponent. In 1952, for example, Eisenhower ran against Hiss; in 1956, Stevenson challenged Nixon; in 1960, Nixon opposed Pope John XXIII; in 1964, the Republicans ran against Bobby Baker; and in 1968, the Democrats challenged Spiro Agnew. Like most either-or arguments, this strawman approach oversimplifies the situation.

To all such examples of ignoring the question, the reasonable response is, "Let's get back to the issue."

CONCLUSION

Most of the fallacies cited can be dissected as examples of induction, deduction, semantic argument, etc. Any false analogy, for example, is deduction with invalid form. Any post-hoc error is induction with an insufficient sample. And any kind of false argument can be called a non sequitur. But special terms do exist for these fallacies, and it is perhaps valuable to have two ways of looking at them.

IDENTIFY THE FALLACY IN THESE ARGUMENTS:

1. So you don't like this story; I suppose you could write a better one.

2. We should not teach communism in the public schools any more than we should teach safe-cracking or arson.

3. Major Claude Eatherly must be honored as a man of up-right conscience. After partaking in the atomic raid on Hiroshima, he left the Air Force and suffered a mental breakdown.

4. Black Power vs. White Power! The war against the White race has already begun. Which side are you on?

5. Arguing from the principle that a person is sick "when he fails to function in his appropriate gender identification," Dr. Charles Socarides, a New York psychoanalyst, concludes that homosexuality is a form of emotional illness.

6. Asked of his union's attitude toward a proposal for work-rule changes, David McDonald responded, "We will never give the steel companies the unilateral right to use a black-snake whip on the backs of our workers."

7. If evolution is true, why has it stopped?

What a Catholic Wishes To Avoid in Marriage

JOHN S. BANAHAN

Tall stories are not the exclusive property of Texans. Men have enjoyed stretching the truth at least as long as they have been able to write. One of the earliest prototypes of Paul Bunyan was a character of Greek mythology named Cyclops. He was a tremendous giant employed in Vulcan's blacksmith shop to forge thunderbolts for Zeus to hurl down from the heavens at the mortals who might defy him. He was a being of gigantic size and immeasurable strength. He was gifted with acute senses. And his only defect was that he had but one eye placed squarely in the midst of his forehead. This weakness was fatal. For he was brought to his knees by one far smaller in stature than he who was clever enough to deprive him of his eyesight. Thus being blinded, his great strength was useless.

In a way, modern man is an image of Cyclops. For though he possesses two eyes and two ears, he has only one intellect. It is this mind of his that gives man the power to look deep into things and understand them. And yet today millions of men have suffered a cyclopean wound. Their mind's eye is blinded. They are deprived of the vision that their intellect should give them.

Tiny objects can deprive us of sight. A cinder or a cataract are infinitesimal but nonetheless they can blind us. And there are things less substantial than these which can darken the light of the mind. A strong emotion has this ability. Quite commonly men are blinded by anger, love, or desire. The company of those blinded by desire is perhaps the largest in world history. Among its membership are such men as Adolf Hitler, Joseph Stalin, and Benito Mussolini. Now, these three men were not the incarnate devils that the cartoonists of the past decade pictured them. They were men of at least ordinary intelligence who were blinded with their desire for power. Desire of wealth can lead men to steal. Desire for liquor can cause drunkenness. Desire for property can bring men to murder. Whenever men are ruled by their desires they become something less than men. Animals have no higher faculties than their desires. But men have within

Reprinted from *Instructions for Mixed Marriages* (Milwaukee: Bruce Publishing Company, 1955), pp. 78–89.

them the spark of divinity—the ability to think and will. The more a man is influenced by his thoughts, the more a man is he. Now, marriage has been made for man, not for animals, and when men forget this the slow cancer of unhappiness threatens their lives.

One of the most prominent signs that man has forgotten his nature is the practice of artificial birth control. Everyone knows that Catholics aren't supposed to use birth prevention devices, but few realize that this applies likewise to the rest of the world. Catholics are not the only ones forbidden to steal or murder. No one should do these things. They are not "Catholic Sins" any more than is artificial birth prevention.

Before we go much farther, let us point this out. There is nothing wrong with birth control! The word "control" implies the correct use of mind and will. It implies that a man acts like a man and not as a blind animal force. The Church favors such control! She encourages men to practice control of their lives, of their faculties, and of their desires. But a further question is just how this control is to be achieved. A man has a right and duty to clothe and feed his family. Suppose he chooses a career of armed robbery to accomplish this end. Certainly the Church would try to dissuade him from adopting such a means of livelihood. But it would be the means that she would criticize, and not the purpose for which he steals. Likewise, with birth prevention by artificial means, she criticizes the measures adopted, not the policy of control of marital relations. The Church has never commanded her members to have two, twelve, or twenty children. The size of a family is something to be determined by husband and wife, not by pastor or bishop. But what the Church says is this: It is improper to use the human faculty of procreation and then deliberately exclude and frustrate its natural purposes by some artificial means. There are three reasons for this condemnation:

I. REASON TELLS US THAT THIS IS WRONG

Nothing that exists in this world is evil. Everything is good. The use of things is not wrong, but the *misuse* of things is. A Cadillac in itself is good. But if I drive it at top speed through a crowded street and bring injury and death to several bystanders, my actions are evil. The auto is still good, but I have misused it.

Or, if I employ a shotgun to shoot not pigeons but people, then the misuse of this weapon is something evil.

Of course, we cannot determine if a thing is misused unless we know its correct use. This is true of the smallest atom and the largest skyscraper. They all have a proper purpose and a correct usage. Our eyes, our ears, and our voices all are designed for definite purposes. When we frustrate these purposes, we do wrong. For instance, our voices have been given us that we might communicate honestly and truthfully what we are thinking. Every time we read a paper or listen to a news analyst, we accept this principle. We trust men to tell us what they think is true. But when we tell a deliberate lie, then we consciously frustrate the purpose for which the power of speech was given us. We have misused this tremendous faculty; we have thereby done wrong.

Paramount among the wonderful activities man is capable of is procreation. Besides the powers to think and will which are replicas of God's faculties, He has given man the ability to co-operate with Him in creating new life. These generative powers are given to all normal men and women for the purpose of perpetuating the human race. It is axiomatic that those who bring such life into existence should assume responsibility for it. And since this obligation is not a light one, mankind must be encouraged to assume it and be rewarded for doing so.

Thus God has attached to this faculty a deep and instinctive drive and a unique physical pleasure. These things are normal and good. There is nothing evil or warped about sex instinct or pleasure. Only their misuse is wrong. Did you ever start to cross a street, then barely see the flicker of an approaching vehicle and find that you have automatically, without thinking at all, jumped back to the safety of the curbstone? If you have had this experience, then you witnessed the subconscious drive all men have of self-preservation. Equal to this in unrelenting intensity is the drive for self-perpetuation, more popularly identified as the sex instinct. This leads mankind to discount the burdens of parenthood and to co-operate again and again with God in bringing human life to exist for all eternity. Besides this, parents experience a unique reward called sexual pleasure. These feelings are attached to the use of the generative faculty. And although all of our senses bring us pleasure, they do not match in any way the sensations evoked by the use of the creative faculty. This is proportionate because none of the others involve us in such tremendous responsibilities. Thus instinct and pleasure co-operate to encourage men to use their generative powers. But observe, the purpose of these faculties is the production of new life, not pleasure. Therefore, when a man deliberately excludes the proper purpose and makes this godlike act of procreation an act of mere pleasure, he does wrong.

Among the sins of man there is no parallel of this. A crime it approximates is an opprobrious custom of the ancient past. In the days when Roman culture had flowered and then began to decay the aristocracy built huge and lovely villas in renowned spas such as Pompeii. There they lived in overnourished luxury. It was then that the practice of all night dinner parties began, made up of twenty or thirty of the richest courses imaginable. And since the human body could not consume such quantity and variety of food, the guests would occasionally retire to a room adjacent to the dining area where they would regurgitate and then return to continue feasting. Such a practice appalls the modern man whose acts parallel the sins of the Romans when he practices artificial birth prevention to enjoy the pleasures of marriage while excluding its proper purpose.

Do not misunderstand! The Church does not say that those who practice planned parenthood today are degenerate. She does not say that they are decadent. But she does say that the two actions are equivalent and that people today can be excused only because they lack the proper information or have not thought deeply on the question. Reason, if correctly employed, should tell all men that this practice is morally wrong.

II. The Bible Tells Us That It Is Wrong

Most Christians today believe in Holy Scripture. Some believe it to be the inspired Word of God, as do Catholics. Others at least admit it to be a collection of profound truths of dubious authorship. But most Christians believe that the statements of the Bible are true.

In the very first book of Holy Writ we find a passage which deals clearly and specifically with this practice. In the Book of Genesis, we can read the tragic story of Onan. In the early days of history, the Jews were a nomadic group with no fixed land to call their own. One of their sociological problems was the care of widows and orphans. In their primitive society, there was no employment suitable for women who had lost their husbands.

Therefore, a law was passed requiring the deceased's brother to marry the widow and care for her and her children. This misfortune befell Onan, and it is recounted that as a result of his dissatisfaction with this regulation he proceeded to practice artificial birth prevention with his new wife. The very next verse of Holy Scripture recounts: "Therefore the Lord slew him because he did a detestable thing."[1]

Notice the two points of this citation:

a) God *detests* this practice. In other words, He regards it as sinful.

b) He detests it to such an extent that He *slew* Onan in punishment. Therefore, this practice cannot be regarded as something merely mischievous or naughty, but as something which is very seriously wrong. Catholics call it mortal sin.

This is not the only mention of artificial birth prevention in the Bible, for the Book of Tobias and certain of the Pauline Epistles[2] abound in instructions on the nature of marriage. However, if you are one who accepts the truth of the biblical quotations the story of Onan should be sufficient.[3]

III. The Church Says It Is Seriously Wrong

A clergyman is as prone to error as the butcher, the baker, or the candlestick maker. Even when said clergyman is a priest, bishop, or even pope, he can still blunder. But the first chapter of this booklet mentioned that there was a percentage of religious teaching that was guaranteed to be true by no less an authority than God Himself, acting through His own institution of which He has said: "He who hears you, hears me."[4] In twenty centuries, this organization has occasionally made public and official statements and given the world assurance that they were true. Among these infallible statements is listed the condemnation of artificial birth control as being a serious sin. There is as much possibility that ecclesiastical teaching on this subject will change as there is that the Church's opposition to murder will change. Birth prevention has always been practiced; it has always been wrong. Possibly it always will be practiced, and if so, it always will be wrong!

[1] Gen. 38:10.
[2] Tob. 6:16; Rom. 1:26.
[3] St. Augustine writes: "Marital relations even with a lawful wife, are unlawful and degrading when the conception of a child is deliberately frustrated. This was the sin of Onan, and God struck him dead because of it" (*De Adulterio*, 2:12).
[4] Lk. 10:6.

WHY?

There are various reasons why people indulge in this practice. Let us enumerate three classes:

a) Those Who Are Selfish. There are married folk who prefer a new Frigidaire or Ford to a filled bassinet. There are wives who fear to lose their figures. There are couples who treasure their adult privacy overmuch. Of course, people who have such a warped and dwarfed appreciation of human life should never be allowed to be parents. Their unborn children are fortunate for there is nothing more pitiful than to be an unwanted child. To them we cite the words of our Saviour who spoke thus to those who maltreated children: "It is better for him to have a great millstone hung around his neck, and to be drowned in the depths of the sea."[5]

b) Those Who Cannot Afford Children. There are several varieties of this excuse.

1. There are the teen-agers who marry though penniless and unemployed! This should not be allowed to happen. Parents, clergy, and judiciary should close ranks in an attempt to prevent boys and girls from entering marriage without the proper financial resources. The mistake having been made, these same authorities should be just as solicitous and co-operative in providing these couples with temporary subsidies.

2. There are those who confuse luxuries and necessities. Some parents feel that their families should be limited to the few whom they can afford to send to college or finishing school. Little do they realize that their children may not wish to attend the schools selected for them. The child that remains unborn might have been the one to treasure and use well the education and physical advantages wasted by the living. Benjamin Franklin was the eighth child of his parents. There were six in the Washington family, and Abraham Lincoln had seven brothers and sisters. The Jeffersons numbered ten, the Madisons twelve, the Longfellows eight, and the Beethovens twelve. There were eight Shakespeares, twelve Tennysons and Scotts, and nine Carlyles. God bestows talent and genius where He wills; it is not arrived at by selective breeding!

3. Those who actually have a serious financial problem. To these the Church will give sympathy, encouragement, and assistance. Sometimes priests are criticized for their interest in trade unionism and collective bargaining. Their policy is founded on

[5] Mt. 18:6.

the belief that a man cannot live the moral life the Church
demands of him unless he receives wages proportionate to his
obligations and dignity as the head of a household. Empty
bellies make poor Christians. The Church is realistic enough
to know that greed and avarice can affect union leaders as well
as the rest of mankind. She knows that her concern for her
people can be twisted by the unscrupulous. But she will continue
to use every possible means to enable parents to afford their
families.

Remember the famous fairy tale of Cinderella? In the closing
chapter, the Prince comes`searching his kingdom for the owner
of the dainty glass slipper. He proffers it to one of the ugly sisters
who lives with Cinderella, who in an effort to make her foot fit
the shoe, cuts off her toes! This is a dreadful way to acquire
footwear of the proper size, but it is rather reminiscent of what
occurs each year in many American homes. Because the size of
the family won't fit the current budget, the family is pared down
a member or two. The Church suggests an alternative solution.
Instead of decreasing the family, why can't men increase their
budgets? Perhaps this is more difficult than purchasing pro-
phylactics at the corner drugstore, but the Church attempts
to give the *correct* solution and not just the easiest one. What is
right is very often difficult!

c) Those Who Are Told That Pregnancy Will Endanger Their
Lives. The sympathy and solicitude of the Church is aroused by
the plight of these worried husbands and wives. But while she
understands the concern of these couples the Church points out
that medical opinion is not infallible. We all know of women
who have defied their physician's orders and safely raised large
families. We do not therefore recommend wholesale rebellion
against all medical authority, but merely point out that sometimes a doctor's diagnosis is incorrect and sometimes perhaps
God Himself suspends the laws He has made for us. Very great
wonders have been worked by the sincere prayers of ordinary
husbands and wives.

However, there certainly are some cases when it is not safe
for a woman to become a mother. What suggestions does the
Church make to a married couple troubled with such a burden?
The only remedy that can be suggested to such people is a life
of virtuous abstinence. This is impossible except for couples who
accept the philosophy that God has made them for eternal happiness and earthly problems are the price we pay for everlasting

felicity. It was impossible for Peter to walk on the waters of the Sea of Galilee until God gave him that ability. God can likewise give married couples the strength to live lives of complete abstinence if such people would devoutly ask it of Him.

DISCUSSION QUESTIONS

1. Pope Paul based *Humanae Vitae*, the encyclical expressing the Church's opposition to artificial birth control, on the natural-law argument. Summarized from the section "Reason Tells Us That This is Wrong," it takes this form:

   Everything in the universe is good and has a proper purpose (a Cadillac, a shotgun, the smallest atom, the largest skyscraper, the human voice, and human generative faculties). When we frustrate these purposes, we do wrong.

   How persuasive is this argument by analogy?

2. The article employs other analogy arguments. Which seem most impressive?

   Modern man is a Cyclops with his reason as his single eye. Emotional desires—like Ulysses' stake—can blind him.

   The person employing birth control techniques is like Hitler, Stalin, Mussolini, and animals in following no higher faculty than his desires.

   A man is wrong to practice either artificial birth control or armed robbery to help support his family.

   Birth control parallels the decadent Roman practice of a person's eating luxurious food, then regurgitating so he could eat some more.

   Practicing birth control to keep one's family at a manageable size is like the action of Cinderella's sister who cut off her toes so she could wear the glass slipper.

   It is possible for a married couple to live a celibate life, just as it was possible for St. Peter to walk on the Sea of Galilee.

3. "Now, marriage has been made for man, not for animals, and when men forget this the slow cancer of unhappiness threatens their lives?" Does the "happiness" theme run through the essay? How is it related to the moral issue?

4. "Reason, if correctly employed, should tell all men that this practice is morally wrong." Discuss the assumptions underlying this statement.

5. The author presents certain of his Biblical arguments in footnote references. Comment on the argumentative advantage of this practice. (It will be revealing to trace the references in the Bible, as well as to read a scholarly commentary on the meaning of the Onan story.)

6. Many responsible Catholics would deny the claim that the Church for twenty centuries has made official statements and given the world assurance that they were true and that "Among these infallible statements is listed the condemnation of artificial birth control as being a serious sin." Discuss the author's claims as argument by authority.

7. In categorizing the "various reasons why people indulge in this practice," is the author illustrating the either-or fallacy?

8. To whom is the author applying Christ's threat against those who mistreat children? Name the fallacy here.

9. How impressive is the argument that many gifted and famous men came from large families? Consider the implications of the argument.

10. "We all know of women who have defied their physician's orders and safely raised large families." Is this a self-evident fact?

This Thing Called Love is Pathological

LAWRENCE CASLER

> Men have died from time to time,
> and worms have eaten them,
> but not for love.
> — Act IV, Scene I, *As You Like It*

Magazines, movies and television teach us the joys of love. Advertisers insist that we must look good and smell good in order to escape loveless solitude. Artists, philosophers and hippies urge their varying versions of Love; and most psychotherapists hold that the ability to love is a sign—sometimes *the* sign—of mental health.

To suggest that this emphasis on lovingness is misplaced is to risk being accused of arrested development, coldness, low self-image, or some unmentionable deficiency. Still, the expanding frontiers of psychology require a reconsideration of love at this time.

We shall be concerned, chiefly, with what is generally called "romantic" love. But many of these observations may be applicable to other varieties as well.

Love, like other emotions, has causes, characteristics and consequences. Temporarily setting aside an inquiry into why, or whether, love makes the world go 'round, makes life worth living, and conquers all, let us consider the somewhat more manageable question of causality. Love between man and woman has many determinants, but instinct is not one of them. Anthropologists have described entire societies in which love is absent, and there are many individuals in our society who have never loved. To argue that such societies and individuals are "sick" or "the exception that proves the rule" (whatever *that* means) is sheer arrogance. Love, when it exists, is a learned emotion. Explanations for its current prevalence must be sought elsewhere than in the genes.

Most individuals in our society, beset by parent-bred, competition-bred insecurity, need acceptance, confirmation, justification. Part of this need is inescapable. Life requires continual decision-making: white vs. red wine, honesty vs. dishonesty, etc. In the

Reprinted from *Psychology Today* (December 1969), pp. 18–20, 74–76.

presence of uncertainty, most of us need to know that we are making the right decisions, so we seek external validation. We are, therefore, absurdly pleased when we meet someone who shares our penchant for Palestrina or peanut butter. Should we find one person whose choices in many different matters coincide with our own, we will value this buttress of our self-esteem. This attachment to a source of self-validation constitutes one important basis for love.

While the relationship between loving and being loved is an intimate one, this is not to say that love is automatically reciprocated. Indeed, it may lead to feelings of revulsion if the individual's self-image is already irretrievably low: "Anyone who says he loves *me* must be either a fool or a fraud." Still, a person is relatively likely to love someone who loves him. Indirect support for this generalization comes from a number of experiments in which persons are falsely informed that they are liked (or disliked) by other members of their group. This misinformation is enough to elicit congruent feelings in most of the deceived subjects. A similar kind of feedback often operates in the elaborate American game of dating. The young woman, for any of several reasons, may pretend to like her escort more than is actually the case. The man, hungry for precisely this kind of response, responds favorably and in kind. And the woman, gratified by this expression of affection, now feels the fondness she had formerly feigned. Falling in love may be regarded, in cases such as these, as a snowball with a hollow core.

Nevertheless, we do not fall in love with everyone who shows acceptance of us. Other needs clamor for satisfaction. And the more needs that one person satisfies, the more likely are we to love that person. One of the foremost needs is called, very loosely, sex. Our love is elicited not simply by the ego-booster, but by the ego-booster with sex appeal.

The mores of our society discourage us from seeking sexual gratification from anyone with whom we do not have a preexisting relationship. As a result, the more ego-boosting a relationship is, the greater the tendency will be for the booster to serve — actually or potentially — as a sex-satisfier. But it is also true that a person who gives one sexual pleasure tends to boost one's ego. Once again, the snowball effect is obvious.

Society emphasizes, furthermore, the necessity for love to precede sex. Although many disregard this restriction, others remain frightened or disturbed by the idea of a purely sexual relationship. The only way for many sexually aroused individuals to avoid frustration or anxiety is to fall in love—as quickly as possible. More declarations of love have probably been uttered in parked cars than in any other location. Some of these surely are nothing more than seduction ploys, but it is likely that self-seduction is involved in many cases.

For most of us, the internal and external pressures are so great that we can no longer "choose" to love or not love. Loving becomes inevitable, like dying or getting married. We are so thoroughly brainwashed that we come to pity or scorn the person who is not in love. (Of course, the pity or scorn may be self-directed, but not for long: anyone who does not have the inner resources to stand alone can usually impose himself upon somebody else who is equally incapacitated.)

Our society, besides being love-oriented, is marriage-oriented. From early childhood on, we hear countless statements beginning, "When (not *if*) you get married . . ." And, just as love is regarded as a prerequisite for sex, it is regarded as a prerequisite for marriage. Consequently, the insecurity and the fear of social punishment that force most of us into marriage provide additional powerful motives for falling in love. (The current value of marriage as a social institution, while open to question, is beyond the scope of this essay.)

To summarize, the *causes* of love are the needs for security, sexual satisfaction, and social conformity. Thus viewed, love loses its uniqueness. Hatred, too, in societies that are as aggression-oriented as ours is love-oriented, may reflect these same needs. To state that love is a superior emotion is to express a current cultural bias. Nothing is good or bad but culture makes it so.

We can study the *characteristics* of love by using techniques of the laboratory psychologist. Several of our emotions trigger specific, distinguishable biochemical reactions. Fear, for example, can be reliably inferred from adrenal and other secretions. However, no physiological indices have been discovered for love. Perhaps there is no biological correlate of love. Perhaps there *is* a correlate, but one so subtle that it has not yet been observed. Or perhaps love is accompanied by other emotions so that its own particular signs are cancelled.

This last possibility seems especially attractive. Love involves need-satisfaction, and need-satisfaction typically is associated (as a cause or an effect) with physical relaxation. But physical relaxation is not a usual concomitant of love. Perhaps the relaxation is being neutralized by sexual arousal or by such tension-producing emotions as anger or fear. The intrusion of either of these latter emotions is easily explicable. The lover may well be angry because he resents his increasing dependency. (Recall that the loved person is likely to be viewed as the actual or potential gratifier of more and more needs—self-esteem, sex, etc.—and therefore becomes more and more indispensable.) A man can come to hate his mistress or his wife as he hates the cigarettes or race track to which he is addicted.

Another likely accompaniment of need-satisfaction is fear. Every increase in dependency increases the fear of losing the source of gratification. There is always the chance of loss through death, but the fear is more usually based, in competitive societies, on the possibility that the loved one will find someone else more gratifying. The fear of loss of the beloved thus fuses with the fear of loss of self-respect. Jealousy, generally regarded as a destructive emotion, thus appears to be a well-nigh inevitable component of love.

While both fear and anger seem to be inextricably involved in love, fear is probably the more fundamental. Indeed, the anger may be viewed as a reaction to fear. This being the case, a working definition emerges: love is the fear of losing an important source of need gratification.

Up to now, my emphasis has been on so-called romantic love. But the same four-letter word is used in an almost infinite variety of other contexts. Besides loving his wife, one may love his parents, his children, his dog, the New York Mets, and God. (We shall return to God later.) One may also, following the lead of psychotherapists and adolescents of all ages, love love. Hopefully, the emotion is somewhat different in each of these cases, but there is considerable overlap. For example, whatever is loved is likely to be a satisfier of multiple needs. Also, it may be that only those experiences that are believed, or feared, to be transitory can inspire love.

Another characteristic shared by many types of love is the primacy of the skin. The mother wishes to touch her child almost constantly, young lovers are obsessed by desire for physical contact, the vain person (the lover of self) continually engages in hair-patting and other self-touching activity. Even the rhesus monkeys in Harlow's experiments demonstrate that whatever love may be, it is likely to be found in the presence of something soft and cuddly.

The skin is richly endowed with nerve endings, and neuro-physiologists have found that the nerve fibers connecting the skin and the central nervous system are better developed at birth than any others. Most of the newborn's experiences are, therefore, tactile. His first contact with his mother is skin contact, and, as other receptive modes develop, they become associated with cutaneous stimulation. Thus, if the baby is held during feeding, he will probably associate skin contact with the satisfaction of hunger. Touching another person acquires linkages with an expanding number of needs and finally becomes an independent source of gratification. The progression may be viewed as beginning with *skin* love, broadening to *kin* love, and culminating in that mildly pathological state of being *in* love.

Recent experiments suggest a relationship between the skin and pleasure centers in the brain. Should this research continue to be fruitful, we will have an explanation of love in terms of the workings of the central nervous system. Meanwhile, we may content ourselves with the observation that when love finds its ultimate physical expression in sexual intercourse, more square inches of skin are stimulated than in any other conceivable joint activity. Love is, undoubtedly, a touching experience.

But love is more than skin deep. If we examine the language of love, we find intimations of yet another of its components. At varying levels of discourse, we encounter such terms as "adoration," "heavenly transport," and "soul kiss." The loved one is an angel, a goddess, a divine creature. Perhaps the most seminal assertion in the Bible is that "God is love." Clearly, the interpenetration of love and religion is too pervasive to be accidental.

The virtual deification of the beloved can be traced to the era of courtly love. In *The Natural History of Love*, Morton Hunt provides several examples: The lady of the troubadors (who was often addressed as "Madonna") was an "inert, icon-like figure." Duke Louis of Bourbon is described as "a very amorous knight, first towards God and then towards all ladies and highborn girls." And one writer of the period portrayed "Lancelot coming to Guinevere's room . . . and then bowing and genuflecting at her door as he leaves, precisely as if before a shrine."

Perhaps the persistent influence of courtly love can be understood in terms of this trinity of love, sex and religion. The linkage of the three has received particularly vivid documentation in religious writings. To give but one instance, St. Theresa of Avila offers this description of a visionary experience:

> I saw an angel . . . in bodily form. . . . He was most beautiful — his face burning as if he were one of the highest angels, who seem to be all of fire. . . . I saw in his hand a long spear of gold and at the iron's point there seemed to be a little fire. He appeared to me to be thrusting it at times into my heart, and to pierce my very entrails: when he drew it out, he seemed to draw them out also and to leave me all on fire with a great love of God. The pain was so great that I cried out, but at the same time the sweetness which that violent pain gave me was so excessive, that I could not wish to be rid of it. . . .

This closely resembles the plea to "sheathe in my heart sharp pain up to the hilt," in a love poem by Coventry Patmore, as well as the phallic "sheathings" and "thrustings" that loom so large in the avid descriptions in *Fanny Hill*. Worthy of note, too, is the fact that a nun who has sexual intercourse is regarded by the Church as an adulteress.

Let us turn now to a consideration of the *consequences* of love. First, being in love makes it easier to have guilt-free sex, to marry, and to view oneself as a normal, healthy citizen of the Western world. Love also tends to alter certain psychological processes. According to a charming quotation that I've been able to trace back no further than its utterance in an old movie called *Mr. Skeffington*, "A woman is beautiful only when she is loved." The statement, however, is not quite accurate. A woman (likewise a man, a worm, a grain of sand) may become beautiful when the perceiver has been primed with LSD, hypnosis, or anything else that can induce hallucinations. In short, love may create the error of over-evaluation. The doting lover is doomed either to painful disillusion or to the permanent delusion that so closely resembles psychosis.

Some may argue that I am speaking of immature infatuation, rather than real love. Mature love, they may insist, is a broadening, deepening experience. This postulation of the salutary effects of love is so pervasive that we must examine its validity. First, there is the matter of evidence. Subjective reports are notoriously unreliable, and experimental studies are nonexistent. The claim that love promotes maturity is unpersuasive without some indication that the individual would not have matured just as readily in the absence of love. Indeed, to the extent that love fosters dependency, it may be viewed as a deterrent to maturity.

I am not asserting that the effects of love always border on the pathological. I *am* saying that the person who seeks love in order to obtain security will become, like the alcoholic, increasingly dependent on this source of illusory well-being. The secure person who seeks love would probably not trap himself in this way. But would the secure person seek love at all?

One inference to be drawn from the material here is that the nonloving person in our society is likely to be in a state of either very good or very poor mental health. The latter possibility requires no extended explanation. One of the standard stigmata of emotional disturbance is the inability to love. Most schools of psychotherapy aim specifically at the development of this ability. Some therapies go so far as to designate the therapist himself as a proper recipient of the patient's newly released love impulses (perhaps on the assumption that if the patient can love his therapist, he can love anybody).

The other part of the statement—that a love-free person can be in excellent mental health—may seem less acceptable. But if the need for a love relationship is based largely on insecurity, conformity to social pressures, and sexual frustration, then the person who is secure, independent, and has a satisfying sex life will not need to love. He will, rather, be a person who does not find his own company boring—a person whose inner resources are such that other persons, although they provide pleasure and stimulation, are not absolutely necessary. We have long been enjoined to love others as we love ourselves. But perhaps we seek love relationships with others only because we do not love ourselves sufficiently.

What would a healthy love-free person be like? One might assume that coldness would be among his most salient characteristics. But a cold person is simply one who does not give us the warmth we want or need. The attribution of coldness says more about the person doing the attributing than it does about the person being characterized. Absence of warmth is responded to negatively only by those insecure persons who interpret it as rejection. (Similarly, a nymphomaniac has been defined as a woman whose sex drive is stronger than that of the person who is calling her a nymphomaniac.)

Would the love-free person be egotistical? Perhaps, but only if that term is relieved of its ugly connotations. To be self-centered does not mean to disregard the worth of other people. It does imply that other people are reacted to within a frame of reference that is centered on the self. There is nothing reprehensible about this. In fact, most psychologists would probably accept the position that we are *all* self-centered. No matter how other-directed our actions may appear, they are functions of *our* perception of the world, based, in turn, on *our* previous experiences. Since every act is a "self-ish" one, evaluative criteria should be applied only to the effects of selfishness, rather than to selfishness, *per se.*

This essay has not been anti-love, but pro-people. I view society's emphasis on love as both an effect and a cause of the insecurity, dependency, and frightened conformity that may be the death of us all. To love a person means, all too often, to use that person. And exploitation, even if mutual, is incompatible with human growth. Finally, like a crutch, love may impede the exercise of our own potential for growth, and thus tend to perpetuate itself.

Perhaps the goal of social reformers should be not love, but respect — for others and, most of all, for self.

DISCUSSION QUESTIONS

1. The author describes a lover as a product of social pressure and sexual frustration and defines a love-free person as honest, secure, and independent. Can the argument as a whole be said to express a common fallacy?

2. Consider the language used to describe the two conditions (love: "dependency," "ego-boosting," "exploitation" vs. non-love: "inner resources," "independent," "excellent mental health"). Distinguish terms which have a specific meaning from those which simply convey a snarl or purr effect.

3. Love is said to derive from the need for security, sex, and social conformity. The author adds, "Hatred, too, in societies that are as aggression-oriented as ours is love-oriented, may reflect these same needs. To state that love is a superior emotion is to express a current cultural bias." Discuss the kinds of definition necessary before one can begin to argue this statement.

4. "We can study the *characteristics* of love by using techniques of the laboratory psychologist." Among the charac-

teristics, the author mentions physical relaxation, anger, fear, and the desire for tactile stimulation. Could one shape a laboratory experiment to demonstrate that love produces these effects? Which fallacy of argument would be likely to result?

5. In discussing what might be called religious love, the author quotes the writings of Morton Hunt, St. Theresa of Avila, Coventry Patmore, and John Cleland (*Fanny Hill*). How persuasive is this argument by authority?

6. The author says that love creates "the error of over-evaluation" as does LSD and hypnosis and that, like alcohol, it can gratify an insecure person. Discuss this either as argument by analogy or as a deductive syllogism.

7. The essay rejects the claim that genuine love (as opposed to infatuation) produces a broadening, maturing effect: "Subjective reports are notoriously unreliable, and experimental studies are nonexistent." Would it be possible to shape a controlled experiment to test this question? Does the lack of experimental data preclude drawing any conclusions in the area?

8. The author refuses to distinguish romantic love from the love one might have for his children, for his dog, for God, for the New York Mets, or for love itself. Is this identification self-evident? Is it subject to evidence?

59 Colleges Indoctrinate Students In Russian By Fed Act

JOHN RARICK, Congressman *(6th district, Louisiana)*

The news announcement read in bold letters:

"RUSSIAN STUDIES WILL BE OFFERED AT
L.S.U. THIS FALL"

One's first thought was, we teach Spanish, French, German, Arabian and other languages . . . why not Russian. Chinese next.

The interested reader continues the article:

". . . Dr. Putnam . . . teaching courses in Russian history from early times to present and and in the intellectual history of the Russian Revolution."

This sounds like the innocent teaching of a foreign language? Better read this more closely.

". . . sufficient courses will be added in the history, economics, government, language and literature of Russia to permit . . . a master's degree."
(Source: *State-Times, New Orleans*, Mon., Sept. 13, 1965)

A most unusual announcement. Not given by any state or federal official. But there's more to this than training an American student in the tongue of a foreign language. Wonder who's calling these signals and why?

This revolutionary, new program at Louisiana State University is but one of 59 such Russian Cultural Centers to be established in the American heartland by the U.S. Office of Education. The master plan is said to be under authority of and financed by the U.S. National Defense Education Act. Can you imagine this so-called progress in education being set up under a law passed by our Congress for the express purpose of preparing the defense of our shores against the communist world conspiracy. At least so some of us thought. But what an imagination!

Pause and think. Where can this but lead to? Where are we to come up with enough adequately trained teachers on Russia to staff 59 schools? But then the announcement carefully made no

Reprinted from *The American Patriot* (October 1965), p. 1.

mention of the nationality of the instructors. Could it be possible that they will be native-born and educated Russians? If not, how long will they have been in America? And then we know that it is unconstitutional to ask a teacher if he or she is a member of the communist party. What connection between Russian at L.S.U. and the teacher-student world exchange program? Can teacher employment be one of the approved solutions as to how to employ the new foreign intellectual immigrants that are to be brought to our shores by LBJ's revised immigration law? Pray tell, how can Russian intellectualism, government and history be taught in a professional degree without at the same time teaching communism? And can communism be taught effectually by other than ideologically-indoctrinated communist professors? Russian at L.S.U. could be but a polite introduction for Russians at L.S.U.

Dare we wonder in what manner our national defense can be improved by wholesale education of our students in Russian culture? Or has business with commie countries grown to the degree that our government must now subsidize communism in education? Where will we obtain the needed textbooks and materials? Printed by union men in the U.S.A. or imported from Moscow?

Could there be any connection between this integration of college campuses with Russians, and the federal president's sought after program to arrange Russian consulates in American cities? More national defense by an invasion by invitation of Russian consular employees and agents with diplomatic immunity from our laws. Don't become upset upon meeting uniformed soldiers of Russia on the street. In a while you can grow accustomed and become tolerant. After all, protocol will demand a display of social friendship and we may even be asked to open our homes in the spirit of comradeship. For this is in the name of peace. A little piece here and a little piece there.

Russian teachers and students on our campuses, communist party leaders protected in the consular buildings and commie agents and soldiers on our streets. And not a shot fired. A policy of national defense by loving our enemy to death.

What strong hearted national leaders we have! Forfeit our own American boys to die by communist steel in Viet Nam but in defense of our homeland send our daughters to socialize with the enemy at L.S.U. and 58 other universities. There's more to this than meets the eye from a routine news announcement. Who's aiding and abetting whom?

DISCUSSION QUESTIONS

1. Distinguish between a program intended to teach courses in Russian culture and one seeking to "Indoctrinate Students in Russian."

2. The author notes that the announcement of the Russian Cultural Centers at L.S.U. and elsewhere (as it appeared in the *New Orleans State-Times*) was "Not given by any state or federal official." Is this an adequate base for his speculation, "Wonder who's calling these signals and why?"

3. "This revolutionary, new program at Louisiana State University is but one of 59 such Russian Cultural Centers to be established in the American heartland by the U.S. Office of Education. The master plan is said to be under authority of and financed by the U.S. National Defense Education Act." Comment on the semantic argument (i.e., snarl words, purr words, and indirect statement) in this passage.

4. Consider the several assumptions underlying the author's speculation
   that the courses would have to be taught
   by native-born Russians or
   by Russians who have not been too long in the country or
   by the "new foreign intellectuals" brought in by President Johnson's revised immigration laws;
   that the courses would necessarily teach communism;
   that this could effectively be done only by "ideologically-indoctrinated communist professors"; and
   that textbooks and materials might have to be imported from Moscow.

5. "What connection between Russian at L.S.U. and the teacher-student world exchange program?" "Could there be any connection between this integration of college campuses with Russians, and the federal president's sought after program to arrange Russian consulates in American cities?" On what evidence does the author infer these connections? What conclusions does he draw?

6. The final paragraphs envision Russian soldiers socializing with coeds at L.S.U., Russian teachers and students on

campuses; communist party leaders in the consulates, and "commie agents" on the streets. Are there any *non sequiturs* in the chain of evidence leading to this speculative conclusion?

Reprinted from *The Thunderbolt* (April 1969), p. 6.

DISCUSSION QUESTIONS

1. The terms of this argument tend to be largely snarl words and purr words:
   White American
   Freedom
   Racial Purity
   Christianity
   Patriotism
   Communism
   Mongrelization
   Jewish Corruption
   Treason
   Are some of these more subject to specific definition than others?

2. Is this a straightforward example of the either-or fallacy?

3. Is there an instance or two of begging the question?

7

Statistics

One-third of Johns Hopkins coeds wed professors.
Smoke Viceroy; it has 20,000 filter traps.
In May, 1968, Americans reported 306 UFO's.
There are 9,000,000 rats in New York City.
My candidate will be lucky to win
15 percent of the vote.

There are a number of ways in which statistics can be used to distort argument. A spokesman can cite impressive averages, irrelevant totals, and homemade figures. He can present his numbers in a context which will make them appear large or small, according to his wish.

A common fallacy involves the use of "average" figures; e.g., average income, average price, average audience size. It is easy to argue from such statistics, because the word "average" can mean three things. What, for example, is the average if a group of fifteen housewives interviewed respond that they watch television 41, 32, 28, 25, 21, 18, 12, 10, 9, 5, 5, 5, 1, and 0 hours per week? From this data, it can be said that the group watched television an average of 14.533 hours per week, or 10 hours per week, or 5 hours per week. The 14.533 figure is the *mean* (the total number of hours watched divided by the number of viewers); the 10 figure is the *median* (the middle number in the list); and the 5 figure is the *mode* (the number which appears most frequently). Each kind of average has its value, according to the kind of data being measured. But all three are available to the spokesman seeking to manipulate an argument.

Questionable data can produce impressive averages. Numbers derived from memory, guesswork, and exaggeration can be averaged with exquisite precision. (The 14.533 figure in the preceding paragraph was calculated after fifteen housewives made rough guesses of their TV viewing time.) Dr. Kinsey interviewed American men and reported that those without a high-school education averaged 3.21 sex experiences per week. The annual FBI report *Crime in the United States*, compiling data from police departments across the country, showed that Baltimore suffered a 71 percent crime increase from 1964 to 1965. But police departments report crimes differently and with different degrees of accuracy. The sensational Baltimore figure derived, not from a huge increase in crime, but from more accurate police reporting in 1965.

Similarly, notable results can be produced from a small sample. Some years ago, a survey reported that 33⅓ percent of all coeds at Johns Hopkins University had married faculty members. Johns Hopkins had but three women students at the time. Similarly, advocates for extrasensory perception like to report cases where a gifted individual (Hubert Pearce, Basil Shackleton, etc.) has produced laboratory results in which the odds were 10,000,000 to 1 against chance as the explanation. Routinely, it is discovered that such cases were *part* of a longer series of tests and that the results of the entire experiment were not given.

And satisfying conclusions can be drawn from an inferred sample. The UFO believer finds significance in the fact that 98 percent of "saucer sightings" have been identified by the U.S. Air Force as aircraft, natural phenomena, and hoaxes; this means the other 2 percent *must be* interplanetary spaceships. Similarly, Administration spokesmen can remain unmoved when millions of citizens organize, petition, and march on Washington protesting the Vietnam war; this means that the vast majority of Americans — i.e., those who did not march, organize, etc. — support the present policy. In argument, the silent majority (or silent minority) always belongs to whoever claims them.

Sometimes an argument is bulwarked with irrelevant statistics. Some years ago, cigarette companies responded to evidence that smoking causes cancer by counting filter traps. Viceroy boasted 20,000 filters ("twice as many as the other two largest-selling brands") until Parliament began claiming 30,000, and Hit Parade overwhelmed both with 400,000. These were impressive figures, but totally pointless: there was no evidence that *any* filter protected one from the pernicious effects of smoking, and no one had defined "filter trap." This practice of putting large numbers to undefined elements is particularly notable in those given to counting communist-front citations, UFO's, and angels.

Even when counting clearly defined entities, a spokesman can offer irrelevant numbers. During the 1960 presidential campaign, for example, Vice President Nixon boasted that more Americans were holding jobs than ever before, and Senator Kennedy charged that more Americans were unemployed than ever before. Neither cared to relate his figures to population growth and admit that there were simply more Americans on the labor market.

The preceding examples indicate that one does not have to make up statistics to create a misleading argument. But, of course, one can make up statistics if he wants to. For example, the temperance spokesman who built an analogy on the claim that there were 10,000 deaths from alcohol poisoning to 1 from mad-dog bites, was using figures which exist nowhere else.

Homemade statistics usually relate to events which have not been measured or which are impossible to measure. Authorities can be suspiciously precise about events too trivial to have been counted. (*Esquire* noted that, as of February 1964, Judy Garland had sung "Over the Rainbow" 10,478 times. Dr. Joyce Brothers reported that "the American girl kisses an average of seventy-nine men before getting married.") And they can be glibly confident about obscure facts. (A *Nation* article said there were 9,000,000 rats in New York City. A Lane cedar chest advertisement warned that moths destroy $400,000,000 worth of goods each year.) With a little practice, one can recognize created statistics on sight.

By careful presentation, a spokesman can make any statistic seem bigger or smaller, as his argument requires. For example, many newspapers reported the 1968 Oberlin College poll which revealed that 40 percent of the unmarried coeds had engaged in sex, that 1 in 13 of these became pregnant, and that 80 percent of the pregnancies were terminated by abortion. Relatively modest statistics appear sensational when given as percentages of percentages of percentages.

More commonly, a person changes the character of a statistic by simple comparison. He relates it to a smaller number to make it appear large and to a larger number to make it seem small. The contrasting figure need have no relevance aside from offering an advantageous comparison. In 1968 when Senator Eugene McCarthy was running in state presidential primaries, for example, his spokesmen would regularly point out that the contest was not in his strongest state, that official duties had limited his public appearances, etc., and that—all in all—he would be lucky to win 15 percent of the vote. Then when the candidate, in fact, won 22 percent, they announced, "He did well. His vote far exceeded expectations." (Russell Baker called this technique "poormouthmanship.") One reverses the process to dwarf a statistic. In the same primaries, when George Wallace— the law and order candidate—had to face the fact that Alabama had the highest murder rate in the nation (11.4 per 100,000 population), it was explained that this figure was not nearly as high as that for Detroit, Los Angeles, and other major cities.

In a summary statement on statistical manipulation, Darrell Huff (*How to Lie With Statistics*, 1954) counsels the business community:

There are often many ways of expressing any figure. You can, for instance, express exactly the same fact by calling it a one percent return on sales, a fifteen percent return on investment, a ten-million-dollar profit, an increase in profits of forty percent (compared with 1935-39 average), or a decrease of sixty percent from last year. The method is to choose the one that sounds best for the purpose at hand and trust that few who read it will recognize how imperfectly it reflects the situation.

In a society subject to political controversy, social argument, and Madison Avenue rhetoric, such misleading statistics are common.

HOW RELIABLE ARE THESE STATISTICAL ARGUMENTS?

1. If you begin having your hair styled, are people going to think you've gone soft? Half the Los Angeles Rams' line has theirs styled. If you want to laugh at them, go ahead. We don't.

2. Last week, the Viet Cong lost 1231 men. American and Vietnamese losses were moderate.

3. In the 1968 Indiana primary, Senator Robert Kennedy won with 42 percent of the vote; Senator McCarthy got 31 percent; and Governor Roger Branigan (representing Vice-President Humphrey) got about 27 percent. A Humphrey supporter analyzed the results: "In the only primary in which Senator Kennedy was opposed by other candidates, nearly 2 out of 3 Democrats preferred someone else."

4. *One in Twenty* by Bryan Magee. Adult, plainly written study of male and female homosexuality.

5. Leo Guild's book *What Are the Odds?* reports that a young person with a broken engagement behind him is "75 percent as happy" as one who was never engaged.

6. When presidential candidate George Wallace toured Chicago in 1968, the crowd on the street was estimated at "20 to 30 thousand" (by liberal students), at "50,000" (by Chicago police), and at "two million" (by Mr. Wallace).

7. Anti-smoking advertisements announce that cigarette smoking, on the average, reduces a smoker's life by 8.3 years, and that every cigarette he smokes takes one minute from his life.

8. Arguing that the period of American Prohibition did reduce the level of crime, a Michigan prohibitionist compared Census Bureau figures for 1910 with 1923, showing that vagrancy decreased 52 percent, larceny 42 percent, assault 53 percent, and disorderly conduct 51 percent. He added that during prohibition there were fewer than two arrests for drunkenness per 100 thousand population, whereas by 1956 there were 1939 arrests for each 100 thousand of population.

Crime Higher in Gun Control Cities

The city of Toledo, Ohio, once garishly described as the wide-open "gun capital of the Midwest," is now being acclaimed by anti-gun spokesmen as a community where a local handgun control law reduced violent crime.

Toledo is being held up to Cincinnati, Los Angeles, and other large cities as a shining example of the wonders that can be worked by gun control.

Without question, violence in Toledo has decreased since the city enacted, in August, 1968, a whole package of anti-crime measures including an ordinance requiring an I.D. card of anyone who would buy or own a handgun. Comparing the first half of 1969 with the first half of 1968, in Toledo murders decreased 57% from 14 to 6; rapes 37% from 51 to 32; robbery 37% from 562 to 352, and aggravated assaults 12% from 210 to 183.

A glowing account of Toledo's conquest of crime was read into the *Congressional Record* (Oct. 20, 1969, p. S12797) by Sen. Joseph D. Tydings (Md.) and has been widely quoted. Those who quote the account seldom stress the seventh paragraph, which frankly says: "Toledo's experience is unique. It may be traceable in part to special restrictions on gun dealers as well as owners, to a tough, well-publicized court crackdown on violators of the control law and to other city efforts against crime."

The "other city efforts" include such things as increasing the 700-man Toledo police force by 100, a sizable increase.

Toledo, population 400,000, is not among the 12 largest cities in the land. Of those 12 cities, four were covered by total firearms registration during the first half of 1969. Four more were under local or State laws requiring permits to buy or transfer handguns. Yet another had an ordinance covering all firearms transfers. Three more, by contrast, had no local or State laws rigidly restricting the sale of firearms.

In the four cities requiring registration of all firearms, murders increased anywhere from six percent (New York City) to 102% (San Francisco). In the four cities covered by handgun controls only, the murder increase varied from two percent (Baltimore) to 53% (Cleveland). In the three cities without firearms restrictions, murders went up 14% in one instance (Los Angeles) and down in the other two (Houston — five percent, Milwaukee — 18%).

Reprinted from *The American Rifleman* (December 1969), p. 43.

The same FBI Uniform Crime Reports that periodically list violence statistics also report the strength of local police departments. From the latter figures, it appears that Houston, Los Angeles, and Milwaukee increased their police forces (1968 compared with 1967) by an average of six percent whereas the other nine largest cities in the U.S. reinforced their police by only two to four percent on the average during that time.

Because factors other than firearms control laws obviously enter into the crime control picture, a detailed comparison of violent crimes in these 12 largest cities is given here. It is based on figures from the FBI Uniform Crime Reports, in turn assembled from city police reports and like sources. So it may be assumed that they are authentic.

The four cities requiring firearms registration of rifles, shotguns and handguns during the first half of this year all reported sharp rises in violence crimes compared with the first half of 1968. They are as follows:

New York City — Murders up six percent from 436 to 464; rapes up 15% from 907 to 1,047; robberies up 23% from 24,255 to 30,002, and aggravated assaults up seven percent from 13,570 to 14,552.

Chicago — Murders up 10% from 288 to 317; rapes up 34% from 482 to 650; robberies up 11% from 8,576 to 9,569. Aggravated assaults decreased two percent from 6,118 to 5,939.

Washington, D.C. — Murders up 42% from 88 to 125; rapes up 50% from 100 to 150; robberies up 45% from 3,491 to 5,096, and aggravated assaults up 15% from 1,489 to 1,725.

San Francisco — Murders up 102% from 36 to 73; rapes up 183% from 85 to 241; robberies up 13% from 2,801 to 3,184, and aggravated assaults up 18% from 1,239 to 1,471.

Another group of large cities, three in the Midwest and one in the East, come under laws requiring permits for handguns to change ownership. Cleveland, Ohio's largest city, passed an ordinance making a permit necessary to purchase (though not to possess) a handgun. A similar law in Detroit is reinforced by a Michigan law requiring a license to buy or carry a handgun. In St. Louis, a Missouri law requires a permit to buy a handgun. In Baltimore, a police order signed by the Police Commissioner, and involving registration of the arm and owner, is necessary to transfer a handgun. Here are crime rates in those four cities for the first half of 1969 compared with the first half of 1968:

Cleveland — Murders up 53% from 76 to 117; rapes up 59%

from 86 to 137; robberies up 61% from 1,440 to 2,327, and aggravated assaults up 70% from 565 to 964.

Detroit—Murders up 13% from 176 to 200, and robberies up 29% from 5,648 to 7,297. Rapes decreased seven percent and aggravated assaults dropped 1%.

St. Louis—Murders up 50% from 83 to 125; rapes up 63% from 188 to 308; robberies up 27% from 1,786 to 2,273, and aggravated assaults up 27% from 1,299 to 1,651.

Baltimore—Murders up two percent from 115 to 118; robberies up nine percent from 4,072 to 4,451; aggravated assaults up 25% from 4,231 to 5,210. Rapes decreased four percent from 321 to 308.

Philadelphia, somewhat in a class by itself, passed a city ordinance in 1965 involving registration of all firearms that change hands or are brought into the city. Pennsylvania has a longstanding State law making it illegal to sell handguns to undesirables. The crime score there:

Philadelphia—Murders up 18% from 107 to 127; rapes up 24% from 203 to 253; robberies up 32% from 1,840 to 2,431, aggravated assaults up 1% from 1,832 to 1,865.

The three largest cities having the least restrictive gun laws are Los Angeles, Houston, and Milwaukee. The figures there:

Los Angeles—Murders up 14% from 158 to 181; rapes up 20% from 829 to 998; robberies up eight percent from 5,440 to 5,918, aggravated assaults up 12% from 6,571 to 7,373.

Houston—Murders decreased five percent from 125 to 118; rapes increased 20% from 154 to 186; robberies increased barely from 2,093 to 2,101, and aggravated assaults decreased 5% from 1,483 to 1,395.

Milwaukee—Murders decreased 18% from 22 to 18; rapes decreased 15% from 44 to 37; robberies decreased 39% from 421 to 254; aggravated assaults decreased 13% from 381 to 330.

Milwaukee was the only one of the 12 most populous cities to show decreases in all forms of violent crime, but decreases were registered in several categories in the other cities without restrictive gun laws.

DISCUSSION QUESTIONS

1. What conclusion is one likely to draw from this essay?

2. The author denies the claim that Toledo's new gun-control law was responsible for the decrease in crime. Name the

fallacy he is rejecting. What is paradoxical about his rejecting this kind of argument?

3. The central argument here discusses crime and gun-laws in "the 12 largest cities in the land." Why did the author choose 12 rather than 8 or 20?

4. "[The argument] is based on figures from the FBI Uniform Crime Reports, in turn assembled from city police reports and like sources. So it may be assumed they are authentic." Is this a reasonable claim?

5. "In the four cities requiring registration of all firearms, murders increased anywhere from six percent (New York City) to 102 (San Francisco). In the four cities covered by handgun controls only, the murder increase varied from two percent (Baltimore) to 53 (Cleveland)." How might these statistics have been presented to make the difference less impressive?

6. The author notes that the three cities without firearms restriction increased their police forces "by an average of six percent whereas the other nine largest cities in the U.S. reinforced their police by only two to four percent on the average during that time." Clarify the meaning here.

7. "Because factors other than firearms control laws obviously enter into the crime control picture, a detailed comparison of violent crimes in these 12 largest cities is given here." How does the second half of this sentence relate to the first?

8. Do the four crimes cited have much relationship to gun-laws? Do they have equal relationship? Is the author arguing that, in San Francisco, rapes went up 183 percent *because* the city requires registration of firearms?

Report by Cancer Society Finds Higher Death Rate for Smokers

WILLIAM L. LAURENCE

A massive report on the statistical relationship between the smoking of cigarettes and an increase in the death rate from various diseases, such as heart disease and cancer of the lung, was presented last week at the annual clinical meeting of the American Medical Association in Portland, Oregon.

The report was presented by Dr. E. Cuyler Hammond, director of statistical research for the American Cancer Society, who described it as "the first real analysis" of information gathered by the society in a huge health study that began Oct. 1, 1959.

Altogether, some 1,078,894 men and women have been enrolled in the study, but the report presented last week was devoted to the data for men only, analyzing the records of 422,094 between the ages of 40 to 79. From this number of men, Dr. Hammond and his colleagues culled, with a high speed computer, 36,975 smokers who were matched in many points in their history, habits and health with 36,975 non-smokers.

FINDINGS CONFIRMED

The results, Dr. Hammond reported, fully confirm findings in previous prospective studies. Death rates were found: (1) to be far higher in cigarette smokers than in men who did not smoke cigarettes: (2) to increase with the amount of cigarette smoking and (3) to be lower in ex-cigarette smokers who had given up the habit for a year or longer than in men who were currently smoking cigarettes at the time of enrollment.

The study also showed that death rates from the following diseases were greatly higher in cigarette smokers than in non-smokers: cancer of the lung; cancer of the mouth and pharynx; cancer of the larynx; cancer of the bladder and the pancreas; gastric ulcer, emphysema (overdistention of the air spaces in the lungs) and aortic aneurysm (dilation of the wall of the main artery).

Reprinted from *The New York Times* (8 December 1963), p. E7.

"Death rates from coronary artery disease," the report states, "were considerably higher in cigarette smokers than in non-smokers and this accounted for nearly half of the difference in the total rates between cigarette smokers and non-smokers.

HIGHER DEATH RATES

"Lung cancer death rates were 11 times as high among current cigarette smokers as among men who never smoked regularly and 18 times as high among very heavy smokers as among men who never smoked regularly. Lung cancer death rates were considerably lower among ex-cigarette smokers who had given up the habit for several years than among current cigarette smokers.

"Death rates were found to be highly related to degree of inhalation of cigarette smoke and age at start of cigarette smoking. Age at start of cigarette smoking appears to be particularly important in this respect."

Non-smokers were matched individually with men who smoked 20 or more cigarettes a day, the two men in each matched pair being similar in respect to: age, height, race, nativity, religion, marital status, residence (rural or urban), certain occupational exposures, education, drinking habits, nervous tension, use of tranquilizers, sleep, exercise, well or ill at time of enrollment, the past history in respect to cancer, heart disease, stroke and high blood pressure.

This kind of evidence was gathered, it was explained, to test the possibility, suggested by critics of previous statistical studies, that the smokers and non-smokers differed from each other in fundamental ways other than smoking and that it was these other differences that accounted for the disparity in the death rates.

The possibility that the association between cigarette smoking and higher death rates might conceivably result from an accidental association, Dr. Hammond said, was extremely unlikely in the light of (1) the quantitative relationship between death rates and the degree of exposure to cigarette smoke; (2) the finding that among ex-cigarette smokers death rates diminish with the length of time since last smoking; (3) the known biological effects of some of the components of cigarette smoke, and (4) pathologic evidence of the effects of cigarette smoking upon bronchial epithelium (tissue lining the air passages leading to the air sacs in the lungs) and the tissues of the lung parenchyma (lungs' air sacs).

Nevertheless, Dr. Hammond said, "we decided to investigate the matter by studying the death rate of cigarette smokers and non-smokers who were alike in respect to many characteristics other than their smoking habits."

During the course of the study, 1,385 of 36,975 cigarette smokers died, while only 662 of the non-smokers died. Of the cigarette smokers, 110 died of lung cancer and 654 died of coronary artery disease, while of the non-smokers only 12 died of lung cancer and 304 died of coronary artery disease.

One to Fifteen

Emphysema accounted for the death of 15 cigarette smokers but only one of the non-smokers. Far more of the cigarette smokers than the non-smokers died of cancer of the buccal cavity (mouth), pharynx, larynx and esophagus; cancer of the pancreas; cancer of the liver, aortic aneurysm and several other diseases.

Following Dr. Hammond's report, the House of Delegates, policy-making body of the American Medical Association, voted to undertake an all-out study on smoking by its education and research foundation, to determine which human ailments are "caused or aggravated by smoking" and which part of the cigarette was responsible. Once before, the A.M.A. attempted to start such a study but dropped it when the U.S. Public Health Service undertook to review the subject. The Public Health Service is expected to release its report in the near future.

DISCUSSION QUESTIONS

1. What is the conclusion to be drawn from this essay?
2. This kind of statistical argument must be analyzed as induction:

    Is the sample sufficient?

    Can a study of 73,950 individuals lead to a reliable conclusion about hundreds of millions of smokers?

    Is four years long enough to get meaningful results from such a study?

    Is the sample representative?

    Why does the test only concern men?

    Why only men aged 40–79?

    Can the study have any relevance for young female smokers?

3. Each pair of subjects (the smoker and the non-smoker) was matched on the basis of age, height, race, nativity, religion, and at least fourteen other areas. How could such factors as height, nativity, or religion be relevant? Why so many areas of comparison?

4. The report reads, "Lung cancer death rates were 11 times as high among current cigarette smokers as among men who never smoked regularly . . . " Is this figure substantiated by the statistics given later in the essay?

5. How reliable as argument by authority is a report made by the American Cancer Society and read to the annual clinical meeting of the American Medical Association?

6. Compare the evidence in this essay with that in the American Tobacco Company's advertisement "Why We're Dropping the New York Times" (p. 146). Which seems more persuasive?

Abby Presents Sex Education Facts

ABIGAIL VAN BUREN

DEAR READERS: In recent months, since I voiced my approval of sex education in the public schools, I have been deluged with letters from well-intentioned readers, urging me to reverse my stand.

"Look what happened to Sweden after THEY introduced sex education into their schools!" they cry.

I have received mimeographed "facts sheets" (some even distributed by CHURCH groups) stating that Sweden is now a "nation of degenerates—leading the world in suicides, alcoholism, divorce, and venereal disease."

I have been advised that "Stockholm is now the abortion capital of the world—that girls and women are flocking there for abortions because they are performed in hospitals with no questions asked."

These same sources inform me that in Sweden in the last two years, the incidence of rape has increased by 55 per cent!

The charge has also been made that "in Sweden the unmarried mother is glorified and rewarded. In fact, the unmarried mother enjoys the same social acceptance as the married mother."

If statistics bore you, skip this column. But if you are interested in knowing what changes have actually taken place in Sweden in comparison to other countries, the following will interest you. These statistics were obtained from the United Nations World Health Organization, whose headquarters are in Geneva, Switzerland.

1. Sweden no longer leads the world in suicides—as she did 17 years ago. The most recent statistics show that Sweden now ranks NINTH among the nations of the world in suicides. Among the European countries with higher suicide rates than Sweden are Austria, Hungary, Denmark, Czechoslovakia and Finland. (In 1968 there were more suicides per 100,000 population in the state of California than in Sweden.)

2. Concerning alcoholism. The people of France and the people of the United States both consume more alcohol per capita than do the people of Sweden.

Reprinted from a column that appeared in the *Mobile Press-Register* (12 January 1970), p. 1-B, and other publications. [©1970 by Chicago Tribune-N.Y. News Synd., Inc.]

3. Concerning divorce. The most recent statistics reveal that in Sweden one out of every six marriages ends in divorce. In the United States, the divorce rate is one out of every three.

4. Concerning abortion. An abortion may not be performed in Sweden unless an application is made, reviewed, and approved by the Royal Medical Board. This is the same system used in the United States by those states which have recently liberalized their abortion laws. Interestingly enough, the requirements for obtaining a legal abortion in Sweden are almost identical to those in the state of Maryland. In recent years, so widespread were the rumors of "easy abortion" in Sweden that many misinformed women did flock to Sweden, hoping to be accommodated, but were disappointed.

5. As for the alleged shocking increase of "rape" in Sweden, the most recent statistics are as follows:

For 1965 and 1966 the "arrest" figures were respectively 87 and 78, showing a decrease of 10 per cent—not an INCREASE of 55 per cent!

In a population of 7,847,395, this works out to approximately 1.1 per 100,000 in 1965 and 1.0 per 100,000 in 1966, one of the LOWEST rates in the world.

By comparison, the United States had 10,734 rape arrests in 1965, [or 5.36 per 100,000 population] and increased 7 per cent to 11,609 in 1966 — or 5.8 per 100,000 population.

6. The facts on venereal disease. The most recent statistics available are for 1967.

The number of cases reported for early syphillis per 100,000 population are:

FINLAND	2.8
UNITED KINGDOM	2.8
SWEDEN	4.3
DENMARK	6.5
UNITED STATES	10.8

7. While the unwed mother in Sweden is not regarded as a "social outcast," neither is she "rewarded and glorified." In Sweden children born out of wedlock are given the same advantages as children born into "families." The reason being that Swedes feel that no child should be made to suffer because his mother is alone, whether she is divorced, widowed or unmarried.

Most of us are inclined to accept as "truths" that which we have heard repeated over and over again. It is for this reason that I have checked out the facts, and present them to you in fairness to a much maligned nation—Sweden.

Very truly yours,
ABIGAIL VAN BUREN

DISCUSSION QUESTIONS

1. Whom is the author answering? Comment on the advantages of responding to random statements from unnamed persons.

2. Three times the essay gives the "most recent statistics": For rape-arrests, these cover 1965 and 1966; for venereal disease, they cover 1967; and for suicide, they cover 1968. Does this suggest the author is selecting her data? Or does it tell something about the U.N. World Health Organization statistics?

3. Sweden is said to rank ninth in suicides among the nations of the world. What would it indicate about sex education in Swedish schools if it ranked first? If it ranked fiftieth?

4. "Concerning alcoholism. The people of France and the people of the United States both consume more alcohol per capita than do the people of Sweden." Does this comparison say anything at all about alcoholism?

5. Why are no statistics offered comparing the number of abortions performed annually in Sweden with the number performed in other countries? Would national sex education tend to raise or lower the number of abortions?

6. The author is answering the claim that higher rates of divorce, rape-arrests, and venereal disease are somehow caused by the introduction of sex education in the schools. Does her response intimate that Sweden's lower rate of divorce, rape-arrests, and venereal disease derive from the introduction of sex education in the schools?

7. Throughout the essay compares Swedish statistics with those related to the United States. Discuss how the author chooses and shapes her evidence to get a desired effect.

8. What do you know about Abigail Van Buren? How reliable is she thought to be as an authority on social problems?

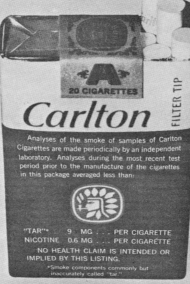

And the same report finds Montclair lowest in "tar" and nicotine of all menthol brands tested.

Just enough in every puff. Just enough bright, lively menthol flavor. Just enough light mild taste.

DISCUSSION QUESTIONS

1. The "Report" referred to appeared in the *Reader's Digest* November, 1966). Speculate why the advertisement refers to it as "a national magazine" rather than by name and date.

2. The *Reader's Digest* specified that the test of filter tip cigarettes was done for the magazine by Foster D. Snell, Inc., in accordance with the methodology approved by the Federal Trade Commission. It did rank Carlton first, with 6.02 mg. tar and 0.39 mg. nicotine. What do you know of the "independent laboratory" which periodically analyzes samples of Carlton cigarettes?

3. Though the *Reader's Digest* did not, the advertisement routinely puts the word "tar" in quotation marks. What difference does this make?

4. Discuss the semantic argument conveyed by the words "Carlton," "Montclair," "bright, lively menthol flavor," and "the light one."

5. What is the implicit conclusion of the advertisement?

6. What is the effect of the line "No health claim is made for either Carlton or Montclair"?

7. Consult the *Reader's Digest* report, and comment on the reason Carlton and Montclair are lowest in tar and nicotine.

8

Exercises for Review

How valid are these arguments? Identify examples of induction, deduction, expert testimony, semantic argument, analogy, argument in a circle, post hoc ergo propter hoc, begging the question, argumentum ad hominem, extension, the either-or fallacy, and statistical manipulation.

1. Of course you support federal aid to education. You're a teacher; you stand to profit on the deal.

2. "Ever wonder why kids instinctively go for soft drinks in bottles?"—Glass Container Manufacturers Institute

3. Register Communists, not Guns!

4. Naval ROTC should be abolished; I'm learning nothing from it.

5. A nationwide poll conducted by *Modern Medicine* reflected the opinions of 28,000 of the 206,000 doctors who receive the magazine. It revealed that 62.8 percent believed that legal abortion should be available on request, that 67.7 percent favored the repeal of laws against private homosexual acts between consenting adults, and that 85.2 percent opposed the unrestricted sale of marijuana.

6. "America's greatest danger is not from without but from the traitors within. It was from these United States that 20 million dollars in gold was carried by Trotsky and 276 revolutionists in their nefarious mission to overthrow the the Czar and take over Russia."—Rollin M. Severance, Prohibitionist candidate for Governor of Michigan, 1958.

7. The major drug companies have been charged with overpricing their products. King Pharmaceutical is not a major company. Therefore, I'll buy its drugs.

8. As you go to the polls to decide this temperance issue, ask yourself, "How does Jesus want me to vote?"

9. I disagree with Abby Van Buren when she says no woman should be forced to have a baby she does not want. A lot of people are forced to have parents they do not like, but we won't let them go about murdering their parents.

10. "There is no proof that sugar confectionery gives rise to dental cavities."—Association International Des Fabricants De Confiserie

11. "Nice Girls *Do* Wear Chantilly!" —A perfume advertisement

12. "Seven out of every ten Americans cheat on their income tax."—Professor R. Van Dyke Ellington

13. In 1936, the *Literary Digest* chose ten million names at random from telephone books and lists of registered automobile owners. The magazine sent pre-election ballots to these persons and received over 2,000,000 responses. The resulting prediction: Landon would defeat Roosevelt.

14. A *Saturday Review* article on the Middle-East carried the sub-title "Do the Arabs Have a Case?"

15. "Obscene material is material which deals with sex in a manner appealing to prurient interest."—Justice Brennan, delivering the opinion of the Supreme Court, *Roth v. United States*, 24 June 1957.

16. *The Husband* (a novel by Sol Stein)—"The dilemma of countervailing demands on the sensual man of good will . . . rich and true . . . modulated with a respectful reserve . . . handled with hardly a false note."—*New York Times*

17. I never knew a University of Alabama varsity football player who could read or write beyond the eighth grade level.

18. *Miss MacIntosh, My Darling* by Marguerite Young: "What we behold is a mammoth epic, a massive fable, a picaresque journey, a faustian quest and a work of stunning magnitude and beauty . . . some of the richest, most expressive, most original and exhaustively revealing passages of prose that this writer has experienced in a long time. . . . It is a masterpiece."—William Goyen, *New York Times*

19. Juvenile delinquency increased over 20 percent from 1947 through 1953, the period of the great rise in comic book circulation.

20. We scientists working with astrological data do not mind being criticized. We know that Newton and Einstein were ridiculed in the past.

21. All this effort to register and confiscate guns will not help us fight crime. Violence arises from the souls of men.

22. On the typical television poll, an early-evening newscaster poses a yes-or-no question, asking viewers to phone one number to vote yes and another to vote no; and a late-evening newscaster gives the result, e.g., 69 per cent support President Nixon's policy concerning Cambodia.

23. Homosexuality is no illness. It is a widespread practice like vegetarianism. The homosexual has a sexual preference for members of the same sex; the vegetarian has an alimentary preference for non-carnivorous foods. In neither case is there any impairment of function or any disease.

24. If you need a loan, call friendly Bob Adams at Household Finance Company.

25. "1,000,000 Doctors Have Quit Smoking Cigarettes. (Maybe they know something you don't.)" – The American Cancer Society

26. *Miss MacIntosh, My Darling* by Marguerite Young: "In fact, this is an outrageously bad book, written by an author with very little of interest to say, and very little skill in saying it . . . wholly unreadable." – *Time*

9

Argument—
Pro and Con

Overpopulated America

WAYNE H. DAVIS

I define as most seriously overpopulated that nation whose people by virtue of their numbers and activities are most rapidly decreasing the ability of the land to support human life. With our large population, our affluence and our technological monstrosities the United States wins first place by a substantial margin.

Let's compare the US to India, for example. We have 203 million people, whereas she has 540 million on much less land. But look at the impact of people on the land.

The average Indian eats his daily few cups of rice (or perhaps wheat, whose production on American farms contributed to our one percent per year drain in quality of our active farmland), draws his bucket of water from the communal well and sleeps in a mud hut. In his daily rounds to gather cow dung to burn to cook his rice and warm his feet, his footsteps, along with those of millions of his countrymen, help bring about a slow deterioration of the ability of the land to support people. His contribution to the destruction of the land is minimal.

An American, on the other hand, can be expected to destroy a piece of land on which he builds a home, garage and driveway. He will contribute his share to the 142 million tons of smoke and fumes, seven million junked cars, 20 million tons of paper, 48 billion cans, and 26 billion bottles the overburdened environment must absorb each year. To run his air conditioner we will strip-mine a Kentucky hillside, push the dirt and slate down into the stream, and burn coal in a power generator, whose smokestack contributes to a plume of smoke massive enough to cause cloud seeding and premature precipitation from Gulf winds which should be irrigating the wheat farms of Minnesota.

In his lifetime he will personally pollute three million gallons of water, and industry and agriculture will use ten times this much water in his behalf. To provide these needs the US Army Corps of Engineers will build dams and flood farmland. He will also use 21,000 gallons of leaded gasoline containing boron, drink 28,000 pounds of milk and eat 10,000 pounds of meat. The latter is produced and squandered in a life pattern unknown to Asians. A steer on a Western range eats plants containing

Reprinted from *The New Republic* (10 January 1970), pp. 13–15.

minerals necessary for plant life. Some of these are incorporated into the body of the steer which is later shipped for slaughter. After being eaten by man these nutrients are flushed down the toilet into the ocean or buried in the cemetery, the surface of which is cluttered with boulders called tombstones and has been removed from productivity. The result is a continual drain on the productivity of range land. Add to this the erosion of overgrazed lands, and the effects of the falling water table as we mine Pleistocene deposits of groundwater to irrigate to produce food for more people, and we can see why our land is dying far more rapidly than did the great civilizations of the Middle East, which experienced the same cycle. The average Indian citizen, whose fecal material goes back to the land, has but a minute fraction of the destructive effect on the land that the affluent American does.

Thus I want to introduce a new term, which I suggest be used in future discussions of human population and ecology. We should speak of our numbers in "Indian equivalents". An Indian equivalent I define as the average number of Indian citizens required to have the same detrimental effect on the land's ability to support human life as would the average American. This value is difficult to determine, but let's take an extremely conservative working figure of 25. To see how conservative this is, imagine the addition of 1000 citizens to your town and 25,000 to an Indian village. Not only would the Americans destroy much more land for homes, highways and a shopping center, but they would contribute far more to environmental deterioration in hundreds of other ways as well. For example, their demand for steel for new autos might increase the daily pollution equivalent of 130,000 junk autos which *Life* tells us that US Steel Corp. dumps into Lake Michigan. Their demand for textiles would help the cotton industry destroy the life in the Black Warrior River in Alabama with endrin. And they would contribute to the massive industrial pollution of our oceans (we provide one third to one half the world's share) which has caused the precipitous downward trend in our commercial fisheries landings during the past seven years.

The per capita gross national product of the United States is 38 times that of India. Most of our goods and services contribute to the decline in the ability of the environment to support life. Thus it is clear that a figure of 25 for an Indian equivalent is conservative. It has been suggested to me that a more realistic figure would be 500.

In Indian equivalents, therefore, the population of the United States is at least four billion. And the rate of growth is even more alarming. We are growing at one percent per year, a rate which would double our numbers in 70 years. India is growing at 2.5 percent. Using the Indian equivalent of 25, our population growth becomes 10 times as serious as that of India. According to the Reinows in their recent book *Moment in the Sun*, just one year's crop of American babies can be expected to use up 25 billion pounds of beef, 200 million pounds of steel and 9.1 billion gallons of gasoline during their collective lifetime. And the demands on water and land for our growing population are expected to be far greater than the supply available in the year 2000. We are destroying our land at a rate of over a million acres a year. We now have only 2.6 agricultural acres per person. By 1975 this will be cut to 2.2, the critical point for the maintenance of what we consider a decent diet, and by the year 2000 we might expect to have 1.2.

You might object that I am playing with statistics in using the Indian equivalent on the rate of growth. I am making the assumption that today's Indian child will live 35 years (the average Indian life span) at today's level of affluence. If he lives an American 70 years, our rate of population growth would be 20 times as serious as India's.

But the assumption of continued affluence at today's level is unfounded. If our numbers continue to rise our standard of living will fall so sharply that by the year 2000 any surviving Americans might consider today's average Asian to be well off. Our children's destructive effects on their environment will decline as they sink ever lower into poverty.

The United States is in serious economic trouble now. Nothing could be more misleading than today's affluence, which rests precariously on a crumbling foundation. Our productivity, which had been increasing steadily at about 3.2 percent a year since World War II, has been falling during 1969. Our export over import balance has been shrinking steadily from $7.1 billion in 1964 to $0.15 billion in the first half of 1965. Our balance of payments deficit for the second quarter was $3.7 billion, the largest in history. We are now importing iron ore, steel, oil, beef, textiles, cameras, radios and hundreds of other things.

Our economy is based upon the Keynesian concept of a continued growth in population and productivity. It worked in an underpopulated nation with excess resources. It could continue to work only if the earth and its resources were expanding at an annual rate of 4 to 5 percent. Yet neither the number of cars, the economy, the human population, nor anything else can expand indefinitely at an exponential rate in a finite world. We must face this fact *now*. The crisis is here. When Walter Heller says that our economy will expand by 4 percent annually through the latter 1970s he is dreaming. He is in a theoretical world totally unaware of the realities of human ecology. If the economists do not wake up and devise a new system for us now somebody else will have to do it for them.

A civilization is comparable to a living organism. Its longevity is a function of its metabolism. The higher the metabolism (affluence), the shorter the life. Keynesian economics has allowed us an affluent but shortened life span. We have now run our course.

The tragedy facing the United States is even greater and more imminent than that descending upon the hungry nations. The Paddock brothers in their book, *Famine 1975!*, say that India "cannot be saved" no matter how much food we ship her. But India will be here after the United States is gone. Many millions will die in the most colossal famines India has ever known, but the land will survive and she will come back as she always has before. The United States, on the other hand, will be a desolate tangle of concrete and ticky-tacky, of strip-mined moonscape and silt-choked reservoirs. The land and water will be so contaminated with pesticides, herbicides, mercury fungicides, lead, boron, nickel, arsenic and hundreds of other toxic substances, which have been approaching critical levels of concentration in our environment as a result of our numbers and affluence, that it may be unable to sustain human life.

Thus as the curtain gets ready to fall on man's civilization let it come as no surprise that it shall first fall on the United States. And let no one make the mistake of thinking we can save ourselves by "cleaning up the environment." Banning DDT is the equivalent of the physician's treating syphilis by putting a bandaid over the first chancre to appear. In either case you can be sure that more serious and widespread trouble will soon appear unless the disease itself is treated. We cannot survive by planning to treat the symptoms such as air pollution, water pollution, soil erosion, etc.

What can we do to slow the rate of destruction of the United States as a land capable of supporting human life? There are two approaches. First we must reverse the population growth.

We have far more people now than we can continue to support at anything near today's level of affluence. American women average slightly over three children each. According to the *Population Bulletin* if we reduced this number to 2.5 there would still be 330 million people in the nation at the end of the century. And even if we reduced this to 1.5 we would have 57 million more people in the year 2000 than we have now. With our present longevity patterns it would take more than 30 years for the population to peak even when reproducing at this rate, which would eventually give us a net decrease in numbers.

Do not make the mistake of thinking that technology will solve our population problem by producing a better contraceptive. Our problem now is that people want too many children. Surveys show the average number of children wanted by the American family is 3.3. There is little difference between the poor and the wealthy, black and white, Catholic and Protestant. Production of children at this rate during the next 30 years would be so catastrophic in effect on our resources and the viability of the nation as to be beyond my ability to contemplate. To prevent this trend we must not only make contraceptives and abortion readily available to everyone, but we must establish a system to put severe economic pressure on those who produce children and reward those who do not. This can be done within our system of taxes and welfare.

The other thing we must do is to pare down our Indian equivalents. Individuals in American society vary tremendously in Indian equivalents. If we plot Indian equivalents versus their reciprocal, the percentage of land surviving a generation, we obtain a linear regression. We can then place individuals and occupation types on this graph. At one end would be the starving blacks of Mississippi; they would approach unity in Indian equivalents, and would have the least destructive effect on the land. At the other end of the graph would be the politicians slicing pork for the barrel, the highway contractors, strip-mine operators, real estate developers, and public enemy number one — the US Army Corps of Engineers.

We must halt land destruction. We must abandon the view of land and minerals as private property to be exploited in any way economically feasible for private financial gain. Land and minerals are resources upon which the very survival of the nation depends, and their use must be planned in the best interests of the people.

Rising expectations for the poor is a cruel joke foisted upon them by the Establishment. As our new economy of use-it-once-and-throw-it-away produces more and more products for the affluent, the share of our resources available for the poor declines. Blessed be the starving blacks of Mississippi with their outdoor privies, for they are ecologically sound, and they shall inherit a nation. Although I hope that we will help these unfortunate people attain a decent standard of living by diverting war efforts to fertility control and job training, our most urgent task to assure this nation's survival during the next decade is to stop the affluent destroyers.

Ecology—The Safe Issue

The editors of RAMPARTS

The environment may well be the gut issue that can unify a polarized nation in the 1970's, writes *Time* magazine. The Hearst Press sees it as a movement "that could unite the generations." And the *New York Times* solemnly predicts that ecology "will replace Vietnam as the major issue with students."

The wishful thinking of a frightened Establishment? Perhaps. But the organizers of the officially-sanctioned April 22 Teach-In movement are doing their best to give life to the media's daydream about the co-optive potential of ecology. If they succeed, thousands of young people across the country will engage in a series of environmental extravaganzas, embellished to capture the excitement of the original Vietnam teach-ins, but structured to encourage the young to forsake the "less important issues" and enlist in a crusade to save the earth.

We think that any analogy between what is supposed to happen around April 22 and the organization of the Vietnam teach-ins is obscene. We think that the Environmental Teach-In apparatus is the first step in a con game that will do little more than abuse the environment even further. We do not think it will succeed.

The originators of the Vietnam teach-ins worked at great odds and against the lies and opposition of government, university administrations and the media. They raised their own money and had offices in student apartments or small storefronts. "Earth Day" came to life in the offices of Senator Gaylord Nelson, received blessings from Nixon's Department of Health, Education and Welfare, was funded by foundations, and has worked out of facilities lent by the Urban Coalition.

Vietnam protestors had to create their own reading lists, fact sheets and white papers; they had to work against the "expertise" of Southeast Asia scholars. The Environmental Teach-In comes pre-packaged; a well-paid and well-staffed national office sends local organizers an official brochure which avoids mentioning the social and economic environment with which Mother Nature has to cope. Friends of the Earth (FOE) provides, through Ballantine Books, a semi-official "Environmental Handbook,"

Reprinted from *Ramparts* (May 1970), pp. 2–4.

which insists that saving the environment "transcends the other issues" and that we should in non-partisan fashion "support a man from any political party if he is a true Friend of the Earth."

Never mind if he's a racist. Don't worry about whether or not he supports American imperialism. This spring the Nixon Administration is busy undoing 15 years of struggle for school integration; the police continue to murder black people in the streets; the American judicial system is disintegrating and, in the eyes of the State, every radical has become a conspirator; the war machine in Washington has made clear its intention to stay in Vietnam indefinitely and to spread its war to Laos. All this—and the Teach-In organizers want to banish everything but environment to the back pages of our minds. They must be blind, or perverse, or both.

How can anyone in this dark springtime believe kind words—about environment or anything else—from the men in power? Once we might have been able to believe that because a President had embraced the civil rights issue, apartheid in the Deep South was dead. But such illusions can hardly be sustained any longer. The Open Housing Act, the chief legislative victory of those years, finds use this season only for its "H. Rap Brown Amendment"—the interstate travel ban on which the Justice Department hung the Chicago 7.

Lyndon Johnson promised that We Shall Overcome. Now Richard Nixon promises to clean up America. Even TV's "Laugh-In" knows the punch-line: "If Nixon's War on Pollution is as successful as Johnson's War on Poverty, we're going to have an awful lot of dirty poor people around."

Haven't we learned after a decade of social struggle that major problems like Vietnam, Race, Poverty—now Environment—can't be packaged separately, each protected from contamination by "other issues"? Even the Kerner Commission realized that white racism was systematic, structural and linked to economic and social institutions. Even the most determined skeptic has now been shown by the Nixon Administration that the Vietnam war was no honest mistake, but the result of a long history of American expansion into Asia and a long-term policy of subjecting poor nations to the imperatives of American investors. To understand why Washington has persisted in its genocidal war in Indo-China, don't look at the politicians who come and go; look at the structures of power and interest that remain.

II

Threats to the environment are no different. At their source is the same division of society—those with power against those without: the corporations, which organize for their own benefit, against the people whom they organize destructively.

Look at the values which galvanize energies and allocate resources in the business system: pursuit of money, enrichment of self, the exploitation of man—and of nature—to generate still more money. Is it surprising that a system seeking to turn everything into gold ends up turning everything into garbage? The market is master. Business makes money meeting consumer demands; it makes even more money creating new demands. More money is spent on advertising and sales promotion in America, on planned obsolescence and consumer manipulation, than on all education—public and private, elementary school through the university. This is pollution of the mind, and it has its own costs. Some students estimate that socially useless, ecologically disastrous waste products make up nearly half of the Gross National Product. Nixon has already predicted a 50 per cent increase in the GNP by 1980, ostensibly to finance new priorities like environmental reform. It would be better if he had questioned how much waste the dynamic American economy will have to produce in the next decade simply to clean up the waste of past decades.

Others, like the organizers of the National Teach-In, tell us that it is in the interest even of the corporate rich to clean up the environment. If all their customers are asphyxiated by air pollution, explain these optimists, business (and businessmen) would expire as well. By this same logic, the military-industrial complex should bar the ABM from its cities, and the corporations, always eager to bring new consumers into the market, should make the war on poverty work. But no businessman, alone or with other businessmen, can change the tendencies of our ultimately ecocidal process unless he puts the system out of business. As long as society organizes production around the incentive to convert man's energies and nature's resources into profit, no planned, equable, ecologically balanced system of production can ever exist. Teach-ins which fail to confront this fact of life do worse than teach nothing. They obstruct knowledge and stand in the way of a solution. They join the struggle on the side which permits them truly to say—not of mankind, but of themselves—"We have found the enemy and he is us."

Perhaps the Teach-Ins could teach better if, instead of their present brochure, they distributed a full-page ad from *Fortune's* special environment issue. Sponsored by the New York State Department of Commerce, the ad pictures Governor Nelson Rockefeller inviting businessmen to come grow with New York. The pitch is simple: "Personal property of manufacturers is completely exempt from taxation in New York . . . During the past eleven years, there has not been one single new business tax in New York." Nowhere does the ad mention New York's long series of new *non-business* taxes. In 11 years in office, Rocky has first imposed, then hiked a new state sales tax; quadrupled the cigarette tax; tripled the gasoline tax; and lowered the minimum income below which poor people are free of the state income tax. Businesses apparently aren't expected to care who subsidizes their growth. But the ad does want them to know that Governor Rockefeller, author of the "soak-the-poor program," considers "economic growth — a continuing expansion of the private economy — to be the indispensable ingredient of all progress."

Rockefeller doesn't say this only because he's a Rockefeller; he says it because he's Governor and every governor wants business to invest in his state. Private business accounts for 85 per cent of the GNP; it must be kept happy and expanding, or, short of revolution, there will be nothing for anyone at all. Regulation of business consequently can never be more than self-regulation, federal intervention into the business sector never more than federal intervention on behalf of the business sector.

But regulation is not the question. We simply don't need any more gross national product, any more unnecessary goods and factories. What we do need is a *redistribution* of existing real wealth, and a *reallocation* of society's resources. Everyone knows what this redistribution and reallocation should do; the crises of the last ten years have made it all so obvious: The poor must have adequate income, the cities must be rebuilt to fit human requirements, the environment must be de-polluted, the educational system must be vastly expanded, and social energies now poured into meaningless pursuits (like advertising and sales promotion) must be rechanneled into humanly edifying and creative activities.

We must, in short, junk the business system and its way of life, and create revolutionary new institutions to embody new goals — human and environmental.

All this sounds utopian. Well, utopias are relative. More

utopian by far than revolution is the idea that the present society, dominated by business, can create lasting, meaningful reforms sufficient, for example, to permit mankind to survive the century.

III

At a recent "survival faire" in San Jose, California, ecology organizers bought a new car and buried it as a symbol of the task which they saw confronting ecology action groups. This was an indication of dangerous political naivete that must be overcome. To buy the car in the first place was to pay the criminal and strengthen him. But this act also pointed the finger of guilt at the consumer, who has only the choice of traveling to work by auto or walking 30 miles to work on the freeway. In opposition to this misdirected gesture of revolt, San Jose's black students angrily demanded that the car be raffled to provide defense funds for their brothers on trial. The blacks made their point very clearly.

In contrast to this Survival Faire, the week after the Conspiracy defendants were sentenced in Chicago, angry students razed the local branch of the Bank of America in Santa Barbara, California. The only bank in the Isla Vista youth ghetto, B of A had long treated young people as a class apart. It had opposed the grape strikers centered in Delano. It had supported, with branches in Saigon and Bangkok and with its leadership of the investment build-up in the Pacific, the American occupation of Southeast Asia. Two of its directors sit on the board of Union Oil, which had for so many months desecrated the once-beautiful beaches of Santa Barbara and destroyed their wildlife. Most important, as the branch manager explained to the press, it had been the major local symbol of capitalism and the business system.

Burning a bank is not the same as putting the banks and their system out of business. To do that, millions of people in this country will first have to wake up to the real source of their misery. The action in Santa Barbara, a community which has seen its environment destroyed by corporate greed, might spark that awakening. If it does, the students who burned the Bank of America in Santa Barbara will have done more to save the environment than all the Survival Faires and "Earth Day Teach-Ins" put together.

Duty, Honor, Country

DOUGLAS MacARTHUR

No human being could fail to be deeply moved by such a tribute as this, coming from a profession I have served so long and a people I have loved so well. It fills me with an emotion I cannot express. But this award is not intended primarily for a personality, but to symbolize a great moral code — the code of conduct and chivalry of those who guard this beloved land of culture and ancient descent.

"Duty," "honor," "country" — those three hallowed words reverently dictate what you want to be, what you can be, what you will be. They are your rallying point to build courage when courage seems to fail, to regain faith when there seems to be little cause for faith, to create hope when hope becomes forlorn.

Unhappily, I possess neither that eloquence of diction, that poetry of imagination, nor that brilliance of metaphor to tell you all that they mean.

The unbelievers will say they are but words, but a slogan, but a flamboyant phrase. Every pedant, every demagog, every cynic, every hypocrite, every troublemaker, and, I am sorry to say, some others of an entirely different character, will try to downgrade them even to the extent of mockery and ridicule.

But these are some of the things they build. They build your basic character. They mold you for your future roles as the custodians of the Nation's defense. They make you strong enough to know when you are weak, and brave enough to face yourself when you are afraid.

They teach you to be proud and unbending in honest failure, but humble and gentle in success; not to substitute words for action; not to seek the path of comfort, but to face the stress and spur of difficulty and challenge; to learn to stand up in the storm, but to have compassion on those who fail; to master yourself before you seek to master others; to have a heart that is clean, a goal that is high; to learn to laugh, yet never forget how to weep; to reach into the future, yet never neglect the past; to be serious, yet never take yourself too seriously; to be modest so that you will remember the simplicity of true greatness, the open mind of true wisdom, the meekness of true strength.

Reprinted from the *National Observer* (20 May 1962). The speech was originally delivered at West Point on 12 May 1962.

They give you a temperate will, a quality of imagination, a vigor of the emotions, a freshness of the deep springs of life, a temperamental predominance of courage over timidity, an appetite for adventure over love of ease.

They create in your heart the sense of wonder, the unfailing hope of what next, and the joy and inspiration of life. They teach you in this way to be an officer and a gentleman.

And what sort of soldiers are those you are to lead? Are they reliable? Are they brave? Are they capable of victory?

Their story is known to all of you. It is the story of the American man at arms. My estimate of him was formed on the battlefields many, many years ago, and has never changed. I regarded him then, as I regard him now, as one of the world's noblest figures; not only as one of the finest military characters, but also as one of the most stainless.

His name and fame are the birthright of every American citizen. In his youth and strength, his love and loyalty, he gave all that mortality can give. He needs no eulogy from me, or from any other man. He has written his own history and written it in red on his enemy's breast.

In 20 campaigns, on a hundred battlefields, around a thousand campfires, I have witnessed that enduring fortitude, that patriotic self-abnegation, and that invincible determination which have carved his statue in the hearts of his people.

From one end of the world to the other, he has drained deep the chalice of courage. As I listened to those songs in memory's eye I could see those staggering columns of the First World War, bending under soggy packs on many a weary march, from dripping dusk to drizzling dawn, slogging ankle deep through mire of shell-pocked roads; to form grimly for the attack, blue-lipped, covered with sludge and mud, chilled by the wind and rain, driving home to their objective, and for many, to the judgment seat of God.

I do not know the dignity of their birth, but I do know the glory of their death. They died unquestioning, uncomplaining, with faith in their hearts, and on their lips the hope that we would go on to victory.

Always for them: Duty, honor, country. Always their blood, and sweat, and tears, as they saw the way and the light. And 20 years after, on the other side of the globe, again the filth of dirty foxholes, the stench of ghostly trenches, the slime of dripping dugouts, those boiling suns of the relentless heat, those torrential rains of devastating storms, the loneliness and utter desolation of jungle trails, the bitterness of long separation of those they loved and cherished, the deadly pestilence of tropical disease, the horror of stricken areas of war.

Their resolute and determined defense, their swift and sure attack, their indomitable purpose, their complete and decisive victory — always victory, always through the bloody haze of their last reverberating shot, the vision of gaunt, ghastly men, reverently following your password of duty, honor, country.

You now face a new world, a world of change. The thrust into outer space of the satellite spheres and missiles marks a beginning of another epoch in the long story of mankind. In the five or more billions of years the scientists tell us it has taken to form the earth, in the three or more billion years of development of the human race, there has never been a more abrupt or staggering evolution.

We deal now, not with things of this world alone, but with the illimitable distances and as yet unfathomed mysteries of the universe. We are reaching out for a new and boundless frontier. We speak in strange terms of harnessing the cosmic energy; of making winds and tides work for us; of creating synthetic materials to supplement or even replace our old standard basics; to purify sea water for our drink; of mining ocean floors for new fields of wealth and food; of disease preventatives to expand life into the hundreds of years; of controlling the weather for a more equitable distribution of heat and cold, or rain and shine; of space ships to the moon; of the primary target in war no longer limited to the armed forces of an enemy, but instead to include his civil populations, of ultimate conflicts between a united human race and the sinister forces of some other planetary galaxy; of such dreams and fantasies as to make life the most exciting of all times.

And through all this welter of change and development your mission remains fixed, determined, inviolate. It is to win our wars. Everything else in your professional career is but corollary to this vital dedication. All other public purpose, all other public projects, all other public needs, great or small, will find others for their accomplishments; but you are the ones who are trained to fight.

Yours is the profession of arms, the will to win, the sure knowledge that in war there is no substitute for victory, that if you lose the Nation will be destroyed, that the very obsession of your public service must be duty, honor, country.

Others will debate the controversial issues, national and international, which divide men's minds. But serene, calm, aloof, you stand as the Nation's war guardians, as its lifeguards from the raging tides of international conflict, as its gladiators in the arena of battle. For a century and a half you have defended, guarded, and protected its hallowed traditions of liberty and freedom, of right and justice.

Let civilian voices argue the merits or demerits of our processes of government: Whether our strength is being sapped by deficit financing indulged in too long, by Federal paternalism grown too mighty, by power groups grown too arrogant, by politics grown too corrupt, by crime grown too rampant, by morals grown too low, by taxes grown too high, by extremists grown too violent; whether our personal liberties are as firm and complete as they should be.

These great national problems are not for your professional participation or military solution. Your guidepost stands out like a tenfold beacon in the night. Duty, honor, country.

You are the lever which binds together the entire fabric of our national system of defense. From your ranks come the great captains who hold the Nation's destiny in their hands the moment the war tocsin sounds.

The long, gray line has never failed us. Were you to do so, a million ghosts in olive drab, in brown khaki, in blue and gray, would rise from their white crosses, thundering those magic words: Duty, honor, country.

This does not mean that you are warmongers. On the contrary, the soldier above all other people prays for peace, for he must suffer and bear the deepest wounds and scars of war. But always in our ears ring the ominous words of Plato, that wisest of all philosophers: "Only the dead have seen the end of war."

The shadows are lengthening for me. The twilight is here. My days of old have vanished—tone and tints. They have gone glimmering through the dreams of things that were. Their memory is one of wondrous beauty, watered by tears and coaxed and caressed by the smiles of yesterday. I listen then, but with thirsty ear, for the witching melody of faint bugles blowing reveille, of far drums beating the long roll.

In my dreams I hear again the crash of guns, the rattle of musketry, the strange, mournful mutter of the battlefield. But in the evening of my memory I come back to West Point. Always there echoes and re-echoes: Duty, honor, country.

Today marks my final roll call with you. But I want you to know that when I cross the river, my last conscious thoughts will be of the corps, and the corps, and the corps.

I bid you farewell.

Domestic Law
and International Order

ELDRIDGE CLEAVER

The police department and the armed forces are the two arms of the power structure, the muscles of control and enforcement. They have deadly weapons with which to inflict pain on the human body. They know how to bring about horrible deaths. They have clubs with which to beat the body and the head. They have bullets and guns with which to tear holes in the flesh, to smash bones, to disable and kill. They use force, to make you do what the deciders have decided you must do.

Every country on earth has these agencies of force. The people everywhere fear this terror and force. To them it is like a snarling wild beast which can put an end to one's dreams. They punish. They have cells and prisons to lock you up in. They pass out sentences. They won't let you go when you want to. You have to stay put until they give the word. If your mother is dying, you can't go to her bedside to say goodbye or to her graveside to see her lowered into the earth, to see her, for the last time, swallowed up by that black hole.

The techniques of the enforcers are many: firing squads, gas chambers, electric chairs, torture chambers, the garrote, the guillotine, the tightening rope around your throat. It has been found that the death penalty is necessary to back up the law, to make it easier to enforce, to deter transgressions against the penal code. That everybody doesn't believe in the same laws is beside the point.

Which laws get enforced depends on who is in power. If the capitalists are in power, they enforce laws designed to protect their system, their way of life. They have a particular abhorrence for crimes against property, but are prepared to be liberal and show a modicum of compassion for crimes against the person — unless, of course, an instance of the latter is combined with an instance of the former. In such cases, nothing can stop them from throwing the whole book at the offender. For instance, armed robbery with violence, to a capitalist, is the very epitome of evil. Ask any banker what he thinks of it.

Reprinted from *Soul on Ice* (New York: Dell Publishing Co., 1968), pp. 128–137. (Originally published by McGraw-Hill.)

If Communists are in power, they enforce laws designed to protect their system, their way of life. To them, the horror of horrors is the speculator, that man of magic who has mastered the art of getting something with nothing and who in America would be a member of good standing of his local Chamber of Commerce.

"The people," however, are nowhere consulted, although everywhere everything is done always in their name and ostensibly for their betterment, while their real-life problems go unsolved. "The people" are a rubber stamp for the crafty and sly. And no problem can be solved without taking the police department and·the armed forces into account. Both kings and bookies understand this, as do first ladies and common prostitutes.

The police do on the domestic level what the armed forces do on the international level: protect the way of life of those in power. The police patrol the city, cordon off communities, blockade neighborhoods, invade homes, search for that which is hidden. The armed forces patrol the world, invade countries and continents, cordon off nations, blockade islands and whole peoples; they will also overrun villages, neighborhoods, enter homes, huts, caves, searching for that which is hidden. The policeman and the soldier will violate your person, smoke you out with various gases. Each will shoot you, beat your head and body with sticks and clubs, with rifle butts, run you through with bayonets, shoot holes in your flesh, kill you. They each have unlimited firepower. They will use all that is necessary to bring you to your knees. They won't take no for an answer. If you resist their sticks, they draw their guns. If you resist their guns, they call for reinforcements with bigger guns. Eventually they will come in tanks, in jets, in ships. They will not rest until you surrender or are killed. The policeman and the soldier will have the last word.

Both police and the armed forces follow orders. Orders. Orders flow from the top down. Up there, behind closed doors, in antechambers, in conference rooms, gavels bang on the tables, the tinkling of silver decanters can be heard as icewater is poured by well-fed, conservatively dressed men in hornrimmed glasses, fashionably dressed American widows with rejuvenated faces and tinted hair, the air permeated with the square humor of Bob Hope jokes. Here all the talking is done, all the thinking, all the deciding. Gray rabbits of men scurry forth from the conference room to spread the decisions throughout the city, as News. Carrying out orders is a job, a way of meeting the payments on the house, a way of providing for one's kiddies. In the armed forces it is also a duty, patriotism. Not to do so is treason.

Every city has its police department. No city would be complete without one. It would be sheer madness to try operating an American city without the heat, the fuzz, the man. Americans are too far gone, or else they haven't arrived yet; the center does not exist, only the extremes. Take away the cops and Americans would have a coast-to-coast free-for-all. There are, of course, a few citizens who carry their own private cops around with them, built into their souls. But there is robbery in the land, and larceny, murder, rape, burglary, theft, swindles, all brands of crime, profit, rent, interest — and these blasé descendants of Pilgrims are at each other's throats. To complicate matters, there are also rich people and poor people in America. There are Negroes and whites, Indians, Puerto Ricans, Mexicans, Jews, Chinese, Arabs, Japanese — all with equal rights but unequal possessions. Some are haves and some are have-nots. All have been taught to worship at the shrine of General Motors. The whites are on top in America and they want to stay there, up there. They are also on top in the world, on the international level, and they want to stay up there, too. Everywhere there are those who want to smash this precious toy clock of a system, they want ever so much to change it, to rearrange things, to pull the whites down off their high horse and make them equal. Everywhere the whites are fighting to prolong their status, to retard the erosion of their position. In America, when everything else fails, they call out the police. On the international level, when everything else fails, they call out the armed forces.

A strange thing happened in Watts, in 1965, August. The blacks, who in this land of private property have all private and no property, got excited into an uproar because they noticed a cop before he had a chance to wash the blood off his hands. Usually the police department can handle such flare-ups. But this time it was different. Things got out of hand. The blacks were running amok, burning, shooting, breaking. The police department was powerless to control them; the chief called for reinforcements. Out came the National Guard, that ambiguous hybrid from the twilight zone where the domestic army merges with the international; that hypocritical force poised within America and capable of action on either level, capable of backing up either the police or the armed forces. Unleashing their formidable firepower, they crushed the blacks. But things will never be the same again. Too many people saw that those who turned the other cheek in Watts got their whole head blown off. At the same time, heads were being blown off in Vietnam. America was embarrassed, not by the quality of her deeds but by the surplus of publicity focused upon her negative selling points, and a little frightened because of what all those dead bodies, on two fronts, implied. Those corpses spoke eloquently of potential allies and alliances. A community of interest began to emerge, dripping with blood, out of the ashes of Watts. The blacks in Watts and all over America could now see the Viet Cong's point: both were on the receiving end of what the armed forces were dishing out.

So now the blacks, stung by the new knowledge they have unearthed, cry out: *"POLICE BRUTALITY!"* From one end of the country to the other, the new war cry is raised. The youth, those nodes of compulsive energy who are all fuel and muscle, race their motors, itch to do something. The Uncle Toms, no longer willing to get down on their knees to lick boots, do so from a squatting position. The black bourgeoisie call for Citizens' Review Boards, to assert civilian control over the activity of the police. In back rooms, in dark stinking corners of the ghettos, self-conscious black men curse their own cowardice and stare at their rifles and pistols and shotguns laid out on tables before them, trembling as they wish for a manly impulse to course through their bodies and send them screaming mad into the streets shooting from the hip. Black women look at their men as if they are bugs, curious growths of flesh playing an inscrutable waiting game. Violence becomes a homing pigeon floating through the ghettos seeking a black brain in which to roost for a season.

In their rage against the police, against police brutality, the blacks lose sight of the fundamental reality: that the police are only an instrument for the implementation of the policies of those who make the decisions. Police brutality is only one facet of the crystal of terror and oppression. Behind police brutality there is social brutality, economic brutality, and political brutality. From the perspective of the ghetto, this is not easy to discern: the TV newscaster and the radio announcer and the editorialists of the newspapers are wizards of the smoke screen and the snow job.

What is true on the international level is true also at home; except that the ace up the sleeve is easier to detect in the international arena. Who would maintain that American soldiers are in Vietnam on their own motion? They were conscripted into the armed forces and taught the wisdom of obeying orders. They were sent to Vietnam by orders of the generals in the Pentagon, who receive them from the Secretary of Defense, who receives them from the President, who is shrouded in mystery. The soldier in the field in Vietnam, the man who lies in the grass and squeezes the trigger when a little half-starved, trembling Vietnamese peasant crosses his sights, is only following orders, carrying out a policy and a plan. He hardly knows what it is all about. They have him wired-up tight with the slogans of TV and the World Series. All he knows is that he has been assigned to carry out a certain ritual of duties. He is well trained and does the best he can. He does a good job. He may want to please those above him with the quality of his performance. He may want to make sergeant, or better. This man is from some hicky farm in Shit Creek, Georgia. He only knew whom to kill after passing through boot camp. He could just as well come out ready to kill Swedes. He will kill a Swede dead, if he is ordered to do so.

Same for the policeman in Watts. He is not there on his own. They have all been assigned. They have been told what to do and what not to do. They have also been told what they better not do. So when they continually do something, in every filthy ghetto in this shitty land, it means only that they are following orders.

It's no secret that in America the blacks are in total rebellion against the System. They want to get their nuts out of the sand. They don't like the way America is run, from top to bottom. In America, everything is owned. Everything is held as private property. Someone has a brand on everything. There is nothing left over. Until recently, the blacks themselves were counted as part of somebody's private property, along with the chickens and goats. The blacks have not forgotten this, principally because they are still treated as if they are part of someone's inventory of assets — or perhaps, in this day of rage against the costs of welfare, blacks are listed among the nation's liabilities. On any account, however, blacks are in no position to respect or help maintain the institution of private property. What they want is to figure out a way to get some of that property for themselves, to divert it to their own needs. This is what it is all about, and this is the real brutality involved. This is the source of all brutality.

The police are the armed guardians of the social order. The blacks are the chief domestic victims of the American social order. A conflict of interest exists, therefore, between the blacks and the police. It is not solely a matter of trigger-happy cops, of brutal cops who love to crack black heads. Mostly it's a job to them. It pays good. And there are numerous fringe benefits. The real problem is a trigger-happy social order.

The Utopians speak of a day when there will be no police. There will be nothing for them to do. Every man will do his duty, will respect the rights of his neighbor, will not disturb the peace. The needs of all will be taken care of. Everyone will have sympathy for his fellow man. There will be no such thing as crime. There will be, of course, no prisons. No electric chairs, no gas chambers. The hangman's rope will be the thing of the past. The entire earth will be a land of plenty. There will be no crimes against property, no speculation.

It is easy to see that we are not on the verge of entering Utopia: there are cops everywhere. North and South, the Negroes are the have-nots. They see property all around them, property that is owned by whites. In this regard, the black bourgeoisie has become nothing but a ridiculous nuisance. Having waged a battle for entrance into the American mainstream continually for fifty years, all of the black bourgeoisie's defenses are directed outward, against the whites. They have no defenses against the blacks and no time to erect any. The black masses can handle them any time they choose, with one mighty blow. But the white bourgeoisie presents a bigger problem, those whites who own everything. With many shackled by unemployment, hatred in black hearts for this system of private property increases daily. The sanctity surrounding property is being called into question. The mystique of the deed of ownership is melting away. In other parts of the world, peasants rise up and expropriate the land from the former owners. Blacks in America see that the deed is not eternal, that it is not signed by God, and that new deeds, making blacks the owners, can be drawn up.

The Black Muslims raised the cry, *"WE MUST HAVE SOME LAND!" "SOME LAND OF OUR OWN OR ELSE!"* Blacks in America shrink from the colossus of General Motors. They can't see how to wade through that thicket of common stocks, preferred stocks, bonds and debentures. They only know that General Motors is huge, that it has billions of dollars under its control, that it owns land, that its subsidiaries are legion, that it is a repository of vast powers. The blacks want to crack the nut of General Motors. They are meditating on it. Meanwhile, they must learn that the police take orders from General Motors.

And that the Bank of America has something to do with them even though they don't have a righteous penny in the bank. They have no bank accounts, only bills to pay. The only way they know of making withdrawals from the bank is at the point of a gun. The shiny fronts of skyscrapers intimidate them. They do not own them. They feel alienated from the very sidewalks on which they walk. This white man's country, this white man's world. Overflowing with men of color. An economy consecrated to the succor of the whites. Blacks are incidental. The war on poverty, that monstrous insult to the rippling muscles in a black man's arms, is an index of how men actually sit down and plot each other's deaths, actually sit down with slide rules and calculate how to hide bread from the hungry. And the black bourgeoisie greedily sopping up what crumbs are tossed into their dark corner.

There are 20,000,000 of these blacks in America, probably more. Today they repeat, in awe, this magic number to themselves: there are 20,000,000 of us! They shout this to each other in humiliated astonishment. No one need tell them that there is vast power latent in their mass. They know that 20,000,000 of anything is enough to get some recognition and consideration. They know also that they must harness their number and hone it into a sword with a sharp cutting edge. White General Motors also knows that the unity of these 20,000,000 ragamuffins will spell the death of the system of its being. At all costs, then, they will seek to keep these blacks from uniting, from becoming bold and revolutionary. These white property owners know that they must keep the blacks cowardly and intimidated. By a complex communications system of hints and signals, certain orders are given to the chief of police and the sheriff, who pass them on to their men, the footsoldiers in the trenches of the ghetto.

We experience this system of control as madness. So that Leonard Deadwyler, one of these 20,000,000 blacks, is rushing his pregnant wife to the hospital and is shot dead by a policeman. An accident. That the sun rises in the east and sets in the west is also an accident, by design. The blacks are up in arms. From one end of America to the other, blacks are outraged at this accident, this latest evidence of what an accident-prone people they are, of the cruelty and pain of their lives, these blacks at the mercy of trigger-happy Yankees and Rebs in coalition against their skin. They want the policeman's blood as a sign that the Viet Cong is not the only answer. A sign to save them from the deaths they must die, and inflict. The power structure, without so much as blinking an eye, wouldn't mind tossing Bova to the mob, to restore law and order, but it knows in the vaults of its strength that at all cost the blacks must be kept at bay, that it must uphold the police department, its Guardian. Nothing must be allowed to threaten the set-up. Justice is secondary. Security is the byword.

Meanwhile, blacks are looking on and asking tactical questions. They are asked to die for the System in Vietnam. In Watts they are killed by it. Now—*NOW!*—they are asking each other, in dead earnest: Why not die right here in Babylon fighting for a better life, like the Viet Cong? If those little cats can do it, what's wrong with big studs like us?

A mood sets in, spreads across America, across the face of Babylon, jells in black hearts everywhere.

Reproduced from an advertisement appearing in *The New York Times Book Review* (29 June 1969), p. 13, and other publications.

The Stupid Machine:
A Review of Jacqueline Susann's
The Love Machine

JONATHAN BAUMBACH

> Perhaps man's only chance of survival
> is to *become* a machine.
> — *The Love Machine*

It is no secret that education in America has a vested interest in stupidity. Our institutions are in business to perpetuate the culture. What one learns in school are strategies of socialization: how to compete, how to fit in, how to give teacher what he wants. Anyone who has taught writing in college has seen the results. Our students write the dead prose of official culture, voiceless, abstract, euphemistic, a language capable of only the most generalized distinctions. Which brings us to *The Love Machine*, currently the best-selling fiction in America.

"This was the kind of love novelists wrote about. It did exist. Her past 'romances' paled in comparison." This is the kind of interior monologue Jacqueline Susann writes. Her prose defines the way her characters experience the world. In almost every creative writing course I've taught, there have been three or four girls who write like Miss Susann—that is write about beautiful non-people leading women's magazine fantasy lives. "Who are these people?" I ask them, and they shrug as if to say, "who is anyone? We grew up in Brooklyn, what do we know about anything?"

The muse of *The Love Machine* is the culture itself. Despite her pretense to sophistication, Miss Susann is, in effect, a primitive. Though she makes a few breathy passes at psychologizing, her narrative is unencumbered by psychology. Her characters go where she moves them, talk for the most part to convey information, experience the world the same way their author does, are interchangeably mindless. It is as if Madame Bovary, stars in her eyes, survived to tell her own story. A novel of manners without nuance, *The Love Machine* shares a common plastic reality with television commercials, Rex Reed, *Guess Who's*

Reprinted from *The Nation* (1 September 1969), pp. 188–190.

Coming to Dinner?, Billy Graham, *Cosmopolitan* and *Playboy*, Richard Nixon, *The Dating Game*, political rhetoric, other popular novels, our schools. As a document of corruption, the novel is essentially — rather touchingly — innocent.

The three heroines seem, for all their protestations of love, less capable of real feeling than their loveless love object, the Love Machine himself, an opportunistic television executive named Robin Stone. Robin's tragic hang-up is to experience sex and love as wholly separate — a rather common circumstance in our culture. Miss Susann's women tend to confuse sex and love — that is, identify love with physical gratification. There's no indication in the novel that Miss Susann doesn't take her heroines at their word. "Her love for Robin refused to find a level. It soared on and on to a peak of feverish infinity." "She wanted Robin so bad she physically ached." When my students write like that I indicate that the language defies belief. "But that's exactly the way it felt," the student will argue, upset at my failure to understand. What happens, of course, is that the prose precedes the experience, fakes it, exists ultimately in lieu of it. Sentimentality is the language of numbness.

"She really loved Gregory but she wasn't *in* love with him." In Faulkner's *As I Lay Dying*, Addie Bundren says: "I knew that the word [love] was like the others just a shape to fill a lack: that when the right time came you wouldn't need a word for that." Miss Susann uses the word relentlessly. "'For the first time in my stinking life I'm really in love.'" "'I know he loves me but I'm just part of his empire.'" "'The whole world loves Lucy, Ed Sullivan and Bob Hope. Tell me, newsgirl, whom do *you* love on television?'"

Reading *The Love Machine* is a numbingly mindless experience. Its effect is narcotic. Miss Susann asks her readers not to think, not to feel, and, before all, not to see — nothing is asked and all is given. In a sense, the book is a collaboration — a shared inhuman cultural fantasy between author and readers, a reinforcement of culture-induced fantasies. Where real literature disturbs, books like *The Love Machine* comfort. It is not only child's play to read but offers gratifyingly easy solutions. After two weeks of psychoanalysis one character discovers that "he had personality problems, but he was not a fag!" The subliminal message of the novel is *stay as stupid as you are*. Stupidity is a way of avoiding pain by ignoring options, a form of inhumanity comparable to Robin's incapacity to feel. "Come to think of it,"

Robin tells Maggie in the voice of wisdom, "I don't think I've ever met a happy adjusted genius."

We are a schizophrenic culture. Our advertisements promote instant gratification, while our institutions—schools, churches, government—tell us to be thrifty, hard working and chaste. So we are programmed by media to live for the moment and programmed by institutions to feel guilty as hell about pleasure. An artifact of the culture, *The Love Machine* has it both ways. The main thrust of the novel is hedonistic—characters hop in and out of bed with one another in various combinations—but the novel opts finally for the middle class puritan verities. "But there's more to life than living this business every second, and making excuses for sexual deviation because we're artists. I want a husband, not a bright young director who smokes pot and makes it with a boy occasionally for kicks."

On the face of it, *The Love Machine* deplores the amoral world it describes. Robin reforms at the end to become his own man, to write his book, to realize self over career; finally, cured of chronic inhumanity, to marry the woman he loves. Integrity and love triumph over hedonism and ambition. *The Love Machine* subscribes to cultural convention so successfully because it believes in it. There is no discernible vision in the novel outside popular culture's vision of itself, no higher intelligence, no other context. As one can see from the quotations, the novel is written in the very language of its world—a language wholly incapable of accounting for human experience, a language geared to genocide. If we had better schools we might have more literate and human best sellers, but then we would be another country.

Little Orphan Annie

"IF THE LAW SUPPOSES 'THAT,' SAID MR. BUMBLE, 'THE LAW IS A ASS.'"—DICKENS. "A STATE WITH DEFECTIVE LAWS WILL HAVE DEFECTIVE MORALS." —SENECA.

OH, THE POLICE HAVE KNOWN FOR WEEKS WHO HIRED THAT GANG TO TRY TO KILL PETE; THE PRICE, THE WHOLE PLAN!

THEN WHY AREN'T THEY ALL IN JAIL, CAPTAIN?

AH, WE'RE LIVING IN A NEW ERA! NOW EVEN ADMITTED VIOLENT CRIME DOESN'T COUNT! THE LEGAL QUESTION IS, HOW THE DICKENS DID THE COPS FIND OUT?

BUT THAT'S CRAZY!

SOME OF US, IN MY BUSINESS, THINK SO, BUT IT'S THE LAW, LADY! WE ALSO KNOW THE MEN IN THAT GROUP OF HIRED KILLERS!

THEY GOT BACK TO THEIR HOME CITY YESTERDAY; BUT BY A RECENT JUDICIAL DECISION IT'S ILLEGAL FOR A COP EVEN TO ASK A SUSPECT HIS NAME!

WHY, THAT'S INCREDIBLE!

NOPE; INVASION OF THE SUSPECT'S CONSTITUTIONAL RIGHT TO PRIVACY, SAID THE LEARNED JUDGE!

WHOSE SIDE ARE THE COURTS ON, ANYWAY?

Escobedo v. Illinois

Certiorari to The Supreme Court of Illinois.
No. 615. Argued April 29, 1964.
— Decided June 22, 1964.

Barry L. Kroll argued the cause for petitioner. With him on the brief was *Donald M. Haskell.*

James R. Thompson argued the cause for respondent. With him on the brief were *Daniel P. Ward* and *Elmer C. Kissane.*

Bernard Weisberg argued the cause for the American Civil Liberties Union, as *amicus curiae,* urging reversal. With him on the brief was *Walter T. Fisher.*

MR. JUSTICE GOLDBERG delivered the opinion of the Court.

The critical question in this case is whether, under the circumstances, the refusal by the police to honor petitioner's request to consult with his lawyer during the course of an interrogation constitutes a denial of "the Assistance of Counsel" in violation of the Sixth Amendment to the Constitution as "made obligatory upon the States by the Fourteenth Amendment," *Gideon* v. *Wainwright,* 372 U.S. 335, 342, and thereby renders inadmissible in a state criminal trial any incriminating statement elicited by the police during the interrogation.

On the night of January 19, 1960, petitioner's brother-in-law was fatally shot. In the early hours of the next morning, at 2:30 a.m., petitioner was arrested without a warrant and interrogated. Petitioner made no statement to the police and was released at 5 that afternoon pursuant to a state court writ of habeas corpus obtained by Mr. Warren Wolfson, a lawyer who had been retained by petitioner.

On January 30, Benedict DiGerlando, who was then in police custody and who was later indicted for the murder along with petitioner, told the police that petitioner had fired the fatal shots. Between 8 and 9 that evening, petitioner and his sister, the widow of the deceased, were arrested and taken to police headquarters. En route to the police station, the police "had handcuffed the defendant behind his back," and "one of the arresting officers told defendant that DiGerlando had named him as the one who shot" the deceased. Petitioner testified, without contradiction, that the "detectives said they had us pretty

---

Reprinted from *Leading Decisions of the Supreme Court* (Scranton: Chandler Publishing Company).

well, up pretty tight, and we might as well admit to this crime," and that he replied, "I am sorry but I would like to have advice from my lawyer." A police officer testified that although petitioner was not formally charged "he was in custody" and "couldn't walk out the door."

Shortly after petitioner reached police headquarters, his retained lawyer arrived. The lawyer described the ensuing events in the following terms:

"On that day I received a phone call [from "the mother of another defendant"] and pursuant to that phone call I went to the Detective Bureau at 11th and State. The first person I talked to was the Sergeant on duty at the Bureau Desk, Sergeant Pidgeon. I asked Sergeant Pidgeon for permission to speak to my client, Danny Escobedo. . . . Sergeant Pidgeon made a call to the Bureau lockup and informed me that the boy had been taken from the lockup to the Homicide Bureau. This was between 9:30 and 10:00 in the evening. Before I went anywhere, he called the Homicide Bureau and told them there was an attorney waiting to see Escobedo. He told me I could not see him. Then I went upstairs to the Homicide Bureau. There were several Homicide Detectives around and I talked to them. I identified myself as Escobedo's attorney and asked permission to see him. They said I could not. . . . The police officer told me to see Chief Flynn who was on duty. I identified myself to Chief Flynn and asked permission to see my client. He said I could not. . . . I think it was approximately 11:00 o'clock. He said I couldn't see him because they hadn't completed questioning. . . . [F]or a second or two I spotted him in an office in the Homicide Bureau. The door was open and I could see through the office. . . . I waved to him and he waved back and then the door was closed, by one of the officers at Homicide.[1] There were four or five officers milling around the Homicide Detail that night. As to whether I talked to Captain Flynn any later that day, I waited around for another hour or two and went back again and renewed by [sic] request to see my client. He again told me I could not. . . . I filed an official complaint with Commissioner Phelan of the Chicago Police Department. I had a conversation with every police officer I could find. I was told at Homicide that I couldn't see him and I would have to get a writ of habeas corpus. I left the Homicide Bureau and from the Detective Bureau at 11th and State at approximately 1:00 A.M. [Sunday morning] I had no opportunity to talk to my client that night. I quoted to Captain Flynn the Section of the Criminal Code which allows an attorney the right to see his client."[2]

[1]Petitioner testified that this ambiguous gesture "could have meant most anything," but that he "took it upon [his] own to think that [the lawyer was telling him] not to say anything," and that the lawyer "wanted to talk" to him.

[2]The statute then in effect provided in pertinent part that: "All public officers . . . having the custody of any person . . . restrained of his liberty for any alleged cause whatever, shall, except in cases of imminent danger of escape, admit any practicing attorney . . . whom such person . . . may desire to see or consult . . . ." Ill. Rev. Stat. (1959), c. 38, § 477. Repealed as of Jan. 1, 1964, by Act approved Aug. 14, 1963, H.B. No. 851.

Petitioner testified that during the course of the interrogation he repeatedly asked to speak to his lawyer and that the police said that his lawyer "didn't want to see" him. The testimony of the police officers confirmed these accounts in substantial detail.

Notwithstanding repeated requests by each, petitioner and his retained lawyer were afforded no opportunity to consult during the course of the entire interrogation. At one point, as previously noted, petitioner and his attorney came into each other's view for a few moments but the attorney was quickly ushered away. Petitioner testified "that he heard a detective telling the attorney the latter would not be allowed to talk to [him] 'until they were done'" and that he heard the attorney being refused permission to remain in the adjoining room. A police officer testified that he had told the lawyer that he could not see petitioner until "we were through interrogating" him.

There is testimony by the police that during the interrogation, petitioner, a 22-year-old of Mexican extraction with no record of previous experience with the police, "was handcuffed"[3] in a standing position and that he "was nervous, he had circles under his eyes and he was upset" and was "agitated" because "he had not slept well in over a week."

It is undisputed that during the course of the interrogation Officer Montejano, who "grew up" in petitioner's neighborhood, who knew his family, and who uses "Spanish language in [his] police work," conferred alone with petitioner "for about a quarter of an hour. . . ." Petitioner testified that the officer said to him "in Spanish that my sister and I could go home if I pinned it on Benedict DiGerlando," that "he would see to it that we would go home and be held only as witnesses, if anything, if we had made a statement against DiGerlando . . . , that we would be able to go home that night." Petitioner testified that he made the statement in issue because of this assurance. Officer Montejano denied offering any such assurance.

A police officer testified that during the interrogation the following occurred:

"I informed him of what DiGerlando told me and when I did, he told me that DiGerlando was [lying] and I said, 'Would you care to tell DiGerlando that?' and he said, 'Yes, I will.' So, I brought . . . Escobedo in and he confronted DiGerlando and he told him that he was lying and said, 'I didn't shoot Manuel, you did it.'"

[3] The trial judge justified the handcuffing on the ground that it "is ordinary police procedure."

In this way, petitioner, for the first time, admitted to some knowledge of the crime. After that he made additional statements further implicating himself in the murder plot. At this point an Assistant State's Attorney, Theodore J. Cooper, was summoned "to take" a statement. Mr. Cooper, an experienced lawyer who was assigned to the Homicide Division to take "statements from some defendants and some prisoners that they had in custody," "took" petitioner's statement by asking carefully framed questions apparently designed to assure the admissibility into evidence of the resulting answers. Mr. Cooper testified that he did not advise petitioner of his constitutional rights, and it is undisputed that no one during the course of the interrogation so advised him.

Petitioner moved both before and during trial to suppress the incriminating statement, but the motions were denied. Petitioner was convicted of murder and he appealed the conviction.

The Supreme Court of Illinois, in its original opinion of February 1, 1963, held the statement inadmissible and reversed the conviction. The court said:

> "[I]t seems manifest to us, from the undisputed evidence and the circumstances surrounding defendant at the time of his statement and shortly prior thereto, that the defendant understood he would be permitted to go home if he gave the statement and would be granted an immunity from prosecution."

Compare *Lynumn* v. *Illinois*, 372 U.S. 528.

The State petitioned for, and the court granted, rehearing. The court then affirmed the conviction. It said: "[T]he officer denied making the promise and the trier of fact believed him. We find no reason for disturbing the trial court's finding that the confession was voluntary."[4] 28 Ill. 2d 41, 45–46, 190 N. E. 2d 825, 827. The court also held, on the authority of this Court's decisions in *Crooker* v. *California*, 357 U.S. 433, and *Cicenia* v.

[4]Compare *Haynes* v. *Washington*, 373 U.S. 503, 515 (decided on the same day as the decision of the Illinois Supreme Court here), where we said:

"Our conclusion is in no way foreclosed, as the State contends, by the fact that the state trial judge or the jury may have reached a different result on this issue.

"It is well settled that the duty of constitutional adjudication resting upon this Court requires that the question whether the Due Process Clause of the Fourteenth Amendment has been violated by admission into evidence of a coerced confession be the subject of an *independent* determination here, see, *e.g.*, *Ashcraft* v. *Tennessee*, 322 U.S. 143, 147–148; 'we cannot escape the responsibility of making our own examination of the record,' *Spano* v. *New York*, 360 U.S. 315, 316." (Emphasis in original.)

Lagay, 357 U.S. 504, that the confession was admissible even though "it was obtained after he had requested the assistance of counsel, which request was denied." 28 Ill. 2d, at 46, 190 N. E. 2d, at 827. We granted a writ of certiorari to consider whether the petitioner's statement was constitutionally admissible at his trial. 375 U.S. 902. We conclude, for the reasons stated below, that it was not and, accordingly, we reverse the judgment of conviction.

In *Massiah* v. *United States,* 377 U.S. 201, this Court observed that "a Constitution which guarantees a defendant the aid of counsel at . . . trial could surely vouchsafe no less to an indicted defendant under interrogation by the police in a completely extrajudicial proceeding. Anything less . . . might deny a defendant 'effective representation by counsel at the only stage when legal aid and advice would help him.'" *Id.,* at 204, quoting DOUGLAS, J., concurring in *Spano* v. *New York,* 360 U.S. 315, 326.

The interrogation here was conducted before petitioner was formally indicted. But in the context of this case, that fact should make no difference. When petitioner requested, and was denied, an opportunity to consult with his lawyer, the investigation had ceased to be a general investigation of "an unsolved crime." *Spano* v. *New York,* 360 U.S. 315, 327 (STEWART, J., concurring). Petitioner had become the accused, and the purpose of the interrogation was to "get him" to confess his guilt despite his constitutional right not to do so. At the time of his arrest and throughout the course of the interrogation, the police told petitioner that they had convincing evidence that he had fired the fatal shots. Without informing him of his absolute right to remain silent in the face of this accusation, the police urged him to make a statement.[5] As this Court observed many years ago:

"It cannot be doubted that, placed in the position in which the accused was when the statement was made to him that the other suspected person had charged him with crime, the result was to produce upon his mind the fear that if he remained silent it would be considered an admission of guilt, and therefore render certain his being committed for trial as the guilty person, and it cannot be conceived that the converse impression would not also have naturally arisen, that by denying there was hope of removing the suspicion from himself." *Bram* v. *United States,* 168 U.S. 532, 562.

[5]Although there is testimony in the record that petitioner and his lawyer had previously discussed what petitioner should do in the event of interrogation, there is no evidence that they discussed what petitioner should, or could, do in the face of a false accusation that he had fired the fatal bullets.

Petitioner, a layman, was undoubtedly unaware that under Illinois law an admission of "mere" complicity in the murder plot was legally as damaging as an admission of firing of the fatal shots. *Illinois* v. *Escobedo*, 28 Ill. 2d 41, 190 N. E. 2d 825. The "guiding hand of counsel" was essential to advise petitioner of his rights in this delicate situation. *Powell* v. *Alabama*, 287 U.S. 45, 69. This was the "stage when legal aid and advice" were most critical to petitioner. *Massiah* v. *United States, supra*, at 204. It was a stage surely as critical as was the arraignment in *Hamilton* v. *Alabama*, 368 U.S. 52, and the preliminary hearing in *White* v. *Maryland*, 373 U.S. 59. What happened at this interrogation could certainly "affect the whole trial," *Hamilton* v. *Alabama, supra*, at 54, since rights "may be as irretrievably lost, if not then and there asserted, as they are when an accused represented by counsel waives a right for strategic purposes." *Ibid.* It would exalt form over substance to make the right to counsel, under these circumstances, depend on whether at the time of the interrogation, the authorities had secured a formal indictment. Petitioner had, for all practical purposes, already been charged with murder.

The New York Court of Appeals, whose decisions this Court cited with approval in *Massiah*, 377 U.S. 201, at 205, has recently recognized that, under circumstances such as those here, no meaningful distinction can be drawn between interrogation of an accused before and after formal indictment. In *People* v. *Donovan*, 13 N. Y. 2d 148, 193 N. E. 2d 628, that court, in an opinion by Judge Fuld, held that a "confession taken from a defendant, during a period of detention [prior to indictment], after his attorney had requested and been denied access to him" could not be used against him in a criminal trial.[6] *Id.*, at 151, 193 N. E. 2d, at 629. The court observed that it "would be highly incongruous if our system of justice permitted the district attorney, the lawyer representing the State, to extract a confession from the accused while his own lawyer, seeking to speak

[6] The English Judges' Rules also recognize that a functional rather than a formal test must be applied and that, under circumstances such as those here, no special significance should be attached to formal indictment. The applicable Rule does not permit the police to question an accused, except in certain extremely limited situations not relevant here, at any time after the defendant "has been charged *or informed that he may be prosecuted.*" [1964] Crim. L. Rev. 166–170 (emphasis supplied). Although voluntary statements obtained in violation of these rules are not automatically excluded from evidence the judge may, in the exercise of his discretion, exclude them. "Recent cases suggest that perhaps the judges have been tightening up [and almost] inevitably, the effect of the new Rules will be to stimulate this tendency." *Id.*, at 182.

with him, was kept from him by the police." *Id.*, at 152, 193 N. E. 2d, at 629.[7]

In *Gideon* v. *Wainwright*, 372 U.S. 335, we held that every person accused of a crime, whether state or federal, is entitled to a lawyer at trial.[8] The rule sought by the State here, however, would make the trial no more than an appeal from the interrogation; and the "right to use counsel at the formal trial [would be] a very hollow thing [if], for all practical purposes, the conviction is already assured by pretrial examination." *In re Groban*, 352 U.S. 330, 344 (BLACK, J., dissenting).[9] "One can imagine a cynical prosecutor saying: 'Let them have the most illustrious counsel, now. They can't escape the noose. There is nothing that counsel can do for them at the trial.'" *Ex parte Sullivan*, 107 F.Supp. 514, 517–518.

It is argued that if the right to counsel is afforded prior to indictment, the number of confessions obtained by the police will diminish significantly, because most confessions are obtained during the period between arrest and indictment,[10] and "any lawyer worth his salt will tell the suspect in no uncertain terms to make no statement to police under any circumstances." *Watts* v. *Indiana*, 338 U.S. 49, 59 (Jackson, J., concurring in part and dissenting in part). This argument, of course, cuts two ways. The fact that many confessions are obtained during this period points up its critical nature as a "stage when legal aid and advice" are surely needed. *Massiah* v. *United States, supra,* at 204; *Hamilton* v. *Alabama, supra; White* v. *Maryland, supra.* The right to counsel would indeed be hollow if it began at a period when few confessions were obtained. There is necessarily a direct relationship between the importance of a stage to the police in their quest for a confession and the criticalness of that stage

[7]Canon 9 of the American Bar Association's Canon of Professional Ethics provides that:

"A lawyer should not in any way communicate upon the subject of controversy with a party represented by counsel; much less should he undertake to negotiate or compromise the matter with him, but should deal only with his counsel. It is incumbent upon the lawyer most particularly to avoid everything that may tend to mislead a party not represented by counsel, and he should not undertake to advise him as to the law." See Broeder, Wong Sun v. United States: A Study in Faith and Hope, 42 Neb. L. Rev. 483, 599–604.

[8]Twenty-two States, including Illinois, urged us so to hold.

[9]The Soviet criminal code does not permit a lawyer to be present during the investigation. The Soviet trial has thus been aptly described as "an appeal from the pretrial investigation." Feifer, Justice in Moscow (1964), 86.

[10]See Barrett, Police Practices and the Law—From Arrest to Release or Charge, 50 Cal. L. Rev. 11, 43 (1962).

to the accused in his need for legal advice. Our Constitution, unlike some others, strikes the balance in favor of the right of the accused to be advised by his lawyer of his privilege against self-incrimination. See Note, 73 Yale L.J. 1000, 1048–1051 (1964).

We have learned the lesson of history, ancient and modern, that a system of criminal law enforcement which comes to depend on the "confession" will, in the long run, be less reliable[11] and more subject to abuses[12] than a system which depends on extrinsic evidence independently secured through skillful investigation. As Dean Wigmore so wisely said:

"*[A]ny system of administration which permits the prosecution to trust habitually to compulsory self-disclosure as a source of proof must itself suffer morally thereby.* The inclination develops to rely mainly upon such evidence, and to be satisfied with an incomplete investigation of the other sources. The exercise of the power to extract answers begets a forgetfulness of the just limitations of that power. The simple and peaceful process of questioning breeds a readiness to resort to bullying and to physical force and torture. If there is a right to an answer, there soon seems to be a right to the expected answer, — that is, to a confession of guilt. Thus the legitimate use grows into the unjust abuse; ultimately, the innocent are jeopardized by the encroachments of a bad system. Such seems to have been the course of experience in those legal systems where the privilege was not recognized." 8 Wigmore, Evidence (3d ed. 1940), 309. (Emphasis in original.)

This Court also has recognized that "history amply shows that confessions have often been extorted to save law enforcement officials the trouble and effort of obtaining valid and independent evidence. . . ." *Haynes* v. *Washington*, 373 U.S. 503, 519.

We have also learned the companion lesson of history that no system of criminal justice can, or should, survive if it comes to depend for its continued effectiveness on the citizens' abdication through unawareness of their constitutional rights. No system worth preserving should have to *fear* that if an accused is permitted to consult with a lawyer, he will become aware of, and

---

[11] See Committee Print, Subcommittee to Investigate Administration of the Internal Security Act, Senate Committee on the Judiciary, 85th Cong., 1st Sess., reporting and analyzing the proceedings at the XXth Congress of the Communist Party of the Soviet Union, February 25, 1956, exposing the false confessions obtained during the Stalin purges of the 1930's. See also *Miller* v. *United States*, 320 F.2d 767, 772–773 (opinion of Chief Judge Bazelon); Lifton, Thought Reform and the Psychology of Totalism (1961); Rogge, Why Men Confess (1959); Schein, Coercive Persuasion (1961).

[12] See Stephen, History of the Criminal Law, quoted in 8 Wigmore, Evidence (3d ed. 1940), 312; Report and Recommendations of the Commissioners' Committee on Police Arrests for Investigation, District of Columbia (1962).

exercise, these rights.[13] If the exercise of constitutional rights will thwart the effectiveness of a system of law enforcement, then there is something very wrong with that system.[14]

We hold, therefore, that where, as here, the investigation is no longer a general inquiry into an unsolved crime but has begun to focus on a particular suspect, the suspect has been taken into police custody, the police carry out a process of interrogations that lends itself to eliciting incriminating statements, the suspect has requested and been denied an opportunity to consult with his lawyer, and the police have not effectively warned him of his absolute constitutional right to remain silent, the accused has been denied "the Assistance of Counsel" in violation of the Sixth Amendment to the Constitution as "made obligatory upon the States by the Fourteenth Amendment," *Gideon* v. *Wainwright*, 372 U.S., at 342, and that no statement elicited by the police during the interrogation may be used against him at a criminal trial.

Crooker v. *California*, 357 U.S. 433, does not compel a contrary result. In that case the Court merely rejected the absolute rule sought by petitioner, that "every state denial of a request to contact counsel [is] an infringement of the constitutional right *without regard to the circumstances of the case.*" *Id.*, at 440. (Emphasis in original.) In its place, the following rule was announced:

"[S]tate refusal of a request to engage counsel violates due process not only if the accused is deprived of counsel at trial on the merits, . . . *but also if he is deprived of counsel for any part of the pretrial proceedings,*

---

[13]Cf. Report of Attorney General's Committee on Poverty and the Administration of Federal Criminal Justice (1963), 10–11: "The survival of our system of criminal justice and the values which it advances depends upon a constant, searching, and creative questioning of official decisions and assertions of authority at all states of the process. . . . Persons [denied access to counsel] are incapable of providing the challenges that are indispensable to satisfactory operation of the system. The loss to the interests of accused individuals, occasioned by these failures, are great and apparent. It is also clear that a situation in which persons are required to contest a serious accusation but are denied access to the tools of contest is offensive to fairness and equity. Beyond these considerations, however, is the fact that [this situation is] detrimental to the proper functioning of the system of justice and that the loss in vitality of the adversary system, thereby occasioned, significantly endangers the basic interests of a free community."

[14]The accused may, of course, intelligently and knowingly waive his privilege against self-incrimination and his right to counsel either at a pretrial stage or at the trial. See *Johnson* v. *Zerbst*, 304 U.S. 458. But no knowing and intelligent waiver of any constitutional right can be said to have occurred under the circumstances of this case.

provided that he is so prejudiced thereby as to infect his subsequent trial with an absence of 'that fundamental fairness essential to the very concept of justice. . . .' The latter determination necessarily depends upon all the circumstances of the case." 357 U.S., at 439–440. (Emphasis added.)

The Court, applying "these principles" to "the sum total of the circumstances [there] during the time petitioner was without counsel," *id.*, at 440, concluded that he had not been fundamentally prejudiced by the denial of his request for counsel. Among the critical circumstances which distinguish that case from this one are that the petitioner there, but not here, was explicitly advised by the police of his constitutional right to remain silent and not to "say anything" in response to the questions, *id.*, at 437, and that petitioner there, but not here, was a well-educated man who had studied criminal law while attending law school for a year. The Court's opinion in *Cicenia* v. *Lagay*, 357 U.S. 504, decided the same day, merely said that the "contention that petitioner had a constitutional right to confer with counsel is disposed of by *Crooker* v. *California*. . . ." That case adds nothing, therefore, to *Crooker*. In any event, to the extent that *Cicenia* or *Crooker* may be inconsistent with the principles announced today, they are not to be regarded as controlling.[15]

Nothing we have said today affects the powers of the police to investigate "an unsolved crime," *Spano* v. *New York*, 360 U.S. 315, 327 (STEWART, J., concurring), by gathering information from witnesses and by other "proper investigative efforts." *Haynes* v. *Washington*, 373 U.S. 503, 519. We hold only that when the process shifts from investigatory to accusatory—when its focus is on the accused and its purpose is to elicit a confession—our adversary system begins to operate, and, under the circumstances here, the accused must be permitted to consult with his lawyer.

The judgment of the Illinois Supreme Court is reversed and the case remanded for proceedings not inconsistent with this opinion.

Reversed and remanded.

MR. JUSTICE HARLAN, dissenting.

I would affirm the judgment of the Supreme Court of Illinois on the basis of *Cicenia* v. *Lagay*, 357 U.S. 504, decided by this

[15] The authority of *Cicenia* v. *Lagay*, 357 U.S. 504, and *Crooker* v. *California*, 357 U.S. 433, was weakened by the subsequent decisions of this Court in *Hamilton* v. *Alabama*, 368 U.S. 52, *White* v. *Maryland*, 373 U.S. 59, and *Massiah* v. *United States*, 377 U.S. 201 (as the dissenting opinion in the last-cited case recognized).

Court only six years ago. Like my Brother WHITE, *post*, p. 495, I think the rule announced today is most ill-conceived and that it seriously and unjustifiably fetters perfectly legitimate methods of criminal law enforcement.

MR. JUSTICE STEWART, dissenting.

I think this case is directly controlled by *Cicenia* v. *Lagay*, 357 U.S. 504, and I would therefore affirm the judgment.

Massiah v. *United States*, 377 U.S. 201, is not in point here. In that case a federal grand jury had indicted Massiah. He had retained a lawyer and entered a formal plea of not guilty. Under our system of federal justice an indictment and arraignment are followed by a trial, at which the Sixth Amendment guarantees the defendant the assistance of counsel. "In all criminal prosecutions, the accused shall enjoy the right . . . to have the Assistance of Counsel for his defense." But Massiah was released on bail, and thereafter agents of the Federal Government deliberately elicited incriminating statements from him in the absence of his lawyer. We held that the use of these statements against him at his trial denied him the basic protections of the Sixth Amendment guarantee. Putting to one side the fact that the case now before us is not a federal case, the vital fact remains that this case does not involve the deliberate interrogation of a defendant after the initiation of judicial proceedings against him. The Court disregards this basic difference between the present case and Massiah's, with the bland assertion that "that fact should make no difference." *Ante*, p. 485.

It is "that fact," I submit, which makes all the difference. Under our system of criminal justice the institution of formal, meaningful judicial proceedings, by way of indictment, information, or arraignment, marks the point at which a criminal investigation has ended and adversary proceedings have commenced. It is at this point that the constitutional guarantees attach which pertain to a criminal trial. Among those guarantees are the right to a speedy trial, the right of confrontation, and the right to trial by jury. Another is the guarantee of the assistance of counsel. *Gideon* v. *Wainwright*, 372 U.S. 335; *Hamilton* v. *Alabama*, 368 U.S. 52; *White* v. *Maryland*, 373 U.S. 59.

The confession which the Court today holds inadmissible was a voluntary one. It was given during the course of a perfectly legitimate police investigation of an unsolved murder. The Court says that what happened during this investigation "affected" the trial. I had always supposed that the whole purpose of a police investigation of a murder was to "affect" the trial of the murderer, and that it would be only an incompetent, unsuccessful, or corrupt investigation which would not do so. The Court further says that the Illinois police officers did not advise the petitioner of his "constitutional rights" before he confessed to the murder. This Court has never held that the Constitution requires the police to give any "advice" under circumstances such as these.

Supported by no stronger authority than its own rhetoric, the Court today converts a routine police investigation of an unsolved murder into a distorted analogue of a judicial trial. It imports into this investigation constitutional concepts historically applicable only after the onset of formal prosecutorial proceedings. By doing so, I think the Court perverts those precious constitutional guarantees, and frustrates the vital interests of society in preserving the legitimate and proper function of honest and purposeful police investigation.

Like my Brother CLARK, I cannot escape the logic of my Brother WHITE's conclusions as to the extraordinary implications which emanate from the Court's opinion in this case, and I share their views as to the untold and highly unfortunate impact today's decision may have upon the fair administration of criminal justice. I can only hope we have completely misunderstood what the Court has said.

MR. JUSTICE WHITE, with whom MR. JUSTICE CLARK and MR. JUSTICE STEWART join, dissenting.

In *Massiah* v. *United States*, 377 U.S. 201, the Court held that as of the date of the indictment the prosecution is disentitled to secure admissions from the accused. The Court now moves that date back to the time when the prosecution begins to "focus" on the accused. Although the opinion purports to be limited to the facts of this case, it would be naive to think that the new constitutional right announced will depend upon whether the accused has retained his own counsel, cf. *Gideon* v. *Wainwright*, 372 U.S. 335; *Griffin* v. *Illinois*, 351 U.S. 12; *Douglas* v. *California*, 372 U.S. 353, or has asked to consult with counsel in the course of interrogation. Cf. *Carnley* v. *Cochran*, 369 U.S. 506. At the very least the Court holds that once the accused becomes a suspect and, presumably, is arrested, any admission made to the police thereafter is inadmissible in evidence unless the accused has waived his right to counsel. The decision is thus another major step in the direction of the goal which the Court seemingly has in mind—to bar from evidence all admissions obtained from an individual suspected of crime, whether involuntarily made or not. It does of course put us one step "ahead" of the English judges who have had the good sense to leave the matter a discretionary one with the trial court.* I reject this step and the invitation to go farther which the Court has now issued.

By abandoning the voluntary-involuntary test for admissibility of confessions, the Court seems driven by the notion that it is uncivilized law enforcement to use an accused's own admissions against him at his trial. It attempts to find a home for this new and nebulous rule of due process by attaching it to the right to counsel guaranteed in the federal system by the Sixth Amendment and binding upon the States by virtue of the due process guarantee of the Fourteenth Amendment. *Gideon* v. *Wainwright, supra.* The right to counsel now not only entitles the accused to counsel's advice and aid in preparing for trial but stands as an impenetrable barrier to any interrogation once the accused has become a suspect. From that very moment apparently his right to counsel attaches, a rule wholly unworkable and impossible to administer unless police cars are equipped with public defenders and undercover agents and police informants have defense counsel at their side. I would not abandon the Court's prior cases defining with some care and analysis the circumstances requiring the presence or aid of counsel and substitute the amorphous and wholly unworkable principle that counsel is constitutionally required whenever he would or could be helpful. *Hamilton* v. *Alabama*, 368 U.S. 52; *White* v. *Maryland*, 373 U.S. 59; *Gideon* v. *Wainwright, supra.* These cases dealt with the requirement of counsel at proceedings in which definable

---

*"[I]t seems from reported cases that the judges have given up enforcing their own rules, for it is no longer the practice to exclude evidence obtained by questioning in custody. . . . A traditional principle of 'fairness' to criminals, which has quite possibly lost some of the reason for its existence, is maintained in words while it is disregarded in fact. . . .

"The reader may be expecting at this point a vigorous denunciation of the police and of the judges, and a plea for a return to the Judges' Rules as interpreted in 1930. What has to be considered, however, is whether these Rules are a workable part of the machinery of justice. Perhaps the truth is that the Rules have been abandoned, by tacit consent, just because they are an unreasonable restriction upon the activities of the police in bringing criminals to book." Williams, Questioning by the Police: Some Practical Considerations, [1960] Crim. L. Rev. 325, 331–332. See also [1964] Crim. L. Rev. 161–182.

rights could be won or lost, not with stages where probative evidence might be obtained. Under this new approach one might just as well argue that a potential defendant is constitutionally entitled to a lawyer before, not after, he commits a crime, since it is then that crucial incriminating evidence is put within the reach of the Government by the would-be accused. Until now there simply has been no right guaranteed by the Federal Constitution to be free from the use at trial of a voluntary admission made prior to indictment.

It is incongruous to assume that the provision for counsel in the Sixth Amendment was meant to amend or supersede the self-incrimination provision of the Fifth Amendment, which is now applicable to the States. *Malloy* v. *Hogan*, 378 U.S. 1. That amendment addresses itself to the very issue of incriminating admissions of an accused and resolves it by prescribing only compelled statements. Neither the Framers, the constitutional language, a century of decisions of this Court nor Professor Wigmore provides an iota of support for the idea that an accused has an absolute constitutional right not to answer even in the absence of compulsion—the constitutional right not to incriminate himself by making voluntary disclosures.

Today's decision cannot be squared with other provisions of the Constitution which, in my view, define the system of criminal justice this Court is empowered to administer. The Fourth Amendment permits upon probable cause even compulsory searches of the suspect and his possessions and the use of the fruits of the search at trial, all in the absence of counsel. The Fifth Amendment and state constitutional provisions authorize, indeed require, inquisitorial grand jury proceedings at which a potential defendant, in the absence of counsel, is shielded against no more than compulsory incrimination. *Mulloney* v. *United States*, 79 F.2d 566, 578 (C.A. 1st Cir.); *United States* v. *Benjamin*, 120 F.2d 521, 522 (C.A. 2d Cir.); *United States* v. *Scully*, 225 F.2d 113, 115 (C.A. 2d Cir.); *United States* v. *Gilboy*, 160 F.Supp. 442 (D.C.M.D.Pa.). A grand jury witness, who may be a suspect, is interrogated and his answers, at least until today, are admissible in evidence at trial. And these provisions have been thought of as constitutional safeguards to persons suspected of an offense. Furthermore, until now, the Constitution has permitted the accused to be fingerprinted and to be identified in a line-up or in the courtroom itself.

The Court chooses to ignore these matters and to rely on the virtues and morality of a system of criminal law enforcement which does not depend on the "confession." No such judgment is to be found in the Constitution. It might be appropriate for a legislature to provide that a suspect should not be consulted during a criminal investigation; that an accused should never be called before a grand jury to answer, even if he wants to, what may well be incriminating questions; and that no person, whether he be a suspect, guilty criminal or innocent bystander, should be put to the ordeal of responding to orderly noncompulsory inquiry by the State. But this is not the system our Constitution requires. The only "inquisitions" the Constitution forbids are those which compel incrimination. Escobedo's statements were not compelled and the Court does not hold that they were.

This new American judges' rule, which is to be applied in both federal and state courts, is perhaps thought to be a necessary safeguard against the possibility of extorted confessions. To this extent it reflects a deep-seated distrust of law enforcement officers everywhere, unsupported by relevant data or current material based upon our own experience. Obviously law enforcement officers can make mistakes and exceed their authority, as today's decision shows that even judges can do, but I have somewhat more faith than the Court evidently has in the ability and desire of prosecutors and of the power of the appellate courts to discern and correct such violations of the law.

The Court may be concerned with a narrower matter: the unknowing defendant who responds to police questioning because he mistakenly believes that he must and that his admissions will not be used against him. But this worry hardly calls for the broadside the Court has now fired. The failure to inform an accused that he need not answer and that his answers may be used against him is very relevant indeed to whether the disclosures are compelled. Cases in this Court, to say the least, have never placed a premium on ignorance of constitutional rights. If an accused is told he must answer and does not know better, it would be very doubtful that the resulting admissions could be used against him. When the accused has not been informed of his rights at all the Court characteristically and properly looks very closely at the surrounding circumstances. See *Ward* v. *Texas*, 316 U.S. 547; *Haley* v. *Ohio*, 332 U.S. 596; *Payne* v. *Arkansas*, 356 U.S. 560. I would continue to do so. But in this case Danny Escobedo knew full well that he did not have to answer and knew full well that his lawyer had advised him not to answer.

I do not suggest for a moment that law enforcement will be destroyed by the rule announced today. The need for peace and order is too insistent for that. But it will be crippled and its task made a great deal more difficult, all in my opinion, for unsound, unstated reasons, which can find no home in any of the provisions of the Constitution.